PROPERTY
DISCARDED

D0936176

NATO's
Nuclear Dilemmas

DAVID N. SCHWARTZ

NATO's
Nuclear Dilemmas

UA
646.3
.S38
1983

THE BROOKINGS INSTITUTION
Washington, D.C.

158331

Copyright © 1983 by
THE BROOKINGS INSTITUTION
1775 Massachusetts Avenue, N.W., Washington, D.C. 20036

Library of Congress Cataloging in Publication data:

Schwartz, David N., 1956–
    NATO's nuclear dilemmas.
    Includes bibliographical references and index.
    1. North Atlantic Treaty Organization.   2. Atomic
weapons.   3. Deterrence (Strategy)—History—20th cen-
tury.   I. Title.
UA646.3.S38   1983   355'.031'091821   83-11911
ISBN 0-8157-7772-8
ISBN 0-8157-7771-X (pbk.)

1 2 3 4 5 6 7 8 9

The excerpts appearing in chapter 5 from Robert R. Bowie, "Strategy and the Atlantic Alliance," *International Organization,* vol. 17 (Summer 1963), are reprinted by permission of the MIT Press, Cambridge, Massachusetts, and the author. Copyright 1963 by the World Peace Foundation and the Massachusetts Institute of Technology.

Board of Trustees

Robert V. Roosa
Chairman
Andrew Heiskell
Vice Chairman;
Chairman, Executive Committee
Louis W. Cabot
Vice Chairman
Vincent M. Barnett, Jr.
Barton M. Biggs
Frank T. Cary
A. W. Clausen
William T. Coleman, Jr.
Lloyd N. Cutler
Thomas Donahue
Charles W. Duncan, Jr.
George M. Elsey
Robert F. Erburu
Hanna H. Gray
Robert D. Haas
Philip M. Hawley
Roger W. Heyns
James T. Lynn
Donald F. McHenry
Bruce K. MacLaury
Robert S. McNamara
Arjay Miller
Herbert P. Patterson
Donald S. Perkins
J. Woodward Redmond
Charles W. Robinson
James D. Robinson III
Ralph S. Saul
Henry B. Schacht
Roger D. Semerad
Gerard C. Smith
Howard R. Swearer
Morris Tanenbaum
Phyllis A. Wallace

Honorary Trustees

Eugene R. Black
Robert D. Calkins
Edward W. Carter
Bruce B. Dayton
Douglas Dillon
Huntington Harris
John E. Lockwood
William McC. Martin, Jr.
H. Chapman Rose
Robert Brookings Smith
Sydney Stein, Jr.

THE BROOKINGS INSTITUTION is an independent organization devoted to nonpartisan research, education, and publication in economics, government, foreign policy, and the social sciences generally. Its principal purposes are to aid in the development of sound public policies and to promote public understanding of issues of national importance.

The Institution was founded on December 8, 1927, to merge the activities of the Institute for Government Research, founded in 1916, the Institute of Economics, founded in 1922, and the Robert Brookings Graduate School of Economics and Government, founded in 1924.

The Board of Trustees is responsible for the general administration of the Institution, while the immediate direction of the policies, program, and staff is vested in the President, assisted by an advisory committee of the officers and staff. The by-laws of the Institution state: "It is the function of the Trustees to make possible the conduct of scientific research, and publication, under the most favorable conditions, and to safeguard the independence of the research staff in the pursuit of their studies and in the publication of the results of such studies. It is not a part of their function to determine, control, or influence the conduct of particular investigations or the conclusions reached."

The President bears final responsibility for the decision to publish a manuscript as a Brookings book. In reaching his judgment on the competence, accuracy, and objectivity of each study, the President is advised by the director of the appropriate research program and weighs the views of a panel of expert outside readers who report to him in confidence on the quality of the work. Publication of a work signifies that it is deemed a competent treatment worthy of public consideration but does not imply endorsement of conclusions or recommendations.

The Institution maintains its position of neutrality on issues of public policy in order to safeguard the intellectual freedom of the staff. Hence interpretations or conclusions in Brookings publications should be understood to be solely those of the authors and should not be attributed to the Institution, to its trustees, officers, or other staff members, or to the organizations that support its research.

Foreword

THE difficulties facing the North Atlantic Treaty Organization (NATO) today over nuclear weapons policy have their proximate source in NATO's controversial December 1979 decision to introduce Pershing II missiles and ground-launched cruise missiles into Western Europe while engaging the Soviet Union in efforts to control them. But the origins of NATO's nuclear dilemmas stem from doubts about the credibility of the U.S. strategic nuclear guarantee to its allies and deep concerns over the proper role of nuclear weapons in NATO defense plans that are nearly as old as the alliance itself.

In this book, David N. Schwartz reviews previous attempts to resolve these issues. His purposes are to explain how NATO arrived at the 1979 decision, to identify the problems facing the allies as they attempt to carry out that decision, and to judge how successful the current effort is likely to be. He also examines several initiatives of the 1957–67 period in detail: the efforts of the U.S. government and General Lauris Norstad to deploy nuclear missiles in Europe between 1957 and 1960; the U.S. proposal for the creation of a multilateral nuclear force for NATO between 1961 and 1964; the debate over the strategy of flexible response, and the subsequent adoption of that strategy by the alliance in 1967; and the creation of the NATO Nuclear Planning Group in 1966–67.

Schwartz, now a research associate in the Brookings Foreign Policy Studies program, prepared this study as a dissertation which he completed while he was a Brookings Research Fellow and submitted in August 1980 to the Department of Political Science at the Massachusetts Institute of Technology. He is especially grateful to the members of his dissertation committee—William W. Kaufmann and Jack Ruina of MIT and John D. Steinbruner of Brookings—for the inspiration and guidance they provided. He also thanks the many other scholars and analysts whose constructive comments and help were invaluable—Jorg Baldauf, John Barry, Richard K. Betts, Robert R. Bowie, Raymond L. Garthoff, Malcolm Hoag, Jiang Enzhu, Catherine McArdle Kelleher, Milton Leitenberg, John J. Mearsheimer, Richard Shearer, Leon V. Sigal, and Strobe Talbott—and the many U.S. government officials, past and present, who, with the assurance of anonymity, gave selflessly of their time and knowledge.

Many Brookings staff members were helpful in providing support for this project. Cristina Gobin, Jan R. Liss, Jacqueline Martin, and Patricia A. O'Brien provided administrative support; Antoinette G. Buena, Ruth E. Conrad, Ann M. Ziegler, and Thomas T. Somuah typed the manuscript; Caroline Lalire edited it; Alan G. Hoden and Clifford A. Wright verified its factual content; Nancy Snyder did the proofreading; and Ward & Sylvan prepared the index. For all these efforts, the author is grateful.

The National Science Foundation and the Pacific-Sierra Research Corporation provided funding for this study in its dissertation stage. Brookings acknowledges with gratitude the subsequent financial support of the Ford Foundation and the Rockefeller Foundation that enabled the project to be completed.

The views in this book are solely those of the author and should not be ascribed to the Ford Foundation, the Rockefeller Foundation, the National Science Foundation, the Pacific-Sierra Research Corporation, or to the trustees, officers, or other staff members of the Brookings Institution.

BRUCE K. MACLAURY
President

May 1983
Washington, D.C.

Contents

For Mom, Dad, and Wendy

ACRONYMS

ABM	antiballistic missile
ACDA	Arms Control and Disarmament Agency
FBS	forward based systems
GLCM	ground-launched cruise missile
HLG	High Level Group
ICBM	intercontinental ballistic missile
IRBM	intermediate-range ballistic missile
ISA	Office of International Security Affairs
LRTNF	long-range theater nuclear forces
MBFR	mutual and balanced force reductions
MIRV	multiple independently-targetable reentry vehicle
MLF	multilateral force
MMRBM	mobile medium-range ballistic missile
MRBM	medium-range ballistic missile
NATO	North Atlantic Treaty Organization
NDAC	Nuclear Defense Affairs Committee
NPG	Nuclear Planning Group
NSC	National Security Council
SAC	Strategic Air Command
SACEUR	Supreme Allied Commander Europe
SACLANT	Supreme Allied Commander Atlantic
SALT	strategic arms limitation talks
SCG	Special Consultative Group
SG	Special Group
SHAPE	Supreme Headquarters Allied Powers Europe
SIOP	single integrated operational plan
SLBM	submarine-launched ballistic missile
SLCM	sea-launched cruise missile

CHAPTER ONE

Introduction

ON OCTOBER 28, 1977, West Germany's irrepressible Chancellor Helmut Schmidt delivered a landmark address to a gathering at London's International Institute for Strategic Studies. The speech touched on many issues, but it will be remembered mainly for its comments on the North Atlantic Treaty Organization (NATO), strategic arms, and Western European defense. SALT (strategic arms limitation talks), Schmidt said,

codifies the nuclear strategic balance between the Soviet Union and the United States. To put it another way: SALT neutralizes their strategic nuclear capabilities. In Europe this magnifies the significance of the disparities between East and West in nuclear tactical and conventional weapons. . . . No one can deny that the principle of parity is a sensible one. However its fulfillment must be the aim of all arms-limitation and arms-control negotiations and it must apply to all categories of weapons. Neither side can agree to diminish its security unilaterally.

It is of vital interest to us all that the negotiations between the two superpowers on the limitation and reduction of nuclear strategic weapons should continue and lead to a lasting agreement. The nuclear powers have a special, an overwhelming responsibility in this field. On the other hand, we in Europe must be particularly careful to ensure that these negotiations do not neglect the components of NATO's deterrence strategy. . . . strategic arms limitations confined to the United States and the Soviet Union will inevitably impair the security of the West European members of the Alliance *vis-à-vis* Soviet military superiority in Europe if we do not succeed in removing the disparities of military power in Europe parallel to the SALT negotiations.[1]

These words catalyzed a process that resulted in the December 1979 decision of NATO to modernize its long-range theater nuclear forces (LRTNF) and to pursue arms-control negotiations with the Soviet Union to limit LRTNF deployments. Some observers have hailed this decision

1. Helmut Schmidt, "The 1977 Alastair Buchan Memorial Lecture," pp. 3–4. Full references to the works cited appear in the bibliography.

1

as NATO's most important in the last fifteen years. It is certainly one of its most controversial.[2]

The main premise of this book is that the LRTNF decision represents the latest response to a complex set of related dilemmas that have plagued the alliance virtually from its inception, dilemmas about the role of nuclear weapons in alliance defense strategy.

Nuclear Dilemmas: Military Dimensions

Some of these dilemmas are largely military, involving the role of strategic nuclear forces for alliance deterrence and defense and the relation between NATO's nuclear and nonnuclear (conventional) forces.

The Strategic Nuclear Forces

Since the mid-1950s NATO has relied—with varying emphasis—on the strategic nuclear arsenal of the United States as the ultimate deterrent to Warsaw Pact aggression against the alliance. Specifically, rather than accept defeat, the United States has pledged to use its strategic nuclear forces against the Warsaw Pact if the conflict reaches a certain point. At times it has threatened to use these weapons early on in any war, even if the initial attack was nonnuclear. At other times it has pledged to use them if NATO found itself incapable of mounting a serious conventional defense against a conventional attack. But at all times it has maintained

2. The terminology here requires a brief explanation. Historically, nuclear weapons have been called either *strategic* or *tactical,* depending on the intended use of the weapons. Strategic weapons are assigned to strike targets relevant to the enemy's overall war-waging capability—military forces, economic and industrial facilities, and even urban population centers. Tactical weapons, in contrast, are intended to support battlefield operations. Some U.S. strategic weapons are deployed in the continental United States; others are deployed elsewhere, such as those on board missile-carrying submarines. Because of the generally shorter range of tactical nuclear weapons, most are deployed close to the areas where they might be used, for example, in Europe. Weapons based in particular theaters of military operations are often also called *theater* nuclear weapons. Long-range theater nuclear weapons, therefore, are weapons deployed in the theater—in this case, Western Europe. Their long range, more than 1,000 nautical miles, makes them suitable for strategic missions against the Soviet homeland, even though most currently deployed theater nuclear weapons are tactical in terms of assigned mission. The Reagan administration recently dropped the term *theater* in favor of *intermediate-range* (see chapter 7, note 1).

that it would respond to a nuclear attack with nuclear weapons, the nature and degree of the retaliation depending on the nature and degree of the Warsaw Pact use of such weapons.

This dependence on the United States has had long-lasting consequences. Most important, it has made the reliability of this pledge, the "nuclear guarantee," a central issue of alliance security. When events or statements throw the reliability of the guarantee into question, the underpinnings of the NATO deterrent become open to doubt. On more than one occasion, this process has led to rancor and tension that has threatened to rip the alliance apart. One enduring goal of American policy within NATO has been to alleviate these doubts, not only because of the intra-alliance tensions they create, but because if unchecked, they could lead to the development of independent nuclear weapons capabilities in other NATO states.

But the reliability of the U.S. strategic guarantee has been difficult to ensure. Not only is it hard for the United States to make the guarantee seem ironclad, but its efforts in the past to do so have raised the opposite fear within the alliance, namely, that the United States could commit its allies to a nuclear war they neither want nor, given their proximity and vulnerability to Soviet nuclear attack, could survive. This fundamental dilemma, dictated by asymmetrical capabilities and vulnerabilities of the members of the alliance and by distinct and disparate assessments of overlapping—but not identical—national interests, forces the United States to walk a thin line between European fear that the American strategic arsenal does not afford protection and fear that it does, with potentially suicidal consequences.

Controversies over Conventional Defense

When the alliance was formed in 1949, some Americans hoped that NATO would develop a strong military posture across the board, including robust nonnuclear, or conventional, forces. Over the next decade several factors worked to undermine these hopes. First, the Soviet nonnuclear threat to Western Europe was incorrectly perceived as so large that efforts to counter it would be futile. The recovering economies of Western Europe, along with the United States, had neither the resources nor the political will to match the 175 Soviet divisions allegedly poised to invade the West. Second—and this was one reason the nuclear guarantee became so important—the United States had nuclear weapons, which when used in battlefield operations would supposedly compensate for NATO's nonnuclear deficiencies, and which when used as a strategic threat would provide a stronger deterrent against a Warsaw Pact invasion than any conventional posture could provide. Third, relying on nuclear weapons as a substitute for nonnuclear strength was far more affordable to budget-constrained NATO governments than trying to achieve adequate nonnuclear capabilities.

All these factors militated against the development of strong conventional forces for NATO during the early years of the alliance. It would be convenient if one could attribute, as some have, a "trip-wire" function to NATO's conventional force posture at that time, a posture that when challenged by Warsaw Pact aggression would serve merely to unleash the strategic nuclear forces. Perhaps this was the theory behind the forces; however, they were too large for this function alone. Yet they were too small to meet serious conventional defense requirements.

Not everyone was satisfied with this state of affairs. Some observers criticized NATO's heavy reliance on nuclear forces and its neglect of conventional forces. They charged that such a posture reduced NATO's flexibility in meeting less-than-ultimate threats. They argued that it lacked fundamental credibility as a deterrent threat. They believed that it simultaneously exaggerated the size of the Warsaw Pact conventional threat and underestimated NATO's capability to deal with it. They pointed to data from exercises and analyses which suggested that manpower deficiencies would not only remain relevant in nuclear battlefield operations but would actually magnify NATO's disadvantage. Finally, they charged that NATO had neglected the problems of controlling a nuclear war in Europe, in particular the pressure that would mount to escalate such a conflict to even greater levels of destruction and the incredible damage Western Europe would suffer even in a "limited" battlefield nuclear exchange.

Attempts to move toward a more serious conventional capability for NATO, particularly in the 1960s, ran into serious trouble. As much as European governments were reluctant to endorse policies that seemed to portend the nuclear decimation of Western Europe, they were equally fearful of moving toward greater reliance on conventional forces. Some saw such a move as an admission of Washington's unwillingness to extend the nuclear umbrella over Europe, while others who were more confident of Washington's intentions feared the Kremlin would misread the move as such an admission. Some saw the move as a cynical attempt to undermine the national nuclear aspirations of other member nations; others, though more generous toward Washington's intentions, challenged the factual validity of its revised assessment of the Warsaw Pact threat. In general, Europeans were convinced that whatever the merits of the new approach put forward in the 1960s by the United States, it simply was not politically or financially affordable. They also clung to the notion, erroneous but understandable given their history and their relative ignorance of the technical facts of nuclear war, that *nothing* could be worse than a replay of World War II. These doubts about the proper role of conventional forces proved just as damaging to alliance cohesion as those about the strategic nuclear guarantee, and just as exasperating for American leadership.

Nuclear Dilemmas: Political Dimensions

The dilemmas posed by nuclear weapons are not just military. There are political considerations that influence the way in which NATO addresses the military problems and that set a general context for the development and resolution of most important issues within the alliance.

The Big Three: London, Paris, Bonn

In political influence, prosperity, and military strength, the United Kingdom, France, and the Federal Republic of Germany stand apart from the other European members of the alliance as a "big three." If NATO is formally an alliance of equals, these three members speak with voices that are louder, if not more influential, than the others, though in recent years Italy has tended to join their ranks. They share a favored political position within the alliance, but they each bring to alliance deliberations a unique set of political perspectives and objectives.

British policies within alliance councils have been heavily influenced by the importance Great Britain places on maintaining a close, special relationship with the United States; by its status as NATO's second independent nuclear power; by its history of Great Power status; by the ambivalence with which its governing elites have viewed its political, military, and economic relations with the Continent; and by its declining importance as a global military and economic power. In addressing the military problems that have been mentioned, Britain walks a fine line between nurturing its trans-Atlantic ties and its trans-Channel ties; it faces the many strategic requirements and responsibilities created by the possession of an independent strategic deterrent; and even though objective measures of its political strength have been in decline for at least a decade, it strives to continue to play a leading role in NATO.

France has historically played an equally important, if more controversial, role in alliance affairs. Emerging from the Second World War with an entrenched national inferiority complex, it regained stature and pride in the late 1950s under de Gaulle. But it did so largely through a pitched political battle with the United States for the leadership of Western Europe. France used its ongoing strategic nuclear program as a political weapon to drive a wedge between the United States and its allies and to serve as a rallying point for French national pride battered by June 1940, Suez, Algeria, and the Indochina War. It lost this political battle and withdrew from NATO's integrated military organization. But it has never renounced its membership in the alliance, and the 1970s have seen a gradual cooling of the passions that raged between Gaullists and Atlanticists in the 1960s. Yet France retains a fiercely independent political perspective on all alliance matters, a perspective that gained greater weight in Europe during the stable, prosperous administration of President Valéry Giscard d'Estaing.

Of the big three, the political position of West Germany has probably been the most complex. The country has always had to balance its various objectives delicately: to play an active and constructive role within the alliance without reawakening the suspicions and resentments of its opponents in World War II; to come to a more stable relationship with East Germany without raising American fears of a leftist or neutralist political shift, and without raising Soviet fears of German revanchism; to seek reunification on terms acceptable to the West, without destabilizing the postwar balance of power; and to pursue all its goals without antagonizing either enemies or friends. Leaders in Bonn are very conscious of Germany's unhappy past and are particularly sensitive to charges of militarism and revanchism; it is only natural, then, that they are reluctant to take on a disproportionate share of the military burden of alliance defense even though their economy would permit them to do so. Especially sensitive are policies relating to alliance nuclear weapons. At the same time, these leaders are sensitive to West Germany's exposed position as the front line of NATO's defense; thus they believe the country has a special stake in alliance defense plans and in the future of détente and arms control. The complexity of meeting these many objectives has grown with Germany's increasingly pivotal role in alliance decisions.

The Other European Members

Just as it is impossible to discuss the big three as a single bloc within the alliance, so it is impossible to discuss the other European members as a bloc. Each has its own distinct security interests, cultural heritage, political traditions, and objectives; each pursues its own policies within the alliance framework. Nevertheless, some crude generalizations are possible. In general, the southern-flank members of NATO—Portugal, Italy, Greece, and Turkey—have rarely been leading participants in the debates over NATO's nuclear dilemmas. Portugal and Greece have tended to act as disinterested observers; Italy and Turkey, when they have been active, have usually supported American initiatives, either to demonstrate loyalty or to have access to modern weapons and thus have a greater political role in the alliance.[3] Denmark, Norway, and Iceland— the Scandinavian members of NATO—have long traditions of strong pacifist domestic political groups, which have effectively limited Scandinavian participation in nuclear matters within the alliance. To this day, the alliance may not stockpile nuclear weapons or station foreign troops on Scandinavian soil, although these governments have usually not resisted American-led NATO initiatives to deploy them elsewhere, and at times have been supportive.

Belgium and the Netherlands have historically had an influence out of proportion to their size and military power within the alliance. Not surprisingly, the two nations were crucial to the formation of the European integration movement. The concept of a Europe transcending nationalistic divisions has great appeal to smaller, exposed nations that are relatively weak in the traditional nation-state system. It has particular appeal in a country like Belgium, where ethnic divisions have long been a source of domestic political weakness and instability. Although NATO was created as a response to specific security problems, it was seen by advocates of European integration as a basis for a future transnational

---

3. This study was written before Spain's entry into NATO. How that country will interact with the other allies, and whether it will find much in common with other southern-flank allies, remains to be seen.

European state. Dutch and Belgian leaders have thus always maintained a keen interest in promoting alliance cohesion and unity. At the same time, powerful elements in Dutch and Belgian political life have considered the pursuit of détente a particularly important NATO goal. Thus these countries have shown great interest in nuclear policies that minimize East-West tensions.

The Role of the United States

Within this complex political environment the United States attempts to lead NATO. The role of leader has devolved quite naturally onto Washington. Unlike the European members, the United States emerged physically unscathed from World War II. In size, military power, and economic potential, it dwarfs any single ally. It is also distant enough from the intra-European quarrels of the past to be able to offer credible leadership to the other members of the alliance.

To a great extent the members have been willing to accord this preeminent role to the United States. Under the American nuclear umbrella, they have been able to recover economically from the war and to achieve high levels of prosperity; Washington's nuclear protection has reduced the perceived need to make the expensive and politically unpopular sacrifices of resources that would be necessary to improve conventional defense.

But this willingness to let the United States play such a large role has been tempered over time by resentment of the relatively unequal political status in which the other members find themselves; by recurring doubts about the reliability or the wisdom of the U.S. strategic guarantee; by suspicion of the motives of American leaders in proposing initiatives to reduce these doubts; and by a longing for greater control over alliance plans and, in some instances, over nuclear weapons.

These problems are further aggravated by a perception that because the United States is not as exposed to the Warsaw Pact threat as some of its other allies, it is less reluctant to take provocative actions that place its allies at a risk disproportionate to its own, and that U.S. leaders therefore take the pursuit of East-West détente less seriously than they should. Yet in trying to reverse this perception, the United States runs another, contrary risk; namely, of inducing fears that it is willing to come to terms with the Soviet Union without accounting fully for the security interests of the allies.

Through painful experience the United States has discovered that it must lead carefully where the nuclear issue is concerned. In general, it has approached the leadership problem in several distinct ways. One way has been to fashion policies to meet the voiced (or perceived) fears and doubts of the allies. This method lets the allies set the agenda of action and define the issues at stake; the United States then strives to address these issues as though they were valid.

This approach has several attractions. It allows U.S. leaders to argue that they are being responsive to the doubts and fears of the allies and that they lead by consensus. It appeals to the democratic instincts bred by the American political system. And it recognizes that the allies' doubts and fears are in some respects legitimate.

There are dangers in this approach, however, because long-term consensus is virtually impossible to achieve. Any initiative designed to accommodate one set of fears almost always gives rise to contrary, and equally frustrating, fears. This result is dictated by the disparities of power between the United States and its allies, by varying degrees of vulnerability to Warsaw Pact aggression, by competing national interests among alliance members, by different political traditions and perspectives, and by Soviet diplomacy.

Another approach has been for the United States to clarify for itself what the defense requirements for the alliance should be, and to challenge the other members of the alliance either to accept these requirements or to propose alternatives. This method has two attractions. One, it is usually easier for the United States to determine what it believes alliance defense requires than to lead on the basis of what fifteen allies, with competing and sometimes inconsistent priorities, believe is required. And two, given the ability of the United States to come to such a determination, this approach puts the burden of proposing alternative policies directly on the other alliance members, who find it easier to disagree with specific policies than to develop coherent, practical alternatives.

But there are also disadvantages to such an approach. Primarily, it opens the United States to charges of leadership by fiat. This approach can worsen the problem by convincing the allies that Washington has no interest in taking seriously the deeply felt views of its allies and by reinforcing resentments that naturally arise out of the unequal status between leader and followers. Moreover, the United States itself may find it difficult to decide on a coherent set of policy objectives with regard to NATO's nuclear dilemmas. If different U.S. agencies pursue differing, and incompatible, policy goals, confusion, suspicion, and tension may result on the other side of the Atlantic.

Successfully leading the alliance on the nuclear issue would be easier if alliance policy were the only foreign policy concern of the United States. Of course it is not. The United States pursues many other foreign policy objectives from the perspective of its own national interest; some of these objectives inevitably conflict with efforts to deal with NATO's nuclear dilemmas. For example, U.S. political and military leaders and virtually all its national security bureaucracy have long held that the spread of nuclear weapons to other countries would be destabilizing and provocative and would increase the likelihood of nuclear war. Within the context of alliance politics, however, this aversion to proliferation has been selective. Although Washington did not actually encourage Britain's efforts to develop nuclear weapons, it did little to block those efforts, and it eventually agreed to comprehensive arrangements for Anglo-American cooperation on nuclear matters. Yet the United States actively sought to derail the French independent nuclear effort, partly because the French were using their program to drive a wedge between Western Europe and the United States, and partly because it was feared that a successful French program would stimulate West German interest in a similar program. Blocking West German nuclear aspirations was a keystone of U.S.-alliance policy in the 1960s; West German nuclear capability would be particularly destabilizing, arousing fears among both friends and enemies about German intentions. It is difficult to imagine a greater provocation, from the Soviet point of view, than a West German nuclear capability.

These antiproliferation motivations have given added impetus to American efforts to resolve doubts about the reliability and credibility of the American nuclear guarantee. If the doubts were not eased, interest in national, independent nuclear arsenals might increase. Conversely, resolving these doubts, making the guarantee more reliable and credible, would remove an important—though not the only—incentive U.S. allies might have to develop their own nuclear capabilities. But efforts to make the guarantee more credible have sometimes run the risk of stimulating proliferation, especially by focusing on ways to give nonnuclear allies a share in the operational control of nuclear weapons. This policy dilemma has repeatedly faced the United States. And the selective application of nonproliferation policy—in particular, the exemption of Great Britain and the inclusion of France and West Germany—has historically created serious intra-alliance tensions.

The Lessons of the Past

Major foreign policy issues of any kind are firmly embedded in a historical framework. Current policies are most often the product of a long and complex chain of events and decisions. To understand policy problems and the range of potential solutions, one must first understand these events and decisions in some detail. That knowledge can guide today's decisionmakers by showing them the rationale behind different policies at different times, by warning them of the consequences of various policy alternatives, by sensitizing them to the degree of flexibility inherent in the policies and issues they inherit from predecessors, and by revealing mistakes to be avoided and successes to be emulated.

The main part of this book consists of an examination of five episodes in which the United States initiated action in part to address NATO's nuclear dilemmas. These episodes include the offer of Thor and Jupiter intermediate-range ballistic missiles (IRBMs) to the allies in December 1957; plans explored and developed by General Lauris Norstad, the Supreme Allied Commander Europe (SACEUR) at that time, to create a mobile land-based medium-range ballistic missile force (MMRBM) for NATO; the U.S. effort between 1960 and 1965 to create a multilateral sea-based MRBM force for NATO; the U.S. effort between 1962 and 1967 to have NATO adopt a strategy of "flexible response"; and the creation of the NATO Nuclear Planning Group in 1966–67. The final chapter deals with the events leading up to NATO's decision, in December 1979, to modernize its LRTNF and to pursue arms control involving LRTNF, and seeks to analyze these events through the perspective of the past.

These episodes differ in many important ways. What makes it possible to consider them as a group is that they each were U.S. initiatives in part designed to address some aspect of NATO's uneasiness over the U.S. nuclear guarantee. No attempt is made to be historically definitive. Rather, the purpose is to show why the United States pursued each initiative, why the Europeans reacted as they did, and why the initiative either succeeded or failed, in enough detail to draw some broad lessons from the 1957–67 period to apply to current issues.

The analysis will highlight several patterns.

—The very act of embarking on an initiative creates substantial pressure on the initiator for success. The initiator—in this case the United States—puts its prestige directly on the line. The perception of NATO as a coherent, purposeful politico-military entity capable of following through on difficult and controversial initiatives is also at stake; thus not only the United States but virtually all members of the alliance eventually come under pressure to succeed. And if one initiative fails, there is even greater pressure for subsequent initiatives to succeed.

—Initiatives that provide hardware to try to solve the nuclear dilemmas of the alliance are more difficult to implement and less likely to have a lasting effect than doctrinal initiatives or initiatives that have no more definite purpose than to stimulate consultative discussions.

—Approaches that challenge the grounds for European fears, forcing the allies to elaborate and to justify those fears, work as well as, if not better than, those that accept such fears as a basis for action.

—Efforts that cater, however indirectly, to latent nuclear aspirations of the allies have been less effective than those that focus on nonnuclear measures in which the allies can take an active role.

These lessons are hardly new. In fact, the United States and the alliance seem to have learned them through a gradual process of painful trial and error during the active 1957–67 decade. But in coming to the December 1979 decision to modernize and to seek limits on long-range theater nuclear forces, NATO seems to have forgotten some of these lessons—with consequences that are explored in the final chapter.

But first it is necessary to set the stage for this excursion into NATO's past. Why did NATO become so reliant on America's strategic nuclear guarantee? And why did that reliance—virtually an addiction—come to be questioned in the crisis in which NATO found itself in December 1957?

CHAPTER TWO

NATO's Nuclear Addiction

WITHIN five years after its establishment in 1949 NATO became firmly committed to a general strategic plan that relied primarily on the use, or threat of use, of American nuclear weapons in defense of Europe to deter Soviet aggression. This commitment had profound and wide-ranging implications for the way NATO members allocated resources to military programs, for operational planning, and for alliance reactions when confronted with the limitations of such plans. The furor over the credibility of the U.S. nuclear guarantee is difficult to understand without an appreciation of why NATO developed this nuclear addiction.

The Postwar Balance of Power

What is now seen as a radical shift in the structure of world power after World War II, from a world dominated by the European Great Powers to a bipolar distribution of power between the United States and the Soviet Union, was not readily apparent in the months following the war.[1] None of the victors could foresee the final shape of postwar Europe. Moscow's occupation of Eastern Europe was widely considered to be temporary, amenable to national and international pressure that would, it was hoped, bring an acceptable resolution to the dilemma of postwar Europe.

1. The following analysis of the early postwar period is based on a selective reading of the vast literature on the outbreak of the cold war. The most helpful books have been Lynn Etheridge Davis, *The Cold War Begins;* Herbert Feis, *Between War and Peace;* and John Lewis Gaddis, *The United States and the Origins of the Cold War, 1941–1947.*

Nor was it apparent just how much the colonial empires on which European claims to Great Power status largely rested had been weakened by the war. In 1945 the British and French empires still extended over most of the globe. Nationalism and the decline of the imperial powers were not yet established facts of the postwar world. But these illusions about British and French Great Power status were only temporary. As the European allies faced up to the intensified problems of colonial administration over restive nationalities, to the myriad economic and political problems of postwar recovery, and to the growing impatience of a U.S. government committed to the dissolution of all overseas empires, they were forced to reconsider the costs and benefits of maintaining their empires. But the deeper realization, foreshadowed by World War I, that European nations were no longer the prime movers in international politics, that they had depended on the United States for their security for longer than they cared to admit, and that they would be increasingly overshadowed by the United States and the Soviet Union in world affairs was difficult for them to accept.

The irony of this situation was the apparent unwillingness of the United States to maintain a strong global presence. The abrupt shift the United States had made after the attack on Pearl Harbor to a broadly internationalist political stance was fragile at best, under stress even during the war from more traditional isolationist elements of the U.S. foreign policy establishment.

As an implicit compromise with these elements, President Harry S. Truman sacrificed continued American global military commitments in order to maintain the highly visible diplomatic role the United States continued to play, especially in the formation and deliberations of the United Nations. Within ten months after the war ended, American forces under arms were cut by almost 50 percent, and most of those remaining were stationed at home.[2] A combination of faith in the ability of the United Nations to settle major international political conflicts, deeply rooted isolationist tendencies, and simple war fatigue was responsible for this retrenchment, which disguised the relative power balance in the world for several years and reinforced European anxiety about the long-term commitment of the United States to the cause of European peace and prosperity.

2. Samuel P. Huntington, *The Common Defense*, pp. 35–36.

The U.S. Nuclear Monopoly

The reality of the postwar situation soon demolished whatever miscalculations existed about the extent of U.S. power and interest in world affairs.

The United States was the only major belligerent to emerge from the war physically unscathed. But more important, it was the only nation with atomic weapons. With them, of course, the United States had brought the war with Japan to a horrifying end. It had shared the full secret of their construction with no other nation. Even Great Britain, largely responsible for the initial steps in producing fission weapons, was not privy to all that went on in the Manhattan Project, the U.S. program that had developed the first nuclear weapons.[3] Within a year after the war, Congress had enacted legislation making cooperation with other countries on nuclear research virtually impossible.[4] No doubt these efforts to protect the secret made it all the more enticing to the recovering European nations.

The American monopoly of nuclear weapons did not eliminate America's problems in the world. While the United States held the monopoly, the Soviet Union embarked on many cold war exploits, including the support of communist revolts in Greece and Turkey, the blocking of free elections in Poland, and the sponsoring of a communist coup d'état in Czechoslovakia. In general, American leaders found it difficult to translate their nuclear monopoly into decisive political advantage in their dealings with an increasingly hostile but nonnuclear Kremlin.

But ever since August 1945 nuclear weapons have held greater political and psychological significance than their actual utility in international politics would seem to justify. To the man on the street, and to many government officials throughout the world, they were the ultimate weapon. They represented a substantial technological achievement. More important, they offered the prospect of Great Power status on the cheap. A few of these weapons, it was assumed, would compensate for

3. For a comprehensive, semiofficial account of Anglo-American cooperation on nuclear weapons development from the British point of view, see Margaret Gowing, *Britain and Atomic Energy, 1939–1945*. For an equally readable account, see Andrew J. Pierre, *Nuclear Politics*, pp. 9–63.
4. Pierre, *Nuclear Politics*, p. 76.

a weaker power's inability to expend the resources necessary to maintain global commitments. These weapons also held out the prospect to the European countries, already resentful of the need for U.S. intervention to settle the two big European wars of the twentieth century, of releasing them from this uncomfortable dependence.

In the open societies of the West, at least, public fascination with nuclear weapons reinforced official interest, as did the secrecy surrounding them. In the public and military mind alike, this fascination was probably stimulated by the unprecedented, unimaginable destructiveness of these weapons. Even though Hamburg, Tokyo, and Dresden all sustained damage from conventional bombardment comparable to the damage in Nagasaki and Hiroshima, the speed and relative ease of nuclear bombardment, and the apparent futility of traditional air defense, place it in a different category. A minority argued that atomic bombs merely differed in degree, not in kind, from conventional ordnance and should be used accordingly. But when the time came for a high-level decision on use, as happened in the Korean War, this position did not prevail. Political decisionmakers have never viewed the nuclear weapon as a mere addition to a usable arsenal.[5] They have tended to treat these weapons with an appropriate mixture of fascination and horror, as has the general public.

Air Power Doctrine

Thus nuclear weapons probably would have captured the imagination of world leaders under any circumstances. But the development in World War II of the doctrine of air power ensured that nuclear weapons would occupy a central place in American military strategy. The importance of the advocates of strategic bombing in developing allied strategy has been described in detail elsewhere.[6] The advent of a superbomb, almost custom-made for strategic use, gave these advocates a decisive argument in persuading the American military establishment of the efficacy of strategic bombing to break the enemy's will to wage war.

5. This point was recognized early by several nongovernmental analysts. See Bernard Brodie, ed., *The Absolute Weapon*.
6. See, for example, Edward Warner, "Douhet, Mitchell, Seversky: Theories of Air Warfare," in Edward Mead Earle, ed., *Makers of Modern Strategy*, pp. 485–503; and Bernard Brodie, *Strategy in the Missile Age*, pp. 71–144.

Significantly, the advocates of air power were not confined to the United States. In Britain an influential group of air power advocates had also arisen before World War II; their influence led to the unprecedented air war against Germany, which included indiscriminate blanket assaults on civilian centers such as Dresden and Cologne.

To air power advocates the results of the air campaign in World War II spoke eloquently for the future usefulness of strategic air power. Though the final assessment of the effectiveness of that campaign was not clear-cut, both the United States and Britain went ahead with postwar military policies to emphasize the air component. Soon after the war the allocation of resources to the U.S. air forces jumped dramatically, and in a short time the U.S. Army Air Forces became a fully independent service. In Britain the Royal Air Force (RAF) Bomber Command grew considerably in size and prestige. In this environment it was natural for attention to focus on the most powerful and destructive ordnance for air delivery. The historic link between the atomic weapon and the air forces of the West is strong and stimulated awareness of the weapon's importance in the immediate postwar period.

The Soviet Threat

These factors alone would have been enough to create enormous political interest in nuclear weapons. But they interacted with perceptions of the Soviet threat to produce an obsession with nuclear power. Soon after the war, it became clear that Soviet postwar demobilization had been much less thorough than expected. U.S. estimates of the Soviet military threat to Western Europe consistently put Soviet military strength at 175 divisions.[7] No particular operational significance was placed on the fact that many, if not most, of these divisions were stationed in the western regions of the USSR, from where they would face quite a long journey to the front across a war-ravaged landscape in preparation for an attack. Furthermore, intelligence during this period was insufficiently complete to assess the actual strength of these divisions. Only much later did it become clear that Soviet divisions were smaller than their Western counterparts and that not all were equally well stocked, equipped, and trained.

7. George H. Quester, *Nuclear Diplomacy: The First Twenty-Five Years*, pp. 26–29.

But from the late 1940s through the early 1960s, the assessment of the Soviet threat argued strongly for almost complete reliance on nuclear weapons for European security. NATO could not hope to match 175 divisions on the ground. There were general doubts that the required manpower for so many divisions existed in the West. Even if it did exist, none of the Western European nations, struggling during this period to reconstitute themselves economically, socially, and politically, were willing to place such a burden on their societies.[8] This led to a sense of hopelessness about building up the conventional forces of the alliance, much to the dismay of Americans like General Omar N. Bradley who were not convinced that nuclear weapons could take the place of conventional force strength.[9] This hopelessness, in turn, fed the remarkably persistent belief that the East-West conventional force ratio inevitably favors the Warsaw Pact.

Truman's Conventional Force Efforts

Even with this background NATO's nuclear addiction was not inevitable.

It took almost four years before a consensus was reached even on the need for a formal security arrangement to protect Western Europe— only after the communist revolts in Greece and Turkey and the coup d'état in Czechoslovakia. Even then, Washington officials were reluctant to involve the United States directly in Western European security arrangements. During the negotiations between Britain and France concluding the Dunkirk Treaty of 1947, and between these two countries and the Benelux nations to form the Western European Union in 1948, the United States assumed a friendly but distant attitude. In the negotiations leading to the formation of NATO, the United States displayed caution about making any concrete military commitments. As at least one close observer has noted, neither the Americans nor the Europeans were clear, even after the North Atlantic Treaty was promulgated, whether NATO would evolve into a military organization or remain a basically political guarantee of American assistance in the event of a war in Europe.[10]

8. See, for example, Robert Endicott Osgood, *NATO*, passim.
9. Ibid., pp. 42–51.
10. Ibid.

In Washington, however, the adoption in April 1950 of NSC 68, the major policy document defining U.S. objectives in the cold war, and the outbreak soon thereafter of the Korean conflict galvanized U.S. policy toward NATO.[11] By September 1950 the signatories had decided that their alliance would indeed become a military organization. At the same time, NSC 68 provided a complete rationale for a broad and comprehensive military buildup.

Significantly, both military and political officials of the Truman administration advocated an across-the-board military buildup. Increases in conventional forces were considered essential to the NATO program. For example, U.S. Army Chief of Staff General J. Lawton Collins argued before Senate hearings in early 1951: "Without adequate army forces on the ground, backed up by tactical air forces, it would be impossible to prevent the overrunning of Europe by the tremendous land forces of the police states no matter what air and sea power we could bring against them. . . . it takes army troops on the ground to repel an invasion on the ground."[12]

Chairman of the Joint Chiefs of Staff General Omar Bradley made a similar point at these hearings. He believed the atomic deterrent was an essential part of the American military posture, but he also stated: "As time goes on, if we can build up the complete defense of Europe to a point where it would not be easy to overrun it, there would be very grave doubt as to whether or not [the Soviets] could; in my opinion, when you reach that stage the chance of war is reduced very, very materially."[13]

Secretary of State Dean Acheson's remarks at the hearings not only present a clear picture of the Truman administration's views on Western Europe's defense in the wake of the Korean conflict but also set forth views echoed by Secretary of Defense Robert S. McNamara a decade later:

11. Department of State, *Foreign Relations of the United States 1950*, vol. 1: *National Security Affairs*. An interesting interpretation of the origins and consequences of NSC 68 can be found in Samuel F. Wells, Jr., "Sounding the Tocsin: NSC 68 and the Soviet Threat," pp. 116–58, and in the response: John Lewis Gaddis and Paul Nitze, "NSC 68 and the Soviet Threat Reconsidered," pp. 170–76. See also the classic, but somewhat dated, account by Paul Y. Hammond, "NSC-68: Prologue to Rearmament," in Warner R. Schilling, Paul Y. Hammond, and Glenn H. Snyder, *Strategy, Politics, and Defense Budgets*, pp. 267–378.

12. *Assignment of Ground Forces of the United States to Duty in the European Area*, Senate Hearings, p. 154.

13. Ibid., p. 135.

Some have asked why we need to do this [build up forces in Europe]—why we can't continue to rely on the deterrent force of our retaliatory air power, and our reserve power elsewhere. Some have argued that this European defense force cannot possibly be made large enough to be effective, while others have argued that this European defense force would be so great a threat to the Soviet Union that it would be provocative. These concerns, although contradictory of each other, have led to a common line of reasoning—that we should not move ahead with our European allies in building a defense force in Western Europe.

Apart from the helpless and defenseless predicament in which this course of action—or more accurately, this course of inaction—would leave us, there are a number of powerful considerations which point to the conclusion that our own security, as well as the security of our allies in Europe, requires vigorous efforts to build an effective defense force in Europe at the earliest possible moment.

One reason why we cannot continue to rely on retaliatory air power as a sufficient deterrent is the effect of time. We have a substantial lead in air power and in atomic weapons. At the present moment, this may be the most powerful deterrent against aggression. But with the passage of time, even though we continue our advances in this field, the value of our lead diminishes.

In other words, the best use we can make of our present advantage in retaliatory air power, is to move ahead under this protective shield to build the balanced collective forces in Western Europe that will continue to deter aggression after our atomic advantage has diminished.[14]

President Truman prevailed over domestic critics and won approval to station U.S. troops in Europe as part of the growing American commitment to NATO. But he did so with the explicit understanding that the Europeans would contribute to the balance of ground forces required to offset Soviet superiority. The United States was sending only a total of six divisions; this force could hardly be expected to hold the Red Army on its own. Several senators even questioned whether such a small force, incapable of holding its own, would be worth the attendant costs and risks; the administration's firmly positive reply was contingent on Europe's help.[15] The Europeans never in fact met the manpower goals they set for themselves during this period, thereby establishing a pattern for later periods.

Tactical Nuclear Weapons

Nuclear weapons, however, were not neglected in defense planning during these years. Throughout Truman's tenure, officials referred to

14. Ibid., pp. 78–79.
15. This is the general sense of virtually all testimony from government witnesses in ibid.

nuclear weapons as the primary deterrent; under Truman the mission of the Strategic Air Command (SAC) was first articulated, and work began on fusion weapons, resulting in the 1952 test of the first fusion device. Truman also approved an initial NATO strategic concept in which nuclear weapons played a central role.[16]

Also relevant to the NATO context was the effect of the Korean conflict. In Korea U.S. army commanders became increasingly frustrated with their inability to fight a decisive ground campaign.[17] Interest turned to the potential of nuclear weapons to generate a decisive outcome on the battlefield. Even before the Korean War, the Joint Chiefs of Staff, stimulated by the interest of army officers and civilian scientists, had begun to study the feasibility of and requirements for tactical nuclear weapons, that is, those designed for use on the battlefield. The outbreak of hostilities in Korea heightened this interest; in fact, high-ranking army officers advocated the use of nuclear weapons in support of UN ground operations.[18] At about the same time, an important study at the California Institute of Technology, Project Vista, pursued under the sponsorship of the army, navy, and air force, examined the technical feasibility of "bringing the battle back to the battlefield," concluded that it could be done, and quickly became the rallying point for advocates of this new concept of nuclear weapons.[19]

This study set off a lengthy debate within the national security community over the direction of the U.S. nuclear weapons program. The choice was seen as between a tactical nuclear capability based on fission technology and a thermonuclear capability based on fusion. The proponents of the latter, SAC air power advocates, charged that efforts to "bring the battle back to the battlefield" were unnecessary and, because of the relative scarcity of fissionable material, a potential threat to the hydrogen bomb project.

Supporters of Project Vista, on the other hand, were skeptical of the

16. An interesting view of early nuclear planning can be found in Anthony Cave Brown, ed., *Dropshot*. For a review of this original NATO concept, see Lawrence S. Kaplan, *A Community of Interests*, p. 68. For a discussion of Truman's efforts on the H-bomb, see Herbert F. York, "The Debate over the Hydrogen Bomb," in Bruce M. Russett and Bruce G. Blair, eds., *Readings from Scientific American*, pp. 9–16.

17. General James M. Gavin describes his and his colleagues' frustrations over Korea in *War and Peace in the Space Age*.

18. Ibid.

19. Several volumes of Project Vista have now been declassified, and they fully agree with earlier public accounts of the project.

universal applicability of air power and saw the development of tactical nuclear weapons as an opportunity for the army to get into the nuclear business, from which circumstances had previously excluded it.[20]

While this conflict of interest, values, and experiences was intense— in no small part responsible for the revocation of the security clearance of Dr. J. Robert Oppenheimer, a Project Vista advocate—both parties in the controversy regarded European security as being intimately linked to nuclear weapons. Even though tactical nuclear weapons advocates never considered conventional capabilities to be as peripheral as air power enthusiasts did, they still thought a pure conventional defense would be helpless against a threat of the perceived magnitude of the Soviet Union. They also attributed to nuclear weapons some tactical advantages over conventional weapons. A tactical nuclear defense, it was argued, would make offensive troop concentrations normally required for conventional breakthrough on the battlefield more risky, since troop concentrations would be attractive targets for nuclear weapons. Furthermore, nuclear weapons would dramatically increase the firepower of individual units, thus reducing the manpower and cost levels required for maintaining a given level of firepower.

Eisenhower's New Look

It was in this environment that the Eisenhower administration decided to use nuclear weapons to justify dramatic cutbacks in relatively costly conventional capabilities, through a series of policies that collectively came to be called the New Look.[21]

The Republican presidential campaign of 1952 had placed heavy emphasis on a balanced federal budget, with Eisenhower himself suggesting that there was room for cuts in the defense budget. When he assumed office, he directed his top aides to reexamine the political and military strategy of the United States with an eye toward economizing wherever possible. After almost six months of careful study and inter-

20. See York, "Debate over the Hydrogen Bomb"; *In the Matter of J. Robert Oppenheimer,* Atomic Energy Commission Hearing; and Robert Jungk, *Brighter than a Thousand Suns,* pp. 260–96.

21. Two excellent accounts of the development of the New Look are Glenn H. Snyder, "The 'New Look' of 1953," in Schilling and others, *Strategy, Politics, and Defense Budgets,* pp. 379–524; and Huntington, *Common Defense,* pp. 64–87.

agency consultation, they produced the basic planning document for the New Look, NSC 162/2, which was approved by the president on October 30, 1953.[22]

NSC 162/2 began by defining a twofold central national security problem: (a) to meet the Soviet threat to U.S. security; and (b) in doing so, to avoid seriously weakening the U.S. economy or undermining its fundamental values and institutions.[23] Within these constraints, it analyzed the security implications of the world political situation for U.S. policy and planning. A complex document, NSC 162/2 contained subtleties notably absent from many of the public pronouncements it engendered. For example, the document argued that the Soviet Union was not likely to attack the United States or NATO deliberately, because these actions "would be almost certain to bring on a general war in view of U.S. commitments and intentions."[24] At some point, it predicted, the United States and the Soviet Union would each have a large enough nuclear retaliatory force to make a first strike by either side unlikely. As a result, it foresaw limitations on the very doctrine it was about to propose—the doctrine of massive retaliation. "Although Soviet fears of atomic reaction should still inhibit local aggression," the document stated,

increasing Soviet atomic capability may tend to diminish the deterrent effect of U.S. atomic power against peripheral Soviet aggression. It may also sharpen the reaction of the USSR to what it considers provocative acts of the United States. If either side should miscalculate the strength of the other's reaction, such local conflicts could grow into general war, even though neither side seeks nor desires it. To avoid this, it will in general be desirable for the United States to make clear to the USSR the kind of actions which will be almost certain to lead to this result, recognizing, however, that as general war becomes more devastating for both sides the threat to resort to it becomes less available as a sanction against local aggression.[25]

But with their eyes fixed on fiscal restraint, the authors of NSC 162/2 viewed the implications of increasing Soviet nuclear capabilities as relevant only over the long term; for the short term it was essential to cut back on manpower and conventional ground forces deployed throughout the world, leaving to friends and allies the task of building

22. See *NSC 162/2: Report to the National Security Council on Basic National Security Policy.*
23. Ibid., p. 1.
24. Ibid., p. 4.
25. Ibid., pp. 4–5.

up the necessary capabilities for local defense. The Eisenhower administration evidently did not foresee the contradictions inherent in stipulating that

since U.S. Military Assistance must eventually be reduced, it is essential that the Western European states, including West Germany, build and maintain maximum feasible defensive strength. The major deterrent to aggression against Western Europe is the manifest determination of the United States to use its atomic capability and massive retaliatory striking power if the area is attacked.[26]

Admitting the latter point undercut the incentives the Europeans might have had to provide conventional forces for their own defense. For if the major deterrent rested with U.S. atomic capability, what purpose was served by expending scarce resources on developing a coherent and strong European ground defense?

The authors of NSC 162/2 recognized this as a potential problem, yet failed to grasp its immediacy. They noted that the allies "tend to see the actual danger of Soviet aggression as less imminent than the United States does, and some have a fatalistic feeling that if it is coming, they will not be able to do much about it. In the NATO countries, many have serious doubts whether the defense requirements can be met without intolerable political and economic strains"[27] Yet the authors failed to provide specific measures to change or shape these perceptions in ways more amenable to American interests. Foreshadowing a persistent flaw in U.S. policy over the past two decades, they viewed these perceptions as an essentially unchangeable aspect of the European security problem.

The Eisenhower administration then set about to explain the policy outlined in NSC 162/2 to an unsuspecting public. The most famous episode of this campaign was the speech delivered by Secretary of State John Foster Dulles on January 12, 1954, before the Council on Foreign Relations in New York City. In rather bold terms he argued that the administration's goal of making collective security "more effective, less costly," of attaining "maximum protection at a bearable cost," drove the United States to place "more reliance on deterrent power and less dependence on local defensive power."[28] To drive the point home, Dulles focused on what he saw as the main problem:

The total cost of our security efforts [in the recent past] at home and abroad, was over $50 billion *per annum,* and involved, for 1953, a projected budgetary

26. Ibid., p. 11.
27. Ibid., p. 13.
28. John Foster Dulles, "The Evolution of Foreign Policy," pp. 107–10.

deficit of $9 billion, and $11 billion for 1954. This was on top of taxes comparable
to wartime taxes; and the dollar was depreciating in effective value. Our allies
were similarly weighed down. This could not be continued for long without grave
budgetary, economic, and social consequences.

But before military planning could be changed, the President and his advisers,
as represented by the National Security Council, had to take some basic policy
decisions. This has been done. The basic decision was to depend primarily upon
a great capacity to retaliate, instantly, by means and at places of our choosing.
. . . As a result it is now possible to get, and share, more basic security at less
cost.[29]

In the weeks that followed, many publicly questioned the wisdom of
such a policy. Several civilian defense thinkers wrote influential essays
exploring the weaknesses of Dulles's pronouncements, thereby generating many critical analyses.[30] They pointed out that the historical record
of U.S. behavior in the postwar world suggested the profound reluctance
with which U.S. leaders had considered the use of nuclear weapons,
thus severely undermining the credibility of the threat to use nuclear
weapons against all but the very gravest "local aggression." Looking
toward the future, the critics wondered how effective such a threat
would be in the face of the ever-growing Soviet strategic arsenal.

These were criticisms that had been largely foreseen in internal U.S.
government deliberations. A careful reading of NSC 162/2 reveals
considerably more subtlety than Dulles's audience at the Council on
Foreign Relations could have recognized. A gap existed between "declaratory" policy and "action" policy that, intentional or not, was
gradually closed.[31] However, Eisenhower and his aides succeeded in
creating the impression, clearly intentional, that the United States was
placing greater emphasis on nuclear weapons to replace the costly
burdens of conventional defense efforts.

This new policy was not merely declaratory; Eisenhower substantially
reallocated resources to correspond more closely with these priorities.
He reduced total military manpower during the first three years of his
first term from 3.45 million to 2.84 million, much of which reflects the
demobilization after the Korean War. At the same time, however, the
air force grew by 20,000 men, the only service to gain in manpower

29. Ibid., p. 108.
30. William W. Kaufmann, "The Requirements of Deterrence," in William W.
Kaufmann, ed., *Military Policy and National Security*, pp. 12–38.
31. This distinction is borrowed from Paul H. Nitze, "Atoms, Strategy and Policy,"
pp. 187–98.

during this period. Similarly, army and navy budgets were slashed during fiscal 1955, while air force expenditures increased by some $800 million.[32] There is no clearer evidence of Eisenhower's commitment in deed to pronouncements and promises of the 1953–55 period.

The most zealous New Look advocates were unable to sustain public enthusiasm for their policies. By 1956, when Admiral Arthur W. Radford, fully in keeping with the substance and spirit of NSC 162/2, proposed to cut military manpower by another 800,000, to beef up reliance on long-range strategic bombers, and to withdraw U.S. troops from Europe, the reaction from Congress and even from other Eisenhower aides was outrage. The administration had reached the limit of politically feasible defense cutbacks.[33]

The British Atomic Program, 1939–57

As the United States began to integrate nuclear weapons into its strategic concepts, Great Britain was gaining nuclear experience that would have significant consequences for the development of NATO's nuclear addiction.[34]

The story of Britain's nuclear addiction, already a central fixture of British national policy by the mid-1950s, is not without elements of pathos. It was the British who first conceived of an atomic bomb project. Refugee German scientists had brought the implications of nuclear fission research to the attention of British scientists and government officials as early as 1939.[35] By 1940 a large scientific study group in England, known as the Maud Committee, had concluded that a fission weapon was probably feasible and certainly desirable.[36] On this basis, the British government authorized research with the object of producing such a weapon. The Maud Committee's report was read with interest by the government and scientific community in the United States. Although not formally in the war, the United States asked to participate in the

32. Dwight D. Eisenhower, *The White House Years: Mandate for Change, 1953–1956*, p. 452.

33. Huntington, *Common Defense*, pp. 93, 99.

34. Excellent sources for this subject are Gowing, *Britain and Atomic Energy*; Pierre, *Nuclear Politics*; and A. J. R. Groom, *British Thinking about Nuclear Weapons*.

35. Gowing, *Britain and Atomic Energy*, pp. 33–42.

36. Ibid., pp. 45–89.

British project, eager to take advantage of the substantial British head start. Equally eager to retain independence in this sphere of national security policy, Britain rejected the American request, agreeing only to exchanges of technical information.[37]

By 1943 this situation was reversed. The British project had bogged down from the outset because of insufficient scientific, technological, and material resources. Britain now turned to the United States with an offer to combine forces in a joint project. By this time, however, the U.S. atomic bomb project had progressed to the point where no outside help was needed. And some important policymakers were reluctant to share the project with Britain for security reasons. Feeling no particular need for Britain's assistance, doubting the reliability of its security system, and resenting its initial haughty rebuff, the United States rejected the offer.[38]

Without adequate resources to complete his project, Prime Minister Winston Churchill continued to petition for collaboration on the Manhattan Project. By the time of the Quebec Conference of 1943, he had won this battle—at the expense of the independent development of Britain's postwar commercial nuclear industry.[39] Even then, the British contribution, though significant, was less than Churchill had hoped. At the end of the war the United States emerged with atomic bombs; the British emerged only with technical knowledge gained from two years of collaboration.

The new prime minister, Clement R. Attlee, tried to gain an extension of the Quebec collaboration agreement, to which the new U.S. president, Harry Truman, felt no special obligation.[40] In late 1945 there still seemed hope for obtaining a British bomb through American assistance. But by 1946 Congress had begun to take a look at nuclear energy, and in a fit of nationalism passed the McMahon Act, which prohibited collaboration with *any* foreign powers on nuclear weapons.

The blow was bitter for Attlee, who then decided to proceed with independent production of a British bomb. In the later 1940s some

37. Groom, *British Thinking about Nuclear Weapons*, pp. 3–5; and Gowing, *Britain and Atomic Energy*, pp. 124 ff.

38. Gowing, *Britain and Atomic Energy*, pp. 147–77.

39. Ibid., pp. 164–77.

40. Pierre, *Nuclear Politics*, pp. 77–86. Indeed, there is some question whether he was even aware of the details of the arrangement, which may have been hidden from him by Major General Leslie R. Groves. See Leon V. Sigal, "The Politics of War Termination in the United States and Japan" (unpublished manuscript).

American-British nuclear collaboration on the basic scientific level was renewed, only to end abruptly when the Klaus Fuchs espionage scandal burst in Britain. At the height of cold war tensions over Berlin and Eastern Europe in 1949, the United States stationed nuclear-capable bombers in England. Their presence made the collaboration of the Strategic Air Command and the Bomber Command, which had grown during the war, easier to extend when the McMahon Act was amended in 1958.

Slowly the British scientific and military communities made their own way, and when Churchill regained office in 1952, he inherited from his predecessor a fission weapon project that was nearly complete. A few months later, Britain detonated its first atomic bomb (some three years after the Soviet Union), thus formally joining the nuclear club. Two years later, when apprised of America's fusion detonation some fifteen months after the fact, Churchill determined to follow this route too. By 1957 Britain had a thermonuclear device.

Even this thumbnail sketch of the early years of the British nuclear weapons program amply illustrates the awkwardness of Britain's position. In a relatively short period—from 1939 to 1942—the United Kingdom had fallen from a position of relative independence to one of clear dependence. Britain would only gradually become accustomed to this new state of affairs. But in the meantime its leaders harbored strong beliefs about the salvation to be found in possessing nuclear weapons. These must be examined in order to explain why London devoted such time and effort, under such adverse circumstances, to developing its own nuclear arsenal.

Aside from its plain desire to defeat Nazi Germany, England had hoped that these weapons would provide tangible, even decisive advantages in the postwar world. This was apparent at the outset of the British nuclear program. The Maud Committee's report included the rather telling comment that "even if the war should end before the bombs are ready the effort would not be wasted, except in the unlikely event of complete disarmament, since no nation would care to risk being caught without a weapon of such decisive possibilities."[41]

The scientists responsible for this assessment were not alone. Sir John Anderson, one of Churchill's chief aides on nuclear matters, remarked: "[Atomic weapons] will give control of the world to whatever

41. Gowing, *Britain and Atomic Energy*, p. 395.

country obtains them first."[42] This view was apparently shared by his boss. According to all reliable sources, Churchill was immediately impressed by these weapons. His reaction to the news of the first successful U.S. nuclear test, while he was at the Potsdam Conference, has been recorded by Herbert Feis. "Stimson," he declared to the U.S. secretary of war, "What was gunpowder? Trivial. What was electricity? Meaningless. This atomic bomb is the second coming in wrath."[43] Churchill's obsession with the growing might of the Soviet Union and the dangers this held for Britain's postwar position, especially given the uncertainties of postwar U.S. behavior, only heightened his interest in the weapons. As Sir John Anderson said, "We cannot afford after the war to face the future without this weapon and rely entirely on America should Russia or some other power develop it."[44]

Attlee, different from Churchill in most other ways, apparently shared the same fears about American retrenchment. When questioned on this subject some years later, Attlee recalled: "We had to hold up our position *vis-à-vis* the Americans. We couldn't allow ourselves to be wholly in their hands, and their position wasn't awfully clear always . . . at that time we had to bear in mind that there was always the possibility of their withdrawing and becoming isolationist once again. The manufacture of the British atom bomb was therefore at that stage essential to our defence."[45]

It requires no great effort to imagine Attlee's bitterness at the decision of the U.S. Congress to clamp down on nuclear collaboration with all foreign powers. Some have even argued that had the United States not precipitately severed its special relationship with Britain—that is, had it not adopted the McMahon restrictions, had it been more willing to implement the Quebec agreement, and had it concerned itself directly with British and European security after the war—Britain might well not be a nuclear power today.[46]

Once British leaders chose to pursue this means to postwar power, they found the logic of massive retaliation even more compelling than U.S. leaders did. Britain was less able to afford a standing army and the

42. Quoted in Groom, *British Thinking about Nuclear Weapons*, p. 9.
43. Feis, *Between War and Peace*, p. 172.
44. Groom, *British Thinking about Nuclear Weapons*, p. 9.
45. Attlee is quoted in Edward Francis-Williams, *A Prime Minister Remembers*, pp. 118–19.
46. Pierre, *Nuclear Politics*, p. 77.

financial and resource burden of maintaining its global commitments
with conventional forces. Even though it agreed to meet the goals set
for its forces at the NATO meeting in Lisbon in February 1952, it was
determined to avoid having to fulfill this commitment.[47] Whether its 1952
atomic policy was the result of an objective military assessment of its
strategic requirements, or rather an attempt to find some way to ration-
alize its inability to fulfill its Lisbon pledge, is impossible to know with
certainty.

This policy, set in mid-1952 by the British chiefs of staff at Churchill's
direction, was formulated in a paper called "Global Strategy."[48] In it
the chiefs essentially argued the NSC 162/2 line, that in a time of great
fiscal restraints, nuclear retaliatory power offered a relatively inexpen-
sive, affordable alternative to a deterrent based on a large standing
conventional army and in fact was *more* suitable for deterrence against
the huge, inevitably superior Red Army. The paper was significant in
part because it predated NSC 162/2 by more than a year.

Air Marshall Sir John Slessor brought "Global Strategy" to Washington in the summer of 1952 in order to brief his American military
counterparts. But the Joint Chiefs were unreceptive. Bradley and others
viewed the report as a transparent excuse for Britain's falling short of its
Lisbon commitments. Unlike their successors, Truman's Joint Chiefs
also were concerned about what seemed like excessive reliance on air
power to deter Soviet actions across a broad spectrum. Nevertheless,
Sir John left copies of the report behind in Washington, copies that may
have influenced the next administration in formulating its New Look
policy.

In Britain it was difficult for the prime minister to implement the new
policy fully. Although the British largely favored developing a hydrogen
bomb—clearly called for by "Global Strategy"—they did not agree
about cutting back the army and navy budgets. But by 1957, because of
the Suez crisis and the continuing dissolution of the empire, even this
was practicable, as Defense Minister Duncan Sandys set out to show.
His 1957 White Paper on Defense, which cut army and navy budgets
substantially, was heralded as a complete shift in British defense policy;

47. At its February 1952 ministerial meeting in Lisbon, NATO agreed to a force
goal of 96 standing divisions by 1954. See Osgood, *NATO*, pp. 87–91.
48. Ibid., pp. 87–89.

it really represented nothing more than the realization of the 1952 "Global Strategy" paper.[49]

By the mid-1950s not only had London overcome many obstacles to arrive at a nuclear capability; it had beaten the United States to the punch in adopting a "New Look" of its own.

NATO's Nuclear Decision

This intense interest in nuclear weapons was bound to have some effect on NATO's defense policy.[50] After all, the United States, with its New Look, was the as yet unchallenged leader of the alliance. And Britain was not alone among European nations in its inability (or unwillingness) to build up to the Lisbon force goals. The almost decade-old obsession with nuclear weapons and the simultaneous reluctance to expend scarce resources and manpower in an allegedly futile attempt to match the conventional forces of the Soviet Union led, by the mid-1950s, to the adoption of a New Look for NATO.

For the military planners at Supreme Headquarters Allied Powers Europe (SHAPE), this entailed the development of a strong tactical nuclear posture. U.S. Army Chief of Staff General J. Lawton Collins had expressed the belief as early as 1952 that nuclear weapons for use on the battlefield would "result ultimately in the ability to do the job with a smaller number of divisions."[51] This was a politically awkward position for the Truman administration, since it threatened to undermine whatever motivation the Europeans might still have had to build up to the Lisbon force goals. But it became the dominant position under President Eisenhower, despite growing evidence that nuclear battle would actually require *more* manpower than conventional battle conditions.

Concurrent with the change in policy—perhaps driving it—was the rapid technical development of nuclear artillery, rockets, and missiles for battlefield use between 1953 and 1955. This development was

49. Laurence W. Martin, "The Market for Strategic Ideas in Britain," pp. 23–41. See also Sir John Slessor, "British Defense Policy," pp. 551–63.
50. This section is based largely on Osgood, *NATO*, pp. 105–26.
51. Ibid., p. 105.

accompanied by an avowed American willingness to share these tactical weapons with NATO allies, in ways as yet unspecified.

Throughout early 1954 General Alfred M. Gruenther, Supreme Allied Commander Europe (SACEUR), presided over a study of the feasibility and desirability of shifting NATO's strategy to place primary focus on nuclear weapons, in the spirit of NSC 162/2. He had apparently already concluded that such a shift was desirable; the resulting report supported his belief. Though never declassified, it was leaked to the press in July 1954. As reported, its conclusions provided ample justification for building a strong NATO nuclear posture:

1. Warfare in the future would inevitably be atomic;
2. The first atomic targets would be armed forces and military installations rather than major centers of population;
3. The peak of destruction would come at the outset of the war;
4. Therefore, the outcome would be determined by the active forces-in-being.[52]

In August SHAPE recommended a major NATO reorganization to adjust for the replacement of high conventional manpower ceilings with new, lower, nuclear-oriented manpower ceilings. This became the basis for the North Atlantic Council's December 1954 decision authorizing NATO military commanders to plan to use nuclear weapons against the Warsaw Pact irrespective of whether the Pact used them. Within a three-year period, it also led to the formal adoption of plans and strategies, in the form of documents MC 70 and MC 14/2, to revise the Lisbon goals downward and to respond to Soviet aggression against NATO by using nuclear weapons at the outset of the conflict.

Deputy Supreme Commander Field Marshall Bernard Montgomery summarized these new plans early on, in a pithily worded address to a gathering at London's Royal United Services Institute in late 1954:

I want to make it absolutely clear that we at SHAPE are basing all our planning on using atomic and thermonuclear weapons in our own defense. With us it is no longer: "They may possibly be used." It is very definitely: "They will be used, if we are attacked." In fact, we have reached the point of no return as regards the use of atomic and thermonuclear weapons in a hot war.[53]

Whether this new policy assumed that a nuclear war would be fought and won primarily on the battlefields of central Europe, or whether it assumed that a NATO nuclear arsenal would be used primarily as a trip

52. Ibid., p. 109.
53. Ibid., p. 110.

wire to trigger a strategic attack by the United States on targets deep in the Soviet homeland, remained for the moment unclear. But greater emphasis was put on the first assumption, which became the focus of much European debate, as seen in chapter 3.

MC 70 and MC 14/2 reflected a substantial shift away from the strategy of the early 1950s. This shift is best highlighted by comparing two statements, one by General Bradley on his understanding of NATO strategy and plans in 1952, the other by SACEUR General Norstad in describing the 1957 version of NATO strategy and plans.

In front of a House Appropriations Committee hearing in 1952, General Bradley described NATO's military objectives as follows:

To build sufficient force as soon as practicable to act as a deterrent to further aggression; to create sufficient power to prevent disaster in the event war is forced upon us; to provide an immediate capability for quick and strong retaliation in case of an attack upon us; and, to produce a firm base upon which to build, as quickly as possible, that power necessary to assure victory should we be forced to engage in all-out conflict. These are our basic objectives—any provisions short of these would invite disaster.[54]

The general evidently believed in the need for military strength across the board and saw a definite role for conventional mobilization to work side by side with nuclear retaliation. For Bradley, maintaining a warm mobilization base to enable NATO eventually to roll back Warsaw Pact troops from occupied territory was the most important requirement.[55]

In his testimony before the Senate Foreign Relations Committee in 1958, SACEUR General Lauris Norstad laid bare the planning assumptions behind document MC 70:

Our capacity for decisive retaliation in case we are attacked continues to be the most effective single element in the deterrent. The bulk of the forces that would carry out this task are national forces, such as the United States Strategic Air Command, the United Kingdom Bomber Command, and certain naval forces. Although they are not directly assigned to NATO, nonetheless all of our planning efforts in Allied Command Europe are based on the conviction that these retaliatory forces are effective, and will continue to be effective.[56]

He then outlined the functions of NATO's "shield"—those forces assigned to hold the front line in Europe. In broad terms it was intended to contribute to the deterrent and to increase NATO's political and military flexibility. But the shield's main task—a "limited but highly

54. *Department of Defense Appropriations for 1952*, House Hearings, pt. 1, p. 204.
55. Ibid., p. 205.
56. *Mutual Security Act of 1958*, Senate Hearings, pp. 186–87.

critical" one—was "to hold an attack until the total weight of the retaliatory power could be brought to bear. . . . I mention this one [task] first, because it is impossible to overemphasize how important is this particular function to our allies in Europe."[57]

Here is the essential difference between NATO strategy before and after the New Look. By 1957, NATO had determined that its ground forces—not conventional, since they were armed with nuclear weapons to offset their supposedly small size relative to those of the Pact—would not seek to achieve the tactical military objective of defeating the enemy on the ground. Instead, those forces would buy the time required to implement strategic nuclear retaliation. NATO's "shield" was relegated to protecting the "sword" of national nuclear arsenals. Whether this strategy could long be acceptable to the allies—or even to Norstad and the United States—is the subject of the next chapter.

57. Ibid., p. 187.

CHAPTER THREE

The Loss of Confidence

NATO HELD its unprecedented heads-of-government summit meeting in December 1957 in an atmosphere of crisis. For the previous five years NATO's strategic plans had become increasingly dependent on strategic nuclear retaliation in response to any Warsaw Pact aggression. Yet neither Europeans nor Americans were now confident that such dependence constituted an adequate deterrent. This crisis of confidence increasingly dominated NATO deliberations over the next decade, driving the United States to embark on many initiatives to restore confidence. Why and how did the crisis come about?

When viewed from the perspective of Washington, the Europeans seemed to have conflicting concerns. On the one hand, they worried that the United States would not execute strategic retaliation in response to aggression against Western Europe; for Washington to do so would be suicidal. On the other hand, they worried about what would happen if the United States did execute a strategic retaliation in response to aggression against Europe, because that could provoke Soviet retaliation against the entire NATO alliance; the Europeans would have had no influence on a decision that would reduce their society to rubble.[1]

The natural American temptation is to dismiss these conflicting fears as a manifestation of European schizophrenia. But this would trivialize and oversimplify the problem. To hold both fears simultaneously was not necessarily a sign of irrationality. More important, different European countries held different views; what appeared to be an internally inconsistent "European" view was often simply conflicting national views. This chapter examines the loss of confidence from the perspective of three major allied governments, France, Great Britain, and West

1. Robert Endicott Osgood, *NATO*, pp. 145–46.

Germany; traces the shift in U.S. and NATO policy as a result of this loss of confidence; and summarizes the effect of the Suez crisis and the launch of sputnik, which placed the confidence issue at the head of the alliance agenda.

France

The French attitude toward the U.S. nuclear guarantee as it developed through 1957 is best understood in the context of the development of French nuclear weapons policy and French participation in NATO.[2]

The events leading up to France's decision to develop its own nuclear weapons began in the early 1930s, with the growth of a sophisticated nuclear scientific community within France. Its leader, Joliot-Curie, pioneered French fission research, and when World War II broke out he offered to aid the Canadian and British atomic weapons research program. That the Americans showed no eagerness to accept French aid can best be explained by fears aroused over Joliot-Curie's dalliance with the Communist party, which foreclosed any French intimacy with the American atomic program and sowed the seeds for even greater constraints on postwar cooperation between the two countries.

Soon after the war Joliot-Curie was placed in charge of the new Commissariat à l'Energie Atomique, created in November 1945 by de Gaulle to direct the French postwar nuclear effort. Throughout the 1945–54 period this effort—the leadership of which fell from Joliot-Curie's hands in 1950 over the issue of his communist ties—consisted almost entirely of basic research and plans for commercial nuclear power development. Though the French military acquired an abiding interest in a French nuclear capability during this period, political leaders after de Gaulle showed little interest in a program to develop it; they were primarily concerned with rebuilding their war-ravaged country and with reconstituting the fabric of French economic and political life.

By 1954, however, conditions had changed sufficiently to lay the

2. Two indispensable sources on this period are Lawrence Scheinman, *Atomic Energy Policy in France under the Fourth Republic,* and Wilfrid L. Kohl, *French Nuclear Diplomacy.* Other useful sources are George A. Kelly, "The Political Background of the French A-Bomb," pp. 284–306; Wolf Mendl, *Deterrence and Persuasion;* and Ciro Zoppo, "France as a Nuclear Power," in R. N. Rosecrance, ed., *The Dispersion of Nuclear Weapons,* pp. 113–56.

groundwork for a massive public and private debate within France over whether to proceed with a nuclear weapons program. By then, France was well along the road to economic recovery. The economic effort required to produce a nuclear arsenal was beginning to appear possible. Moreover, Great Britain had joined the United States and the Soviet Union in the nuclear club. As a result, French officials were becoming increasingly sensitive to what they considered France's secondary status within NATO, particularly with respect to its ally across the channel. To make matters worse, France was involved in a costly and ultimately unsuccessful military effort to retain control over Indochina. When France requested U.S. aid during the siege of Dien Bien Phu, the United States considered using nuclear weapons to help break the siege and then backed off from any direct support.[3] Finally, the effort to rearm Germany and to bring it into NATO was well under way. During the volatile debate over the proposal to include a rearmed Germany in a new European Defense Community, all France's old fears of its traditional enemy resurfaced, causing a proposal to be shelved that, ironically, had been initiated by the French government.[4]

With these events as background, a heated public and private debate erupted in France between 1954 and 1956 over whether France should develop its own nuclear weapons. Seeing the opportunities afforded by the events of 1950–54, military officers took an active part in promoting French nuclear status. Among the many articles to appear at this time by such generals as Paul Stehlin and André Beaufre, the writings of General Pierre Gallois stand out in their forcefulness and influence.[5]

Gallois' argument rested on two related points. He first argued that once a nation possessing nuclear weapons becomes vulnerable to nuclear attack from enemy countries, its ability to extend the nuclear deterrent to its allies is eliminated; the threat to commit actions tantamount to nuclear suicide in defense of other nations is unreliable—that is, no political leader could be counted on to do this—and thus incredible. In

3. General Maxwell D. Taylor, *The Uncertain Trumpet*, p. 24; and Kelly, "Political Background of the French A-Bomb," p. 287.

4. For a quick overview of the controversy surrounding the European Defense Community proposal, see Osgood, *NATO*, pp. 92–98.

5. Gallois's writings of the 1950s are almost all in French, having appeared in journals like *Révue de Défense Nationale*. For the purpose of this chapter, his 1961 book, *The Balance of Terror*, has been used. It is generally agreed that the views expressed there are identical to those expressed in the late 1950s.

The Balance of Terror General Gallois restates the theme that ran through his (and others') arguments in the mid-1950s:

Since the United States itself is vulnerable to Soviet ballistic missiles, the automatic nature of American intervention is less certain. If, therefore, America were to come to the support of a friendly nation, she would be placed in a difficult situation from a military point of view. She would either have to destroy her adversary's reprisal forces—and such an operation would be all the less feasible because these forces, long since alerted, would be protected by underground storage or mobility—or else suffer their terrible effects. To annihilate the Soviet cities would present no operational difficulties but would not paralyze the Soviet reprisal, which would be launched at once. Threatened with enormous damages if she were to come to the aid of Great Britain, America might hesitate. And once the likelihood of American intervention was in doubt, the U.S.S.R. would recover a share of its freedom of action with regard to the United Kingdom.

It is, in fact, plausible for the potential aggressor to make the following calculation: if seriously threatened a powerful adversary would probably use his megatons of destruction in retaliation. But in a question of intervening for the sake of another country, even a friendly power, hesitation is particularly likely, for the laws of nuclear strategy are unfavorable to such intervention.[6]

The second part of Gallois' thesis is that since nuclear offensive forces are likely to become increasingly invulnerable and hence unattractive targets for strategic retaliation, deterrence (or "dissuasion") rests on the counter-city potential of a nation's nuclear arsenal.

Confronting Soviet (or American) power, all nations are in the same class. Whether they possess, tomorrow, a thousand Atlas, Titan, or Minuteman missiles, like the United States, or fifty Thor missiles like Great Britain, they could base their security only on an anti-city strategy. In other words, faced with an alternative of servitude or invasion, a nation could gamble on dissuasion for its independence. But it would have to run the risk of being annihilated, for if it failed the policy of dissuasion would lead to total destruction. And this is as true for the Great Powers among themselves as for the Small and Medium Powers in relation to the Great Powers.[7]

Arguments like these provided a strategic rationale on which to proceed with the development of a French nuclear arsenal. But they were not the only ones; political constituencies favored French nuclear independence for six reasons:

1. Nuclear weapons were a symbol of national prestige in the international community.

2. They would provide France with greater leverage and input into the setting of Western strategy.

6. Gallois, *Balance of Terror*, pp. 139–40.
7. Ibid., p. 199.

3. With respect to other issues, possession of nuclear weapons would provide France with political leverage.

4. Nuclear weapons would reverse the trend toward Anglo-American domination of NATO.

5. They would boost the morale of a French officer corps shattered by the experience of Dien Bien Phu.

6. They would give France a greater voice in the increasingly prestigious arms-control discussions between East and West.[8]

The opponents of the adoption of a French nuclear force favored four arguments:

1. Nuclear weapons were immoral in their indiscriminate destructiveness.

2. The French economy was too weak to withstand the drain on resources necessary for a serious weapons effort; more fruitful efforts would be in the direction of developing a full-scale nuclear energy program.

3. France could afford to build no more than a primitive nuclear arsenal incapable of fulfilling political or strategic objectives.

4. The development of a French nuclear force would put even greater distance between France and the rest of NATO, and could also, by stimulating similar efforts in other NATO nations, seriously erode alliance unity.[9]

These arguments notwithstanding, France's formal decision to proceed with a nuclear weapons program was not simply a result of a resolution of this public and private debate. In retrospect it appears that by 1955 a substantial momentum had developed within the bureaucracies and the military to produce nuclear weapons, a momentum slowed neither by the debate nor by the weakness and political indecisiveness of the previous few governments of the Fourth Republic.[10] By December 1956 the government of Guy Mollet had made a formal, if secret, commitment to proceed with a nuclear weapons program and had established a committee within the Commissariat à l'Energie Atomique to implement this decision. In late 1957 the French government went public with its decision.

8. Kelly, "Political Background of the French A-Bomb," p. 292. See also Kohl, *French Nuclear Diplomacy*, pp. 29–44.

9. Ibid.

10. This is the argument advanced by Scheinman, *Atomic Energy Policy in France*, pp. 94–95, and supported by Kohl, *French Nuclear Diplomacy*, p. 7.

It is tempting to view the Gallois arguments about the credibility of the American nuclear guarantee as the main justification for the development of a French nuclear force. But as subsequent events demonstrated, the political arguments set forth above (which took on new and important nuances with de Gaulle's return to power in 1958) were at least as important as the strategic arguments made by the French military. In any event, executive leadership was so ineffectual during the last years of the Fourth Republic that elaborate political and strategic justifications were not needed to ensure the December 1956 decision. Even so, as the public debate raged in France the prolific pens of the French military placed these arguments on center stage, both within France and within the alliance as a whole. They set the intellectual context for American initiatives that were to come.

The nuclear debate in France was influenced in no small way by its general position within the alliance.[11] In the aftermath of World War II, French political and military planners saw two future threats to French security: the Soviet Union and West Germany. Throughout the later 1940s, as the Western Europeans began to seriously consider plans for ensuring Western European security, France insisted on plans that took *both* potential threats into account. The Dunkirk Treaty of 1947 was directed against both the Soviet Union and Germany; and only because of American and Belgian intervention did the Brussels Pact of 1948, which established the Western European Union, avoid including anti-German language in its text.[12]

France was thus understandably sensitive about bringing West Germany into NATO. When the French government initiated discussion of a European Defense Community that would include West Germany, it suffered a severe political defeat at the hands of its own National Assembly. Its acquiescence to German entry into NATO in 1955, and to Bonn's subsequent rearmament, was a grudging acceptance of several unpleasant realities: Anglo-American dominance of the alliance; the military requirements of defense along the central front; and the growing Western acceptance of the new Germany back into the family of nations.

11. For a broad review of the many issues confronting France within the context of the alliance during this period, see Edgar S. Furniss, Jr., *France, Troubled Ally.* See also Furniss, "France, NATO, and European Security," pp. 544–58.
12. The full story of the Western European Union and the Dunkirk Treaty, from the U.S. perspective, can be found in U.S. Department of State, *Foreign Relations of the United States, 1948,* vol. 3: *Western Europe.*

France extracted a price for its acquiescence—Bonn's public commitment never to produce nuclear weapons on its own soil.

Even with this pledge in hand, France strove to change these unpleasant realities. How it would proceed to do so was left for the Fifth Republic under de Gaulle, who had a clear and compelling alternate vision and the strength to chart a new course.

So by 1957 France had embarked on its own nuclear weapons program, justified in part by vocal claims that the U.S. nuclear guarantee could not be counted on, and fed by resentment over the subordinate role allegedly forced on it by Anglo-Saxon domination of the alliance.

West Germany

The loss of West Germany's confidence in the U.S. nuclear guarantee by 1957 was the result both of broad trends in the development of West Germany within the Atlantic alliance and of specific events like the Carte Blanche military exercise of 1955.

There were many political reasons for West German accession to the North Atlantic Treaty Organization in 1954.[13] Important to stress was Chancellor Konrad Adenauer's fundamental objective of bringing his country into the Western bloc on an equal basis with other members. At the same time, his quest for German reunification placed sensitive constraints on how far Adenauer could afford to move in an anti-Soviet direction. He also had to work against the constraints imposed by the legacy of World War II, in particular the reluctance of the rest of Western Europe to permit untrammeled German rearmament. This reluctance, which in France defeated the idea of a European Defense Community with West Germany as a member, was one of the main reasons for

13. The amount of literature on West Germany's admission into NATO, on its policies on rearmament and nuclear weapons, and on general foreign policy issues during the 1950–57 period is vast, reflecting a general preoccupation with the central problem of Germany in any discussion of Western security. The following works are a small but representative sampling of this literature: Gordon A. Craig, "NATO and the New German Army," in William W. Kaufmann, ed., *Military Policy and National Security*, pp. 194–232; Craig, "Germany and NATO, 1950–58," in Klaus Knorr, ed., *NATO and American Security*, pp. 236–59; Catherine McArdle Kelleher, *Germany and the Politics of Nuclear Weapons;* James L. Richardson, *Germany and the Atlantic Alliance;* and Hans Speier, *German Rearmament and Atomic War.*

Germany's explicit pledge, on accession to NATO, not to produce its own nuclear weapons.

This is not to imply that the Adenauer government had previously been contemplating such manufacture. Under the Allied occupation German scientists had been effectively prohibited from pursuing any but the most basic kind of nuclear research. Though these controls were gradually lifted after the formation of the Federal Republic of Germany, German scientists continued to operate as if controls were in effect. There is no evidence throughout the early 1950s of any political interest in these weapons; Adenauer was content to remain virtually ignorant about this revolution in military technology. Both he and his party focused efforts in the military sphere on rebuilding a national consensus for a new German army—no mean feat, considering the prevailing antimilitary attitude of the German population and decimation and demoralization of the German officer corps.

To this end, Adenauer and the military used the Lisbon force goals to provide a basis for rebuilding West Germany's conventional armed forces within an integrated NATO command. For Germany, these goals called for 12 standing army divisions: from 1955 on this objective dominated Germany's efforts to contribute to the alliance. Preoccupied with this task, Germany seemed to take little notice of the changes in military strategy heralded by nuclear weapons or of the changes in alliance strategy adopted under the New Look. NATO's 1954 decision to introduce nuclear weapons into NATO Europe, and to begin integrating them into alliance defense plans, went without much comment in German circles. The embryonic German Defense Ministry, headed by Theodore Blank, went about planning its 12 divisions as if nuclear weapons had not been invented, in spite of the growing literature available to German leaders about the constraints atomic warfare would place on ground warfare organization and operations.

Operation Carte Blanche pulled the proverbial ostrich's head out of the sand. The rather dramatic revelation in press and parliament that a simulated NATO operation using 355 nuclear weapons in defense of Western Europe had "resulted" in 1.7 million German deaths and 3.5 million Germans wounded forced the issue of NATO's nuclear strategy onto the German consciousness. A volatile debate in the Bundestag ensued. Opposition leaders pointed to the futility of German rearmament in determining the outcome of a nuclear war in Europe. It seemed manifestly obvious to them that any war in Europe involving nuclear weapons would result in unmitigated disaster for the German people.[14]

The Adenauer government stuck by its plans to rearm, insisting that the possibility of nuclear operations on German soil did not render a strong conventional defensive capability superfluous. At first the government even denied the need to reexamine its ground force planning assumptions in light of the possible characteristics of a nuclear battlefield. But because of exposure to the burgeoning academic and public literature on nuclear ground campaigns, or because of exposure to NATO planning documents on West Germany's formal accession to the alliance, the government gradually accepted the need to revise these assumptions. By the end of 1955 the Defense Ministry had decided to reduce the size of West Germany's divisions to give them greater mobility, to create logistical and command flexibility so as to permit detachment of smaller units from the main body of the division, and to institute various other changes designed to make the new West German army compatible with NATO's New Look.[15] But the Adenauer government, while able to prevail in this first round of the German debate, had only pushed the opposition temporarily underground. The debate was to resurface two years later in more vitriolic form.

Throughout the 1955–56 period Adenauer and Blank seemed confused about the implications of the New Look for West Germany. As late as August 1956, Adenauer believed that nuclear weapons could not compensate for conventional strength in a war with the Warsaw Pact.[16] To this extent he had evidently not absorbed the main implication of the New Look. At the same time, he apparently believed that membership within NATO would *remove* West Germany from the theater of operations during a NATO–Warsaw Pact war.[17] His reasoning on this point was never clear; perhaps he believed that any war between the two blocs would quickly become a strategic war between the United States and the Soviet Union. From the narrowly construed West German national interest, this was a highly desirable alternative to a shooting war, either nuclear or conventional, taking place on German territory. Yet such a

14. Speier, *German Rearmament and Atomic War*, pp. 182–84.

15. Ibid., p. 192.

16. Ibid., pp. 15, 47. See also Kelleher, *Germany and the Politics of Nuclear Weapons,* p. 47.

17. Speier, *German Rearmament and Atomic War*, pp. 182–83.

position would obviate the need for a strong German conventional force. That Adenauer did not accept this conclusion is ample evidence of the confused state of German thought on strategic affairs during this period.

In mid-1956 the public leak of Admiral Radford's plan to withdraw U.S. troops from Europe forced the Adenauer government to come to terms with these issues. The prospect of the withdrawal of U.S. troops from Germany angered Adenauer, especially because he had come away from a recent meeting with Eisenhower with assurances to the contrary. It finally dawned on Adenauer and his advisers that even though the Radford plan had no official support from the U.S. chief executive, it reflected a fundamental change in U.S. (and NATO) strategy, away from a reliance on conventional forces and toward a reliance on deterrence by threat of nuclear retaliation. For a while Adenauer clung to his position that nuclear weapons would not compensate for conventional weakness; but under pressure from the military, from some of his own aides, and from the U.S. government, he did an about-face in late 1956. He appointed Franz Joseph Strauss to replace Blank at the Defense Ministry; Strauss was noted for his early appreciation of the new strategy and for his forceful advocacy of a German role in the disposition of alliance nuclear weapons. In December 1956 the Adenauer government joined Britain and France in requesting access to U.S. nuclear weapons under NATO auspices.

The motivations behind this shift by Adenauer are complex. Perhaps German officials, particularly Strauss, did share some of the French fears about the reliability of the U.S. guarantee. However, Adenauer's program of reunifying Germany within the Western bloc, and of undermining the extreme nationalist tendencies that had brought disaster on the German nation, led him to be reluctant to call the American security guarantee into question. Binding West Germany closely to the U.S. strategic objectives was one way—the only way perceived at the time— to pursue this program with any success.

Another important consideration was Adenauer's goal of maintaining West Germany as an equal partner within the alliance. Denying the German army access to powerful weapons available under various control arrangements to other NATO armies would place Germany in an inferior position. This argument was used repeatedly by government officials to justify new German interest in access to nuclear weapons.

Finally, the Carte Blanche exercise demonstrated the potentially disastrous implications of a nuclear war on German soil. No doubt

Adenauer and his aides felt that some German control over the circumstances in which nuclear weapons would be used would be essential to protect German interests. It would also provide the government with at least one way to address the opposition's fears about West Germany's fate in a NATO–Warsaw Pact conflict.

This background helps in understanding the circumstances surrounding the controversial nuclear flirtation between France and West Germany in 1957.[18] In early 1957 France, West Germany, and Italy began secret discussions to coordinate and integrate production of defense-related equipment. As part of this series of discussions Defense Minister Strauss met in Paris with Maurice Bourges-Manoury, the French defense minister. Afterward, Strauss and his staff were treated to a tour of French military bases, including the French rocket test base in the Sahara. As a result of these contacts, there emerged a series of informal agreements on cooperation between the two countries on development and production of modern weapons. Apparently the package included German technical and financial assistance for a joint Franco-German effort to develop nuclear weapons on French territory, hence circumventing West Germany's pledge to forgo nuclear production on its own soil. In return, an arrangement would be established to secure German access to some of these weapons during a crisis. Although the series of talks eventually concluded in a formal agreement in 1958 to pool efforts on research and development of short-range rockets, ground force vehicles, tanks, and other military equipment, the issue of joint atomic production remained, according to French Premier Jacques Chaban-Delmas, "reserved." For his part, Strauss fed rumors by stating that though West Germany had no current interest in such an effort, this position was by no means permanent. When de Gaulle came to power in June 1958, he quickly called a halt to the discussions, which by all accounts were still in the exploratory phase.

That the Franco-German nuclear flirtation never led anywhere can be attributed to political hesitancy on both sides. For their part, the French were still hoping for American aid on their nuclear program; to come to a formal understanding at this time was considered premature insofar as it would antagonize the United States and jeopardize whatever hopes France held out for this aid. For the Germans to enter a nuclear deal

18. The details of this flirtation are found in Kohl, *French Nuclear Diplomacy*, pp. 54–61; and Kelleher, *Germany and the Politics of Nuclear Weapons*, pp. 149–53.

with the French would have required a serious break with the United States, which Adenauer wished to avoid for many reasons. It would also have eventually required creating some sort of public consensus in support of Franco-German nuclear cooperation, a process that, during early 1958, would have been politically divisive and probably unsuccessful, as the debate in early 1958 over arming the German Bundeswehr with nuclear weapons under joint U.S.-German control was amply to demonstrate.

During this particular period—that is, pre-sputnik—the German public debate over nuclear weapons did not center on the *reliability* of the nuclear guarantee. It is entirely possible, however, that Germans like Strauss were sensitive to this issue well before it became such a volatile public issue in 1958. In Strauss's dealings with his French counterparts, it is difficult to imagine that the subject, as elaborated by General Gallois and others, did not arise. Yet, as suggested earlier, there were many reasons for the relative German silence on this point, most notably Adenauer's firm belief in the need for maintaining a close, trusting relationship with the United States, to permit full German integration into the alliance. Another was the divided state of German political attitudes on NATO's nuclear strategy. Strauss and his followers were eager to accept NATO's New Look, with enhanced reliance on tactical nuclear weapons as a compensation for conventional weaknesses and as a trip wire for U.S. strategic retaliation. Others in Adenauer's party who might have doubted the wisdom of such a strategy, because of Carte Blanche, fully supported the government's efforts to build a new German army. Still others, in the opposition and among the public, found the whole prospect of war in Germany, conventional or nuclear, so distasteful that they condemned even nonnuclear preparations for war. These, then, were the most important constraints on vocal German opposition to NATO's strategic planning. Close observers of the German political scene were aware, however, of how near to the surface were the latent fears and doubts about NATO's New Look.

Great Britain

By 1957, as noted, Britain was the world's third nuclear power, and NATO's second. The process by which Britain came to find itself in this position has already been examined. But between 1954 and 1957 events and debates took place that altered British attitudes toward nuclear weapons and proved significant for future British policy.

In 1954 the British, along with the rest of the world, first learned of the American detonation of a fusion device, some fifteen months after the event. At once dismayed at America's obsessive secrecy, and envious of the destructive potential and military implications of thermonuclear weapons, Churchill and his aides came to an almost immediate decision to proceed with a British hydrogen bomb project.[19]

The debate in the House of Commons over this decision—which stands as one of the most extensive, informed public debates on nuclear issues in Britain, or anywhere else for that matter—fell along familiar lines.[20] Those who favored the government decision pointed to the immensely greater destructive power of hydrogen weapons, which would for the first time place Britain on equal terms with the two superpowers in sheer destructive potential. They also argued that the American guarantee, while currently secure, could become less so over time. Britain would therefore be wise to have these deterrent weapons in its own arsenal. Churchill's famous words opening the 1955 debate underscored the importance he placed on the deterrent effect of the new weapons: "Then it may well be that we shall, by a process of sublime irony, have reached a stage in this story where safety will be the sturdy child of terror, and survival the twin brother of annihilation."[21]

The minority opposed to the government position predictably based its opposition on the high cost of the proposed project; the possibility that Britain would become a more attractive target for Soviet preemption after it had deployed a thermonuclear arsenal; the moral issues raised by the threat of indiscriminate retaliation against innocent civilian populations; and the argument that the American guarantee, in its immense size and technical superiority, would protect Britain far better than any arsenal Britain itself could afford.

The opponents of government policy were, however, in the minority, and Churchill was able to win parliamentary support for his position. During the next few years Britain's reliance on thermonuclear weapons became a justification for an across-the-board cutback in other military expenditures. The famous Sandys 1957 White Paper on Defense, which

19. Andrew J. Pierre, *Nuclear Politics*, pp. 89–94.
20. The full debate makes for fascinating reading. See *Hansard Parliamentary Debates* (Commons), 5th ser., vol. 537, cols. 1893–2012.
21. Ibid., col. 1899.

heralded this cutback, was hardly revolutionary in its adoption of deterrence through massive retaliation. Though its presentation and rhetoric suggested otherwise, this White Paper was a direct descendant of the 1952 "Global Strategy" paper.[22] But it did have an operational bite that previous White Papers had lacked. It announced an end to Britain's long-standing policy of national military service; a five-year plan to cut the size of the military forces from 690,000 to 375,000; a cut in forces in Europe within a year from 77,000 to 64,000; and the cancellation of plans for a supersonic manned bomber so as to focus efforts on long-range ballistic missile technology.[23] On the other hand, Sandys's explicit reliance on an independent national nuclear arsenal as a deterrent drew approving notice in Paris and further stimulated German interest in access to nuclear weapons.

François de Rose, a French strategic analyst and one-time ambassador to NATO, commented later:

The publication of the White Paper demonstrated that the British effort, above all a political effort and an effort for prestige with the aim among other things of reestablishing the privileged cooperation with the United States which had existed during the war, responded in 1957 to a military necessity. The intervention of the U.S. being no longer certain, England had to have at her disposal the means of strategic reprisal, in the event that she should be threatened by nuclear annihilation.

For France this was the moment when more and more vigorous pressures intervened on the part of political and military elements in order that a decision be taken to produce the atomic weapon.[24]

And the White Paper gave Adenauer the opportunity to advance the argument for arming the Bundeswehr with nuclear weapons, in keeping with the late 1956 German shift to the New Look.

That the 1957 White Paper did not receive a more critical reception on its release in April is curious, since the British government's growing reliance on massive retaliation was coming under increasing criticism from opposition and nongovernmental experts.[25] These analysts took up arguments familiar to Americans from the various U.S. critiques of

22. As mentioned in chapter 2, Sir John Slessor and Laurence W. Martin both make this point: Sir John Slessor, "British Defense Policy," pp. 551–63; and Laurence W. Martin, "The Market for Strategic Ideas in Britain," pp. 23–41. See also Pierre, *Nuclear Politics,* pp. 87–101; and H. A. DeWeerd, "Britain's Changing Military Policy," pp. 102–16.

23. Pierre, *Nuclear Politics,* p. 96.

24. Cited in Kohl, *French Nuclear Diplomacy,* p. 41.

25. Pierre, *Nuclear Politics,* pp. 101–11.

Dulles's massive retaliation doctrine. First, they argued that the Sandys doctrine was not credible:

So far, massive retaliation, despite its shortcomings and failure to halt aggression in Korea and Indo-China, has been a fairly effective deterrent because the Russians have been incapable of striking back massively, particularly at the United States. With this situation changing, massive retaliation, although still an effective deterrent against an all-out attack by the Communists, is no longer effective against the much more likely threat of local aggression by Soviet and satellite armies, because the Communists might well expect the United States to refrain from action which is becoming akin to suicide. Increasingly, therefore, our present policy is in danger of being interpreted as bluff—if indeed it does not prove to be one—for any aggression between an all-out war and a very minor one; and it leaves much room for misunderstanding and Communist exploitation.[26]

Second, they argued that an independent nuclear arsenal program like the one on which the government was embarked would not increase Britain's political influence over enemies and allies or enhance Britain's international prestige. Such well-known writers as Alastair Buchan, a correspondent for the London *Observer,* and Denis Healey, the Labour party defense specialist, argued that Britain's influence over events in the rapidly decolonizing third world would depend more on the efficacy of British diplomacy than on a British mini–Strategic Air Command; that British nuclear weapons had not stayed Dulles's hand in the Suez crisis of 1956; that conventional weaknesses in NATO were more pressing; and that the British dependence on American technology would *increase* rather than decrease as the British nuclear arsenal became operational.[27]

To replace the Sandys strategy, some of these critics endorsed a strategy that came to be known as graduated deterrence.[28] As elaborated by Sir Anthony W. Buzzard, such a policy would deliberately distinguish between tactical nuclear responses to aggression, in which low-yield atomic weapons would be used against military targets, and strategic nuclear responses, which would involve high-yield (thermonuclear) attacks on enemy cities. As a deterrent against less-than-all-out local aggression, NATO would threaten tactical nuclear retaliation; if enemy aggression continued unabated, then the alliance could threaten strategic

26. Perhaps the most influential assault on massive retaliation in the British debate was marshaled by Sir Anthony W. Buzzard, "Massive Retaliation and Graduated Deterrence," pp. 228–37. The quotation is from p. 230.
27. Cited in Pierre, *Nuclear Politics,* p. 106.
28. See Buzzard, "Massive Retaliation and Graduated Deterrence."

nuclear responses. Since tactical nuclear responses would not necessarily compel enemy retaliation against Western cities—in fact, they might give the enemy incentives to avoid escalation to counter-city strikes—the tactical nuclear threat would appear to be more credible and hence better able to deter aggression in a wide range of contingencies.

Those who made this argument were vague about whether graduated deterrence was primarily a doctrine that the United States should adopt to strengthen its guarantee to the West, or a doctrine that Britain should adopt to make its own deterrent more credible, or a doctrine that required nuclear forces controlled by a centralized NATO command in order to function. They were also vague about the role of conventional forces in a graduated deterrent; the implicit assumption seems to have been that purely conventional resistance to Warsaw Pact aggression would be ineffectual, so NATO should plan to center its response around tactical nuclear weapons. Though not certain that warfare on the tactical level could be prevented from escalating to a strategic war involving the mutual annihilation of cities, these critics showed some confidence in being able to do so:

It is far from certain that we would not succeed in maintaining these limitations during at least the early stages of any nuclear war, which is really what matters. Moreover, once our distinctions were established, and thus could grow in the minds and plans of both sides, the risks of the limitations breaking down in war would gradually diminish as the years went by. Finally, even if our limitations should break down in war, would anything have been lost by making the attempt to uphold them? Little or nothing, surely, provided only that we never lose sight of the risk of this happening, and avoid becoming "trigger-happy" with our tactical atomic weapons.[29]

This particular criticism of massive retaliation, shared by influential American observers of NATO affairs, served as one stimulus to a subtle but important shift in NATO strategy from primary reliance on strategic nuclear retaliation to a more flexible—if still nuclear—deterrent based on graduated tactical nuclear retaliation. No doubt the development of a new theoretical justification for tactical nuclear weapons relieved those who had originally argued for them as compensation for conventional manpower inferiority—an argument increasingly open to question as the results of NATO nuclear exercises were analyzed. The influence of graduated deterrence in British defense policy was slower in coming. At the time of the December 1957 NATO meeting, Britain was still firmly

29. Ibid., p. 235.

committed in policy declaration and resource expenditure to the course outlined by Sandys earlier in the year: to reduce reliance on conventional forces and to enhance Britain's strategic nuclear retaliatory capabilities. Much of the reason for this attitude is to be found in the legacy of the Suez crisis. But before that legacy is examined, it is necessary to briefly summarize the U.S. debate, which influenced many of the European arguments.

The American Shift

In October 1957 Secretary of State John Foster Dulles wrote the following in a widely noted article in *Foreign Affairs*:

The United States has not been content to rely upon a peace which could be preserved only by a capacity to destroy vast segments of the human race. Such a concept is acceptable only as a last alternative. In recent years there has been no other. But the resourcefulness of those who serve our nation in the field of science and weapon engineering now shows that it is possible to alter the character of nuclear weapons. It seems now that their use need not involve vast destruction and widespread harm to humanity. Recent tests point to the possibility of possessing nuclear weapons the destructiveness and radiation effects of which can be confined substantially to predetermined targets.

In the future it may thus be feasible to place less reliance upon deterrence of vast retaliatory power. It may be possible to defend countries by nuclear weapons so mobile, or so placed, as to make military invasion with conventional forces a hazardous attempt. . . . Thus the tables may be turned in the sense that instead of those who are non-aggressive having to rely upon all-out nuclear retaliatory power for their protection, would-be aggressors will be unable to count on a successful conventional aggression, but must themselves weigh the consequences of invoking nuclear war.[30]

Dulles seemed to be implying that the threat of massive retaliation had never presented much of a deterrent to an aggressor intent on conventional success: by implication, he argued that only the recent development of small-yield battlefield nuclear weapons would deter such an aggressor.

U.S. declaratory policy on nuclear weapons and deterrence had thus shifted away from pure massive retaliation. This shift, coming as it did during the growing crisis of confidence, had important implications for U.S. policy in NATO and for NATO's own deterrent policy. By

30. John Foster Dulles, "Challenge and Response in United States Policy," p. 31.

December 1957, as will be seen, SACEUR General Norstad had enunciated an even more dramatic shift away from NATO's New Look.

It is difficult to know conclusively why Dulles made his shift. Dulles
left no memoirs—and Eisenhower's memoirs seem to ignore the change.
It is a reasonable assumption, however, that the tremendous debate
inspired by Dulles's 1954 speech had had a gradual effect on high-level
governmental thinking.

Almost all critics of massive retaliation believed that the lack of
credibility in the threat of massive retaliation against any but the most
devastating all-out nuclear attack on American cities was a crucial flaw
in the policy. This criticism, developed early on in the academic debate
by Bernard Brodie and William Kaufmann, noted that neither America's
previous record of responses to local communist aggression, nor the
state of American public opinion, nor the somewhat confused and
contradictory public declarations of high-level governmental officials
would give the Kremlin reason to believe the United States would
actually use "massive retaliatory power" in response to local aggression
"at times and places of [its] own choosing." The credibility of the U.S.
threat would grow increasingly questionable over time as the Soviet
Union and others developed nuclear arsenals capable of delivering
devastating attacks against American urban-industrial targets. The U.S.
posture was clearly unsatisfactory, not only as declaratory policy but as
planning and procurement guidelines. In Kaufmann's words, a policy so
obviously incredible would "result only in deterring the deterror."[31]

Although critics agreed broadly on the flaws of massive retaliation,
they did not agree on what constituted a workable alternative. Some
argued that besides a capability for massive retaliation, the United States
should have a "limited war" capability based primarily on nonnuclear
weapons, doctrines, and tactics. Others argued for a limited war capability based on plans and doctrines for using relatively low-yield nuclear
weapons on the battlefield in support of traditional military operations.[32]

---

31. Kaufmann's critique first appeared in 1954 as a monograph from Princeton
University's Center for International Studies and was later reprinted as a chapter, "The
Requirements of Deterrence," in Kaufmann, ed., Military Policy and National Security;
see especially pp. 17–23. Hard on the heels of the Kaufmann critique came Bernard
Brodie, "Unlimited Weapons and Limited War," pp. 16–21, and Henry A. Kissinger,
"Military Policy and Defense of the 'Grey Areas,' " pp. 416–28.

32. The open sources for this debate are vast. A useful annotated compendium of
the sources can be found in Morton H. Halperin, Limited War in the Nuclear Age, pp.
133–84. This compendium should be read along with Robert Endicott Osgood, Limited
War, for an overview of the "schools of thought" on limited war in the nuclear age.

Those who emphasized nonnuclear capabilities argued that in a war against the Warsaw Pact an overriding NATO goal would be to prevent the war from degenerating into an all-out nuclear conflict, which would be so destructive as to negate any political objectives. Particularly if aggression was initiated without the use of nuclear weapons, the threat of massive retaliation would probably not deter the aggressor. Some other threat must be made. The threat of a solid conventional defense, at least in the initial stage, would provide a credible deterrent against conventional aggression. A successful conventional defense would be more amenable to control during battle. Political authorities have had some experience in associating nonnuclear military operations with political objectives, experience totally lacking in the nuclear realm. If successful, a conventional defense would place the burden of making the agonizing decision to use nuclear weapons on the enemy. In this situation the enemy would have little assurance that the war would not quickly become an all-out nuclear exchange involving the strategic arsenals of both sides—a powerful incentive against bringing the conflict over the nuclear threshold. If unsuccessful in its conventional defense, NATO would still have recourse to its nuclear arsenals. Such a posture would provide a reliable deterrent against a wide range of possible aggression.[33]

Others argued that, given the size of the conventional forces facing NATO's central front, it was unrealistic to expect members of the alliance to make the tremendous sacrifices of resources needed to provide a reliable conventional defense. They viewed nuclear firepower at the tactical level as one way to offset the alleged nonnuclear inferiority of the alliance. But they also saw some distinct military advantages in a posture that relied heavily on tactical use of nuclear weapons. Successful conventional Warsaw Pact operations, these analysts argued, would virtually require concentration of Warsaw Pact troop formations along axes of attack, thereby providing attractive targets for tactical nuclear strikes. Moreover, nuclear weapons could be used effectively against military targets well behind the forward edge of the battle area. Logistics networks and issues of communication would be severely disrupted by tactical nuclear strikes. In short, tactical use of nuclear weapons would

---

33. These ideas are reflected in several thoughtful essays, including William W. Kaufmann, "Limited Warfare," in Kaufmann, ed., *Military Policy and National Security*, pp. 102–36; Malcolm W. Hoag, "The Place of Limited War in NATO Strategy," in Knorr, ed., *NATO and American Security*, pp. 98–126; and Paul H. Nitze, "Atoms, Strategy and Policy," pp. 187–98.

be extremely effective in undermining the coherence and strength of a conventional Warsaw Pact attack.

The proponents of this position recognized that using such weapons in NATO's defense would make unprecedented demands on NATO leaders. To avoid provoking a Warsaw Pact nuclear response against Western cities, the tactics would have to signal to the Warsaw Pact the willingness of the alliance to spare Soviet and Eastern European civilian populations. Such tactics would require careful selection of targets so as to minimize the possibility of striking Warsaw Pact urban centers. They would also require reliability and accuracy of delivery. Finally, they would require technological modifications of nuclear ordnance to minimize widespread nuclear damage and fallout that could affect large civilian populations. Lower yields and airbursts were held to be the technical prerequisites of a feasible tactical nuclear doctrine that would reduce Warsaw Pact incentives to retaliate against NATO urban areas.[34]

Advocates of tactical nuclear weapons ran into criticism from those who wondered whether the proposed cure would not be worse than the disease. Simulations and studies had only confirmed the lessons of Carte Blanche, that using tactical nuclear weapons to defend Western Europe would destroy much of Europe in the process. Some doubted whether the tacit signaling designed to give the Warsaw Pact an incentive to avoid Western cities would be received clearly in a period of intense political and military crisis. Even if it were, they doubted that the high-yield, relatively inaccurate Warsaw Pact theater nuclear weapons would technically permit the Soviet Union to carry on the relatively pristine battlefield nuclear operations envisioned by tactical nuclear advocates.

Finally, and perhaps most important, many critics questioned the wisdom of relying on NATO's ability to fight a war under the historically unprecedented circumstances of nuclear conflict. The most sophisticated critics did not argue that nuclear weapons could not be used to complement traditional battlefield operations. They did, however, express concern that some advocates of the tactical use of nuclear weapons displayed more confidence than the facts warranted. Any step over the nuclear threshold would place alliance leaders in an uncertain sort of conflict, one for which no previous experience provided guidance. Since

34. One exponent of these ideas was Kissinger. See Henry A. Kissinger, *Nuclear Weapons and Foreign Policy*, and "Force and Diplomacy in the Nuclear Age," pp. 349–66. See also Bernard Brodie, "Nuclear Weapons: Strategic or Tactical?" pp. 217–29.

it was so difficult to predict how such a conflict might evolve, and how it might end, it seemed safer to prepare for a conventional conflict in which the rules of the game were better understood and to contemplate only reluctantly the use of these terrible weapons if the conventional battle seemed lost.[35]

Making a sharp distinction between these two alternatives to massive retaliation, however, oversimplifies a complex, multifaceted debate. For one thing, some influential participants in the debate, including General Maxwell D. Taylor, argued that NATO should have a strong capability for both types of warfare, nonnuclear and tactical nuclear.[36] For another, interservice rivalries played an important role. The air force, jealously guarding its mission of strategic nuclear strikes, was reluctant to concede that other capabilities were needed to provide an effective deterrent. General Curtis LeMay reflected this thinking when he admitted he was unable to see why a capability that could deter large-scale war would not also deter smaller-scale aggression. If a tactical nuclear posture was in fact necessary for NATO's security, then the air force wanted a role in nuclear delivery through tactical air forces assigned to NATO; it did not want merely to support an army operation by means of nuclear close air support. Navy officials were also reluctant to concede the main nuclear role to the army when the navy was competing with the other services for its own enhanced piece of the nuclear pie. Such was the formidable resistance that faced the frustrated Taylor in his push for an effective dual capability.

Separating the debate into two opposing schools also runs the risk of ignoring the aspects on which all critics of massive retaliation agreed. Chief among these was the undesirability of a strategic nuclear policy that confined the U.S. leadership to two choices, either to do nothing or to launch an all-out strategic nuclear attack against Soviet military and urban-industrial targets. It was generally agreed that to constrain the president's freedom of action to these two choices would be to place him in an untenable situation in a crisis. Against any threat except the imminent destruction of the entire military and urban-industrial target base of the United States, the president would be unlikely to do anything at all. As a result, the Soviet leadership would be free to make less

---

35. See, for example, James E. King, Jr., "Nuclear Weapons and Foreign Policy," pp. 16–18.

36. See Taylor, *Uncertain Trumpet*, pp. 178–80.

catastrophic threats. A more effective strategic deterrent would be a posture capable of responding to a presidential order to attack a restricted set of Soviet targets, to reduce enemy military capabilities as well as give the Kremlin incentives not to respond against Western cities. As will be seen in the discussion of flexible response during the Mc-Namara years, this rationale for pursuing limited strategic retaliatory options was to play an important part in U.S. policy toward NATO.

The debate outlined here was not without its effect on the Eisenhower administration. In 1957 a panel of experts was commissioned to examine the problems of deterrence and survival in the nuclear age and to bring its findings directly to the president. Its final report, known as the Gaither Report for its director, H. Rowan Gaither of the Ford Foundation, was a general critique of the administration's defense program and gave the following advice on alliance nuclear policy:

Augment our and Allied forces for limited military operations, and provide greater mobility, to enable us to deter or promptly suppress small wars which must not be allowed to grow into big ones. The Panel suggests that a study be undertaken, at the national rather than at a service level, to develop current doctrine on when and how nuclear weapons can contribute to limited operations. . . .

As long as the U.S. population is wide open to Soviet attack, both the Russian and our allies may believe that we shall feel increasing reluctance to employ SAC in any circumstance other than when the United States is directly attacked. To prevent such an impairment of our deterrent power and to ensure our survival if nuclear war occurs through miscalculation or design, we assign a somewhat lower than highest value, in relation to cost, to a mixed program of active and passive defenses to protect our civil population.[37]

However, the precise effect that the Gaither Report, the interservice discussion, or the debate in the more academic circles had on the thinking of Eisenhower and Dulles is not known. As already seen, Dulles in his *Foreign Affairs* article in October 1957 took the position of the tactical nuclear advocates. But it is possible to overstate the effect of the debate on the objective status of U.S. and NATO force posture. NATO had begun to introduce nuclear weapons into its regional forces as early as 1954; by the time of the Dulles article, many nuclear systems had already been deployed with American NATO forces on the Continent. These

37. *Deterrence and Survival in the Nuclear Age (The "Gaither Report" of 1957)*, Committee Print, p. 18. See also Morton H. Halperin, "The Gaither Committee and the Policy Process," pp. 360–84, for a detailed examination of the report's genesis and consequences.

included nuclear artillery and gravity bombs, Mace and Matador cruise missiles, and nuclear capable antiaircraft missiles.

As mentioned before, the justification for this arsenal at the time was that it could compensate for NATO's conventional inferiority. No deeper rationale seemed necessary, given the momentum of the New Look. What followed in the way of doctrinal elaboration can be seen not so much as a rational attempt to determine the requirements of NATO's posture, but as a rationalization of procurement and deployment decisions that had developed a life of their own.

The Effect of the American Debate

Nevertheless, the American debate over NATO's conventional and nuclear posture had two important consequences. First, rather than inspire confidence, the debate seemed to feed many of the European fears. According to one European observer,

American intellectuals started a chain reaction by pointing out that Europe might not be satisfied with the American guarantee of its defense, once the Soviet Union had attained the ability to destroy American cities. This made us wonder whether the Russians might think the possible loss of New York would be too much for the Americans to risk in defense of Paris. So finally we did come to be worried over what the Russians would believe the Americans thought the Europeans should think.[38]

Whether the cause and effect noted here is quite so simple is debatable. As already seen, Europe needed no prompting from the United States to voice many of these concerns. Nevertheless, the writings of Henry Kissinger and others, which openly questioned the reliability of the U.S. guarantee, were no doubt read and pondered by influential European statesmen.

The second consequence was a change in thinking at SHAPE. Up till 1957 the main justification for a NATO "shield" of continental ground forces was that it would act as a trip wire to nuclear retaliation against the Warsaw Pact. But SACEUR General Norstad began to doubt the wisdom of such a posture, for many of the reasons cited above. In a remarkable policy speech in Cincinnati in November 1957—a speech apparently not previously cleared through political channels—Norstad

38. Cited in Timothy W. Stanley, *NATO in Transition*, p. 159.

introduced additional reasons for NATO's shield, which have come to be known as the "pause concept."

The might of our strategic retaliatory forces vastly reduces the dangers of a general war. The aggressor knows that to start such a war would invite his own destruction. However, there remains the risk of a war by accident, by miscalculation. A probing operation to achieve political advantage—a border incident, negligible in itself—might flare out of control. And here lies the value of the Shield Force, deployed along NATO's frontier—a frontier which is not an imaginary line, a mere geographical concept like the Tropic of Capricorn. It is an actual, physical line that runs for more than 4,000 miles through the villages, forests, and the farms of Europe. If this critical line, which the 15 NATO nations have vowed to defend, is held with reasonable force, then force must be used to breach it. The decision to apply that force would be terrible in its implications. It must consider not only the Stout Shield in immediate defence, but the sharp sword of our strategic retaliation. The Shield Force thus serves to complete the deterrent, to integrate all the elements that compose its strength.[39]

His subsequent testimony to Congress clarified this concept: "In order to penetrate our defense, force would have to be used, which we feel would bring a pause long enough for consideration not only of the opposition of the shield forces, the force actually on the spot, but also of the retaliatory forces behind them."[40]

Norstad also gave another reason for the shield in his Cincinnati speech:

In an era of nuclear plenty and of delivery means adequate in number and in effectiveness, the NATO Shield provides us with an option more useful than the simple choice between all or nothing. Should we fail to maintain reasonable Shield strength on the NATO frontier, then massive retaliation could be our only response to an aggression, regardless of its nature. There is real danger that inability to deal decisively with limited or local attacks could lead to our piecemeal defeat or bring on a general war. If, on the other hand, we have means to meet less-than-ultimate threats with a decisive, but less-than-ultimate response, the very possession of this ability would discourage the threat, and would thereby provide us with essential political and military manoeuverability.[41]

Norstad's comments were clearly an attempt to move away from the view that massive retaliation alone could serve as NATO's deterrent. A strong local defense against certain kinds of Warsaw Pact aggression could "give pause" to Soviet leaders, who would then have to make the awesome decision whether to press on and incur American strategic

39. "Text of General Norstad's Cincinnati Speech," p. 27.
40. *Mutual Security Act of 1958*, Senate Hearings, pp. 200–01.
41. "Text of General Norstad's Cincinnati Speech," p. 27.

retaliatory wrath. Norstad also saw the shield as a prime instrument in providing flexible alternatives to deal with less-than-ultimate attacks. But the Norstad shield was *not* conventional. Norstad made this point explicitly in the 1958 hearings, in which he stated that "the Shield forces can no longer be considered as 'conventional forces,' a point I should like to emphasize, for although they retain a conventional capability, their minimum size requires that they be equipped with the most modern weapons, including nuclear weapons, deployed and available on a wide basis throughout the NATO forces."[42]

General Norstad was to become a staunch advocate of a NATO capability to launch nuclear strikes deep into Soviet territory in strategic missions. At the same time, however, he took the shield requirements seriously. For example, Norstad pursued, and eventually won endorsement of, a five-year NATO program (known as MC 70) to create a 30-division standing for the NATO shield.[43] The actual degree to which SHAPE planning reflected declaratory policy is difficult to determine; Osgood argues that the logistical requirements for a ninety-day war on the Continent, which drove much of SHAPE planning during this period, may reflect some serious hopes for the shield as a pause-creating force.[44] In any case, declaratory policy at SHAPE had shifted, if not toward acceptance of conventional deterrence and defense, then at least away from the rhetoric of massive retaliation that had guided General Norstad's predecessors.

The Effect of Suez and Sputnik

The basic outlines of the Suez crisis are well known. Concerned about Egyptian President Nasser's rise to power, and about his intentions regarding the Suez Canal, the British and French governments hatched an elaborate scheme to conquer the canal zone with the help of the Israeli army. Because of poor planning and even poorer timing, British and French forces were unable to accomplish their objectives, even though Israeli forces captured the entire Sinai Peninsula. The British and French, particularly British Prime Minister Anthony Eden, had counted on tacit

42. *Mutual Security Act of 1958,* Senate Hearings, p. 187.
43. Osgood, *NATO,* pp. 118, 161.
44. Ibid., p. 162. See also F. W. Mulley, *The Politics of Western Defence,* p. 197.

U.S. support for the operation, but at the crucial moment Dulles and Eisenhower made public their lack of enthusiasm for the adventure and even threatened to place intolerable financial pressure on the British pound if the United Kingdom, France, and Israel did not agree to stop hostilities. In the face of explicit U.S. opposition, ominous threats from the Soviet Union, and a military operation plagued by delays and lack of coordination, Eden, French Prime Minister Guy Mollet, and Israeli leader David Ben-Gurion had no choice but to back down.

The American position in this affair was bound to affect perceptions significantly not only in London and Paris but throughout Europe. The reliability of American support for interests considered vital by the European allies was now open to question. One need only glance at Eden's memoirs to sense the feelings of bitterness and betrayal aroused by the sharp reactions of Eisenhower and Dulles. It is hardly an accident that the Sandys 1957 White Paper on Defense, coming four months after the resolution of Suez, justified the pursuit and maintenance of the independent British deterrent as a hedge against the unreliability of the U.S. guarantee of British security interests. All the more galling was the apparent American nonchalance regarding the overt nuclear threats against Britain and France made by the Soviet Union at the height of the crisis.[45]

The French response was similar. A 1958 Rand Corporation study of the attitudes of the French government toward nuclear weapons drew these conclusions from the Suez crisis:

At the time of the Suez Affair, the French leaders (first the government, then the parliament) came to realize to what extent France would be at the mercy of the Russians in case she were abandoned by the Americans (this despite the reassuring words of SACEUR). France either could rely on American bombs for protection (but then she would be at the mercy of the Americans in Africa and would be forced to abandon Algeria) or else, if she wished to keep Algeria, she would have to acquire atomic weapons and thus be in a position to resist Soviet pressures alone. The Suez Affair clearly showed the parliament members the profound divergencies between American and French policy in the Mediterranean and Africa and the necessity of acquiring an atomic arsenal if France was not to be compelled to align her policy with that of the United States.[46]

As a result of Suez, the French Commissariat à l'Energie Atomique, in charge of research and development for nuclear energy, and the

45. Hans Speier, "Soviet Atomic Blackmail and the North Atlantic Alliance," pp. 307–28.
46. Cited in Kohl, *French Nuclear Diplomacy,* p. 36.

Ministry of National Defense agreed to a program to work out the details and allocate responsibilities for France's nuclear weapons development.[47] Within the next several months the government also made other moves to facilitate the final decision to pursue nuclear weapons.

French resentment over Suez was further increased by the apparent eagerness of the Eisenhower administration to patch up the Anglo-American breach. The new British prime minister, Harold Macmillan, gave this reparation the highest priority. In March 1957 Anglo-American cooperation was set back on track, this time by the offer of U.S. Thor intermediate-range ballistic missiles to Britain under dual-key arrangements. The United States would provide the missiles and keep custody of the warheads; the British would pay for base construction and man the missiles.[48]

There is little public evidence to document the reactions of either West Germany or the other European allies to the events over Suez in 1956. Perhaps Adenauer and his aides felt both relief about not having to participate in such a disruptive affair and fear over the possible effect of the crisis on Western unity. But it must also be remembered that West Germany's interest in some access to American tactical nuclear forces within NATO was aired at the same time, presumably influenced by Suez; it may simply have been Adenauer's overwhelming political debt to Dulles that prevented him from talking openly about German doubts.

The second event that prompted the crisis of confidence surrounding the December 1957 meeting of NATO heads of government was the launch of sputnik. Much has been written about the panic reaction in Washington to the announcement in October 1957 that the Soviets had succeeded in launching the first earth-orbiting space satellite. If in general terms sputnik was a dramatic symbol of the technological superiority of the Soviet Union in a particularly threatening military area, it also symbolized in specific terms the ever-growing vulnerability of the United States to Soviet strategic attack. This second aspect would hardly have been lost on Europeans and Americans alike, who had been worrying for years about the implications for NATO deterrence of a United States vulnerable to strategic missile attack. Sputnik was the event that had been foreseen and feared. The doubts that had grown slowly over the previous three or four years now had to be faced.

47. Ibid.
48. Michael H. Armacost, *The Politics of Weapons Innovation*, pp. 191–97. See the next chapter for details.

CHAPTER FOUR

Missiles for Europe, 1957–60

EVENTS that took place between 1955 and 1957 had thus raised the debate over NATO's nuclear policies to full-blown crisis. Suez and its aftermath shook to the core the confidence of the allies in America's willingness to support European foreign policy goals and objectives. The launch of sputnik in October 1957 shook America's confidence in its ability to maintain a technological edge over the Soviet Union, an ability that had smugly been taken for granted before the launch. There was widespread agreement in Washington on the need for some kind of initiative to counteract the negative effect of these events.

The Origins of the Thor-Jupiter Offer

Suez and sputnik took place against the background of the Eisenhower administration's efforts to bring the United States into the missile age. In early 1954 a scientific panel headed by the Princeton mathematician Dr. John von Neumann reported to the president on the feasibility of reducing the size and weight of nuclear weapons so that they could be launched atop intercontinental ballistic missiles (ICBMs). Because of this report and of subsequent tests that confirmed the panel's findings, work on the liquid-fueled Atlas ICBM was accelerated.[1]

In July 1954 President Eisenhower asked James R. Killian, president of the Massachusetts Institute of Technology, to form a panel of scientific experts "to direct a study of the country's technological capabilities to meet some of its current problems."[2] Killian complied and by February

1. Edmund Beard, *Developing the ICBM*, pp. 157–94.
2. James R. Killian, Jr., *Sputnik, Scientists, and Eisenhower*, pp. 67–68.

1955 had put together the panel's report, which examined the broad technological balance between the United States and the Soviet Union, projected trends in that balance, and drew out the implications of these trends for national security requirements. Among the many recommendations of the report were ones to accelerate even further the ICBM program and to launch a program to develop intermediate-range ballistic missiles (IRBMs) for early deployment either on the European continent or at sea. Eisenhower later shared Killian's assessment that this report was the initial stimulus for the development of the Thor, Jupiter, and Polaris missiles.[3]

IRBMs seemed attractive to the Killian panel largely because technical factors promised to make IRBM development faster than ICBM development. Because of their shorter (1,500-mile) range, IRBMs do not require the same high rate of acceleration as ICBMs. And their fuel load is lighter, which means that, all things being equal, the payload can be heavier. Finally, shorter ranges create fewer problems for designing precision inertial guidance systems, which were then in their infancy. High-acceleration rocket engines, lightweight nuclear payloads, and high-precision inertial guidance systems were all feasible and under development as part of the ICBM program. But estimates at the time suggested that it would be 1962 before an operational ICBM with these advanced components could be developed and that Soviet efforts in ballistic missile technology might require an earlier response. IRBMs could be produced sooner; hence Killian's and Eisenhower's interest in them.

The subsequent story of interservice rivalry between the air force and the army over which service would be allowed to produce and deploy the IRBMs is a classic.[4] Time and again the decision to choose between the two services was postponed; Secretary of Defense Charles Wilson had no stomach for such a difficult choice. What made the decision even more difficult, aside from the bitter interservice rivalry, was the irony that the air force IRBM, Thor, was virtually identical to the army IRBM, Jupiter. Both would be liquid-fueled; both would have 1,500-mile ranges; both would be stationary and based above ground. The main difference was in the position of the missile before launch: the Thor stood vertically;

3. Ibid., pp. 70–79. See also Dwight D. Eisenhower, *The White House Years: Waging Peace, 1956–1961*, p. 208.
4. The full, fascinating story is in Michael H. Armacost, *The Politics of Weapons Innovation.*

Jupiter was deployed in a semihorizontal mode. Since there was no militarily significant difference between the two, Wilson had little basis for decision. As development proceeded, it became clear that Thor would be operational before Jupiter; therefore some, like Killian, pushed for a decision to cut the Jupiter program. But still no decision was reached. In the end sputnik made the decision for Wilson's successor, Neil McElroy: both missiles would be produced.

The decision to proceed with the development of a 1,500-mile-range IRBM implied that the weapons would have to be deployed on forward bases, either in Europe or at sea. So the decision, once taken, virtually guaranteed that efforts to negotiate European deployments would be forthcoming. These efforts began on the technical-military level as early as the end of 1956, when military staffs from the U.S. Air Force and Britain's Royal Air Force discussed the possibility of Thor deployment on British bases. It is not clear who initiated the discussions, but both services were willing partners. In March 1957 these discussions were brought to the highest political level at the Anglo-American summit conference in Bermuda, where Eisenhower and Macmillan came to a tentative agreement to deploy Thor missiles on British bases in exchange for Eisenhower's commitment to seek amendments to the 1954 Mc-Mahon Act that would facilitate British access to American data on nuclear weapons technology.

British interest in having the new IRBMs deployed on its own bases can be explained in several ways. First, agreement on such deployments would begin to reestablish the special relationship between London and Washington that had been strained during the Suez crisis. Second, this was the period in which Defense Minister Duncan Sandys was preparing his 1957 White Paper on Defense, which emphasized reliance on the nuclear deterrent. Access to the most advanced ballistic missile technology would make this decision more politically and militarily justifiable. It might also have been felt that access to the new American missiles, in conjunction with the expected amendment of the McMahon Act, would have beneficial spin-offs for the new national land-based ballistic missile program upon which Britain was about to embark, the Blue Streak.

On the American side, Eisenhower had many incentives for offering the missile to the British. He was well aware of the basing constraints imposed by the 1,500-mile range of the missile. IRBMs required European basing, and Britain was an obvious candidate. Also, he was probably as eager as Macmillan to set the Anglo-American relationship back on an intimate course. Moreover, if some sort of cost-sharing arrangement could be worked out with Macmillan, it would fit well into Eisenhower's cost-cutting philosophy.

Just how detailed the March 1957 Bermuda agreement was remains unclear. In view of subsequent events, it seems likely that the details were left to be worked out later. One thing certain is that the agreement aroused little public controversy at the time. In its initial form, at least, the Thor offer was *not* an American initiative in response to a grave alliance crisis. It was not embedded in any grand, overarching intellectual rationale. Technological considerations meshed well with the pragmatic political objectives of both countries. Or, as the most careful student of the Thor arrangement wrote, "What strategy required, economics encouraged, and politics permitted!"[5] The whole arrangement, in fact, seemed casual, almost an "old boys' " understanding between the U.S. Air Force and the RAF.

By the fall of 1957, however, the casual approach had given way to a greater sense of urgency. The Gaither Report had recommended an acceleration in the development and deployment of IRBMs on overseas bases—even before the launch of sputnik.[6] The sense of urgency in developing a broad, effective response to the Soviet missile launch can be imparted only by some of the more candid memoirs of the period, like that of James Killian, the man whom the president chose as his "missile czar," in response to the Soviet ballistic development.[7] In one sense the decision to make a formal offer to enter into bilateral negotiations with any interested ally at NATO's heads of government meeting in December 1957 should be seen as part of a much larger package of U.S. defense initiatives developed in response to sputnik, not all of which were designed to allay specifically European fears.

Nonetheless, the American plan provoked strong behind-the-scenes resistance, in advance of the formal offer, on the part of almost all the other allies. So strong were these private responses that on December 10, less than a week before the Paris conference, Secretary of State Dulles was compelled to assure the allies that "there is no desire on the part of the United States to press these missiles in the hands or on the

5. Ibid., p. 191.
6. *Deterrence and Survival in the Nuclear Age (The "Gaither Report" of 1957)*, Committee Print, p. 37.
7. Killian, *Sputnik, Scientists, and Eisenhower*.

territory of any country that doesn't want them."[8] The heads of government who assembled on December 16 did agree in principle, however, to deployments of IRBMs in Europe, pending further exploration and determination of the military requirements for IRBMs on the territory of specific countries by SHAPE officers. Placing the burden of requesting deployments on the shoulders of SACEUR was probably the most expedient face-saving move Dulles and Eisenhower could have chosen, since General Norstad, an admired and respected SACEUR, was in an excellent position to judge the political problems raised by such a request.

What were the general reasons for initial resistance to the American offer? Some were plainly political. These missiles were to be based above ground and would have high political visibility to both the Soviet Union and to pacifist domestic political groups in each basing country. Thus not only would the missiles result in increased tension between the host country and the Soviet Union; they would also provide a convenient focus for domestic political opposition.

The technological characteristics of the Thor missiles created another problem. Their above-ground basing and liquid fuel would make them vulnerable to Soviet preemption, which, given the status of NATO defenses at the time, would probably come without warning. They would soon look primitive in comparison with other systems under development in the United States, particularly Polaris, which had none of the vulnerability problems associated with stationary, above-ground liquid-fueled missiles.

Nevertheless, Norstad went quietly to work sounding out possible candidates for deployment—France, West Germany, Italy, the Netherlands, Turkey, and Greece. At the same time, negotiators immediately began to complete the details of the Anglo-American agreement of March 1957.

The Reaction in Britain

The details of the March 1957 agreement in Bermuda began to emerge only after the heads of government meeting in December. The final agreement, formally announced on February 22, 1958, called for the stationing of sixty Thor IRBMs on four British bases under a carefully

8. Armacost, *Politics of Weapons Innovation*, p. 188.

worded joint arrangement, in which the authority to launch the missiles required "joint positive decision" by the two governments. Although the RAF Bomber Command would man the four bases, "all nuclear warheads so provided shall remain in full United States ownership, custody, and control." This decision reflected concern about security of command and control and about U.S. statutes related to the McMahon Act that restricted the provision of nuclear weapons to other countries.[9]

Even before the negotiations had concluded, sharp debate stirred the British political community. In early January the Labour party's spokesman for foreign affairs, Aneurin Bevin, issued a harsh criticism of the emerging deal, stating that the view of the Soviet Union implicit in the U.S. offer would find "scarcely any support" throughout Europe.[10] Also on the political left, influential journals began to speak out against the agreement. One such periodical, *The Statesman,* declared that "Britain, it seems, can be trusted to commit national suicide in America's defense, but not to share America's secrets," a rather blunt reference to the difficulties Eisenhower was encountering in trying to have the McMahon Act amended in Britain's favor.[11]

Macmillan immediately went on the offensive. In a nationwide broadcast he addressed himself to a vigorous justification of his foreign policy and the Thor deal in particular. He focused on the military necessity of the weapons and on the arrangements that would prevent Britain from unwilling involvement in a general nuclear war: "If bases for nuclear rockets are the up-to-date equivalent for bomb-carrying planes, then our whole defense policy, our whole strategy, becomes meaningless unless we have those bases. And we will have exactly the same veto upon the use of rockets as we have on the use of bombs from airplanes."[12]

In the week after the formal announcement, the national debate picked up considerable steam. There were four main groups of critics. First, some on the far left, including many Labour members of Parliament, opposed the deal because they wanted Britain to lead the world by the example of unilateral nuclear disarmament. Second, other Labour MPs, and a considerable public following, favored the deployment of Thor IRBMs in Britain only if disarmament talks with the Soviet Union, at that time being pursued by Macmillan, failed to achieve anything

9. *New York Times,* February 25, 1958.
10. Ibid., January 3, 1958.
11. Cited in ibid.
12. Ibid., January 5, 1958.

meaningful. Third, people across a wide political spectrum were concerned that Thor, as a relatively vulnerable product of the first phase of U.S. ballistic missile technology, would become obsolescent before it could actually be deployed. Fourth, some expressed skepticism about the government's claim to an effective veto over launch in times of crisis.

The first group of critics has a long tradition in Britain and at that time was a vocal, if ineffectual, source of political pressure. It used the Thor issue as only one component of a general peace campaign, which, for example, included the demand to ban all aircraft patrol flights over Britain that carried nuclear weapons.[13]

The second group received unwitting assistance from the British government. Throughout this period Macmillan was developing what was to become a long-term Conservative policy of encouraging a dialogue with Moscow over disarmament issues. He thus found himself in the uncomfortable position of having to strike a balance between those who wanted to deploy Thor irrespective of the Russian response and those who wanted to pursue Macmillan's own policy of dialogue before committing Britain to this particular military course.

The third group found its strongest support in the front bench of the Labour party, which repeatedly raised the obsolescence issue in the parliamentary debate. A related issue raised by these opponents was the difficulty encountered by the Eisenhower administration in amending the McMahon Act.[14]

The fourth group became less important when the details of the agreement were made public. The dual-key arrangement, by which Britain controlled release of the missile while the United States controlled the installation and the arming of the warheads, gave Britain an effective veto over launch.

Against the arguments of these groups, Macmillan used two counterarguments: the deployment of Thor would probably be only temporary, until American ICBM technology had progressed to the point where IRBMs were redundant and unnecessary; and the development of the IRBM option must not proceed throughout Europe so as to rigidify the cold war divisions of Europe. This second aspect of Macmillan's counterattack was easily reconciled with his desire for maintaining a continuing dialogue with the Soviet Union on security matters. What it

13. H. A. DeWeerd, "British Unilateralism," in R. N. Rosecrance, ed., *The Dispersion of Nuclear Weapons*, pp. 101–12.

14. Armacost, *Politics of Weapons Innovation*, pp. 195–96.

amounted to was quiet but firm opposition to the deployment of long-range, and later medium-range, ballistic missiles on West German soil—a position never put to the test by either the United States or SACEUR. Implicit also was the notion that because of its distance from the central front, Britain would be both politically and militarily the best place for Thor deployments in Europe.

On February 27, 1958, the government's position was accepted by Parliament, 317 to 261, with the strenuous efforts of Defense Minister Duncan Sandys paving the way for the final victory. Though this acceptance did not end public debate over the matter—protests and marches against the bases continued sporadically over the next several months—it did mark the end of serious attempts to reverse the Thor decision. Within the next year Britain received its first delivery of the missiles.

The French Reaction

In 1957 the French political scene was in a state of transition and crisis stemming from the Fourth Republic's chronic inability to maintain stable coalition governments and from growing frustration with France's colonial problems. The government was also in the process of reassessing its relations with Washington and London in the wake of the Suez affair. Unlike Britain, France had decided to move away from reliance on U.S. political and military guarantees. The significance of this decision was enhanced some months later when General de Gaulle reemerged as France's leader and made this turn from the United States a central part of the Gaullist world view.

Within this context, France's decision to develop its own nuclear arsenal already troubled American leaders. But the decision struck a deeply resonant chord with French voters, who never protested it. The Anglo-American rapprochement in March 1957 and the launch of sputnik in October had set the stage for the negative French reaction to the IRBM offer at the December NATO meeting. It was the French who persuaded undecided and confused European allies to press for the limited "commitment in principle" in the wording of the final communiqué.[15] When Norstad canvassed the French over IRBMs, and in subsequent contacts between U.S. officials and the French government,

15. Ibid., p. 199.

the French set three conditions for IRBM deployment under NATO auspices on French soil. First, the decision to use IRBMs based on French soil must be shared under the dual-key arrangement. This condition was not problematic: the British had successfully negotiated this provision in their agreement. France, however, insisted on a second condition: it must receive technical assistance from the United States to enable it to produce its own missile arsenal. Neither Eisenhower nor Dulles—nor, for that matter, Norstad—intended to let this offer become a vehicle for France to pursue its own national nuclear aspirations. Third, France insisted that as part of the deal the United States would have to help finance French missile production, a totally unacceptable condition for the United States.[16]

U.S.-French talks took a turn for the worse when de Gaulle returned to power in mid-1958. De Gaulle added many other requirements: specific political quid pro quos, technical assistance on French nuclear warhead design, and further comprehensive assurances of France's right to participate in any decision to launch. Adding fuel to the fire, when Eisenhower finally succeeded in having the McMahon Act amended, only Britain was allowed to benefit from liberalized access to nuclear weapons data. The result was obviously discriminatory against France. Finally, the deal proposed to France seemed to place the weapons under the authority of SACEUR, while British-based IRBMs would remain under bilateral U.S.-British command.[17]

The anger aroused in France by the perceived shortcomings of the IRBM offer to France when compared with the British deal, combined with the many political obstacles de Gaulle placed in the way of agreement and the American opposition to a French national nuclear arsenal, assured that negotiations between the two countries would remain unproductive. In 1959, after some eighteen months of frustrating negotiations, the French formally rejected the American offer. By that time their rejection surprised no one.

The West German Debate

The American IRBM offer in December 1957 was received in Bonn with a mixture of apprehension and confusion. For a while it was unclear

16. Wolf Mendl, *Deterrence and Persuasion*, pp. 56–57.
17. Armacost, *Politics of Weapons Innovation*, p. 200.

whether the United States intended to press Bonn to base either Thor or Jupiter missiles on its territory. At first Norstad seemed to discount this possibility; but in late February he denied that West German deployments had been excluded from consideration. Yet he must have been aware of Adenauer's position, formulated even before the December 1957 meeting, that although IRBMs and MRBMs were essential to counter the Soviet military threat, the Thor or Jupiter system would be inappropriate for deployment on the territory of the Federal Republic. Militarily, the inherent vulnerability of a stationary, liquid-fueled missile based above ground would be heightened by placement on the front line of NATO defenses. Such placement not only could lead to military instability in crises but would probably have domestic political repercussions that would be difficult to manage. Politically, deployment of missiles with ranges capable of reaching Soviet territory would leave West Germany open to Soviet charges of politically provocative behavior, hence endangering progress on one of Adenauer's top priorities, the reunification of Germany.[18] The Soviets made this linkage explicit during the course of alliance deliberations.

Because of these problems, and Norstad's sensitivity to them, West Germany was never formally asked to participate in IRBM deployments. Nevertheless, another proposal made at the December 1957 meeting, which Defense Minister Franz-Joseph Strauss followed up in March 1958, touched off a big debate in West Germany, one that was to affect West Germany's policies not only during this period but for some time to come.

At the December meeting, the alliance agreed to the formation of a NATO nuclear stockpile. The IRBM warheads were considered part of that stockpile. Nuclear weapons assigned to national armies under dual-key arrangements were also a part. On his return from a trip to the United States to survey U.S. programs for tactical nuclear weapons, Defense Minister Strauss announced his intention to equip the West German armed forces with Matador C nuclear-capable pilotless cruise missiles and some 300 Nike-Ajax air defense missiles, both under dual-key arrangements with the United States.

There followed one of the most vitriolic, emotional political debates in the history of postwar Germany. Arrayed on one side of the issue

18. Catherine McArdle Kelleher, *Germany and the Politics of Nuclear Weapons*, p. 131.

were the cabinet, headed by Adenauer with Strauss as defense minister, and the members of Adenauer's Christian Democratic party. The Christian Democrats used two arguments to justify their position. First, a failure to obtain what were euphemistically termed the "most modern weapons" would seriously undermine the government's ability to place the Federal Republic on an equal footing with other NATO European members and could negatively affect the morale and the fighting effectiveness of the armed forces. Second, these weapons were needed to help SACEUR meet his established requirements for greater nuclear capabilities in the European theater.

The opposition, led in the Bundestag by the Social Democrats, consisted of student groups, professors, clergy, and a wide but ill-defined segment of the general public. Polls indicated that some 80 percent of the West German population opposed atomic missile bases of any kind on German territory. The broad antinuclear coalition, called *Kampf dem Atomtod* (Campaign against Atomic Death), included a variety of political ideologies: the strictly pacifist elements were joined by those who were simply against nuclear weapons, as well as by those who favored reunification over other objectives and those who favored closer ties between Bonn and Moscow.[19]

In the Bundestag the debate was short but violent. Adenauer led off the debate by declaring that his government would not oppose nuclear weapons for the Federal Republic if the Atlantic alliance required it. He expressed his concern for NATO solidarity, and for the equality of West Germany within NATO, if the Bundestag repudiated an alliance requirement.[20]

Social Democratic leaders Fritz Erler and Erich Ollenhauer and a young representative named Helmut Schmidt led the opposition attack. They based their arguments not only on the vulnerability issue but also on the political issue of what nuclear arming would do to the cause of disarmament and disengagement agreements with the Soviet Union. The session of March 22, 1958, was particularly volatile, with unprecedented personal abuse being hurled back and forth between Strauss and Schmidt. In the end, the government won its case, passing the following resolution on March 25 by a vote of 275 to 161, with 26 abstentions:

19. Ibid., pp. 80–121.
20. Gordon A. Craig, "Germany and NATO: The Rearmament Debate, 1950–1958," in Klaus Knorr, ed., *NATO and American Security*, pp. 236–59.

In accordance with the requirements of this defensive system [the North Atlantic defense community] and in light of the armament of the possible opponent, the armed forces of the Federal Republic must be so equipped with the most modern weapons that they are able to fulfill obligations assumed by the Federal Republic within the NATO framework, and to make, in an effective manner, the necessary contribution to the securing of peace.[21]

Not content to let the matter rest with the Bundestag resolution, the *Atomtod* movement immediately took its cause to the streets, with mass demonstrations, rallies, and even calls for a general strike. The Social Democrats, confident of widespread public support, tried to administer a referendum in various districts on the question of nuclear armament for the Federal Republic.

In response, the government effectively blocked the referendum process through legislative and judicial measures. (There was a legitimate constitutional question about whether national referenda could in fact be administered.) It also spearheaded a public-relations campaign that emphasized the security requirements of the Federal Republic within NATO and U.S. custody and control over the actual nuclear warheads under standard dual-key arrangements. Using this two-pronged approach, Adenauer and Strauss were successful in settling the issue in the government's favor by the end of the summer.

The Other Allies

When Norstad canvassed the other European allies after the December 1957 NATO meeting, he found few countries eager to accept the IRBM offer. Denmark and Norway had already developed policies, current to this day, banning the stationing of nuclear weapons on their territories. In Belgium and Holland some interest had been shown, but in the end there was enough domestic political opposition in both countries to foreclose their participation. Among the remaining countries, only Italy, Greece, and Turkey were seriously considered for deployment, Portugal being too far from Warsaw Pact territory for IRBM deployments to be militarily justifiable.

In Italy the response to the American offer was positive, but there was some hesitation about the cost involved, especially since the British

21. *New York Times*, March 26, 1958. See also Kelleher, *Germany and the Politics of Nuclear Weapons*, p. 113.

experience made it clear that the host country would have to finance a large part of IRBM deployments. Negotiations dragged out on this issue, but on March 26, 1959, the United States and Italy came to an agreement for deployment of fifteen Jupiter missiles on Italian bases. The Italian government would build the bases and man them; the United States would sell the missiles to Italy and would retain custody of the warheads, much as it did in the British deal.[22]

The timing of the offer for Greece was not fortunate. Greek elections were taking place in mid-1958, and anti-Americanism was a popular political theme. The Karamanlis government was known to be friendly to the United States but because of election politics was constrained in how openly it could show its support. The result was decided disinterest in IRBMs for Greek deployment.[23]

Turkey was perhaps the most eager of all the recipients of IRBM offers. The Turkish government agreed early on to deploy two squadrons of Jupiter missiles, some thirty missiles, on Turkish bases under the same type of arrangement as was worked out for Italy.[24]

The Soviet Response

Even before the December 16, 1957, NATO meeting, Moscow was beginning to criticize the potential deployments. For several months it unleashed a diplomatic barrage against the offer, directing threats against each of the potential recipients. Some threats amounted simply to a warning that deployment of IRBMs on the territory of a given country would make it a more attractive target for nuclear devastation should war break out. Other threats were directed against particular objectives of potential host countries; for example, as already mentioned, Moscow told West Germany that progress on reunification would be stalled, perhaps permanently, if Bonn went forward with IRBM deployments.[25]

It is difficult to determine the precise influence of these diplomatic initiatives. They might have strengthened some countries, like Iceland or the Netherlands, against deployment. And West Germany would

22. Armacost, *Politics of Weapons Innovation,* p. 202.
23. *New York Times,* April 13, 1958.
24. Armacost, *Politics of Weapons Innovation,* p. 202.
25. For example, see *New York Times,* January 15 and 27, 1958; February 8 and 19, 1958; March 7 and 8, 1958; and April 1, 1958.

probably not have been asked to participate even if the Soviet Union had not launched its diplomatic offensive. Nevertheless, as Michael Armacost pointed out, the vociferous threats mounted against potential host countries probably created general public apprehension about the offer and contributed to Adenauer's difficulties on related matters.[26]

Mobile MRBMs: The Norstad Plan

The offer of Thor and Jupiter IRBMs to interested NATO allies constituted only a small part of a broader American response to sputnik. As mentioned before, the December 1957 heads of government meeting came to another critically important decision: to establish a nuclear stockpile for NATO.

The concept of such a stockpile seems to have originated with SACEUR General Norstad, who began developing the rationale for creating one as early as 1956.[27] The concept was straightforward. Forces assigned to NATO might require access to nuclear weapons at some point in a conflict with the Warsaw Pact. To assure that they would be given access when necessary, under appropriate political authority, a stockpile of nuclear weapons would be created for NATO, under SACEUR, that would supply relevant units with warheads after the North Atlantic Council authorized their release. Under the stockpile arrangement, delivery systems could be given to the allies in advance, so that once the weapons were released, it would be necessary only to match warheads with the already-deployed delivery systems.

Part of the impetus for this concept derived from the December 1956 North Atlantic Council ministerial meeting. At that meeting France announced its decision to pursue its own nuclear arsenal and succeeded in getting allied support for a request to the United States to supply NATO countries with nuclear weapons. Such a request could not be granted by the United States without a major revision of its legislation regarding the control of and access to nuclear weapons. As a result, the stockpile concept was developed; it stepped around the need for revising

26. Armacost, *Politics of Weapons Innovation,* pp. 203–04.
27. See John D. Steinbruner, *The Cybernetic Theory of Decision,* pp. 174–78. See also the authoritative account in Charles J. V. Murphy, "NATO at a Nuclear Crossroads," pp. 85 ff.

the McMahon Act, while moving a good way toward meeting the European request. It also provided a way of planning for deployment and use of weapons that were already being stockpiled in Europe by American forces.[28]

The offer of IRBMs fit well into the stockpile concept. As such, SACEUR General Norstad supported the deployment and lent his offices to the negotiation of the agreements just examined. However, during 1957 Norstad and his staff at SHAPE had been studying ways to implement the stockpile concept and had identified a requirement for a mobile medium-range ballistic missile system for deployment in Europe.[29] The requirement was based on the need to counter similar Soviet deployments in the theater and on the need to modernize NATO's tactical interdiction forces, which till then consisted almost entirely of fighter-bomber aircraft that would have increasing problems in penetrating Soviet air defenses.

The IRBMs being deployed in Britain, Italy, and Turkey would not fulfill this requirement, for many of the reasons already suggested. First, they were being deployed on fixed sites above ground, which made them extremely vulnerable to Soviet attack and attractive targets for preemption. Second, they were liquid-fueled and hence at low states of readiness. Third, too few of them were being deployed; SACEUR required anywhere from 300 to 700 medium-range ballistic missiles to cover the targets he wanted to be able to cover through his own command during a war.[30]

When the IRBM negotiations were drawing to a close, SHAPE became the focus of a series of consultations between Britain, France, and West Germany mediated by SACEUR.[31] These consultations during 1959 focused on an agreement by which the United States would provide a consortium of British, French, and West German firms with blueprints and technical data to begin production of a new mobile medium-range ballistic missile to be deployed under SACEUR's command, with the warheads to be provided under the stockpile arrangement. The consul-

28. Steinbruner, *Cybernetic Theory of Decision*, pp. 174–78; and Murphy, "NATO at a Nuclear Crossroads."
29. Ibid.
30. Exactly how these numbers were derived is unclear. See Steinbruner, *Cybernetic Theory of Decision*, p. 185.
31. Ibid., p. 184. In a recent interview with the author, Norstad stated that formal negotiations never took place, but that he raised the issue in bilateral discussions in Bonn, Paris, and London.

tations were drawn out by French insistence that France have the right to extend production of these missiles beyond what SACEUR required so as to meet its own national requirements. A compromise agreement was reportedly reached between West Germany and France, which would have provided for missile production for national purposes beyond the level of SACEUR's requirements.

It is unlikely that the Eisenhower administration had a direct role in these consultations, considering its opposition to any aid to the French national nuclear effort.

The consultations continued until August 1959 without any clear agreement on the specifications of the new missile. But in August the U.S. ambassador to NATO, William Draper, presented the recommendations of the panel he had headed at President Eisenhower's request to examine the problems facing the U.S. military assistance program.[32] The Draper Committee recommended, among other things, that the Polaris missile under development in conjunction with the U.S. fleet ballistic missile program be offered as a land-mobile MRBM to fulfill Norstad's MMRBM requirement. Progressing well through its development phase, the missile was admirably suited to Norstad's requirements from a technical standpoint. Readily adaptable to a land-mobile launcher, it would be relatively invulnerable to a Soviet preemptive missile attack. Fueled with solid propellant, it could be kept at a high state of readiness without the dangers associated with highly volatile liquid fuels. Finally, its medium range would give it the capability to strike targets deep within the Soviet Union from deployment locations in West Germany.

President Eisenhower authorized putting the Draper recommendation before the NATO Council in December 1959. Throughout 1960 negotiations continued at SHAPE, this time adapting the production formula based on the consortium of 1959 to production of Polaris. It is unclear whether members of the consortium would have been allowed to produce extra missiles for national purposes. It is also unclear to what degree the control over the missiles and warheads had been worked out and to what degree it was subject to the stockpile arrangements described above. But in a sense these issues are irrelevant, because the consultations never bore fruit.

The reasons that Norstad failed to realize his MMRBM requirement are complex. In this first place, the U.S. defense bureaucracy raised a

32. Steinbruner, *Cybernetic Theory of Decision*, p. 185.

series of strategic and military arguments against MMRBMs. For example, however mobile they were, they would still be vulnerable to capture or destruction during ground operations. This vulnerability would create tremendous pressure for their use before capture or destruction by enemy forces. Furthermore, it was conceivable that such pressure would mount before either side had used nuclear weapons. Surely the West would want to be more deliberate in any decision to initiate the use of nuclear weapons. To make matters worse, warning systems to detect preemptive attack were virtually nonexistent, creating even more pressure for early use of these weapons.

Another problem raised by American critics was the relatively small size of the projected deployments. Even if 700 MMRBMs were deployed, it was argued, SACEUR would still have to rely heavily on the national strategic forces of the United States for target coverage. Some argued that, given the extra funds involved in creating a separate NATO strategic nuclear force, it would be more efficient simply to let U.S. strategic nuclear forces—already programmed to grow substantially over the next several years—satisfy the mission requirements SHAPE had identified.

The practical and political problems of arranging for the transport of Polaris missiles and launchers over public roads in densely populated areas of Western Europe were also not insignificant. Would the roads actually be strong enough to support Polaris convoys? Would the visibility of the convoys in such a deployment mode create political problems among the host countries by arousing local opposition to the deployments?

Not only were Americans concerned about security from Warsaw Pact attack; some feared that a system like the MMRBM could be overcome by NATO national military forces and used unilaterally without the authority of alliance decisionmakers or appropriate NATO commanders.

Finally, some Americans objected to the whole idea of negotiating a sharing arrangement for strategic nuclear weapons with the allies, on the grounds that such an arrangement would exaggerate the importance of these systems in the overall NATO deterrent, and distract the allies from potentially more useful expenditures on conventional ground and air forces.

Certainly all these objections, held not only by academics and bureaucrats but by the Joint Committee on Atomic Energy, which would have to pass judgment on U.S. participation in any such NATO nuclear sharing scheme, contributed to the demise of Norstad's MMRBM proposal. Another contributing factor was probably Norstad's increasing distance from the main centers of decisionmaking in Washington. As early as 1957 he had aroused controversy and confusion within the United States and NATO over his pronouncement of the pause doctrine. He had also met with strong rebuff in a premature attempt to shift NATO doctrine toward greater flexibility and greater recognition of the importance of conventional forces within NATO's overall capabilities. Perhaps leaders in Washington, increasingly irritated by his maverick behavior, wanted to undermine his position and objectives, yet at the same time felt constrained, because of Norstad's general popularity among European leaders, against doing so openly. Thus they were willing to let Norstad conduct his negotiations at SHAPE and were even willing to give him support at various times, but deliberately did little to bring the initiative from the bargaining table to the implementation stage.

This interpretation is admittedly speculative. It is proposed in ignorance of exactly how close to agreement these secret negotiations came; whether France ever agreed to participate in MMRBM deployments without demanding some aid to its own nuclear program; whether the United States ever agreed to allow production of Polaris for European use to be extended beyond SACEUR's requirement to meet national requirements; or whether the myriad technical problems that are part of any negotiation over a weapons system were ever resolved satisfactorily in the eyes of the participants. Nevertheless, the interpretation above is plausible and would help to explain why a proposal apparently taken so seriously by major allies never moved off the drawing board.

There is, however, an additional explanation: those who found something to question in the Norstad plan were able to come up with an alternative, which they carried through negotiations between 1962 and 1965: the multilateral force, discussed in the next chapter.

Conclusions

Any explanation of why the United States pursued the IRBM initiative must include many reasons, not all related to fears about the U.S. strategic guarantee. For example, the fact that an IRBM was pursued at all by the United States virtually guaranteed some sort of European deployment; and the fact that the IRBM was pursued at all was directly due to the faster development projected for it over that of the ICBM. But in many ways the IRBM offer was motivated by fears about the potential implications of the sputnik launch, implications that might lead to greater questioning of the U.S. strategic guarantee and leadership ability.

In some ways the United States had already received hints that the allies were entertaining such doubts, especially after the December 1956 North Atlantic Council ministerial meeting, in which the allies petitioned the United States for access to nuclear weapons. The response was the creation of the NATO nuclear stockpile arrangement, which later became the foundation both for the IRBM initiative and Norstad's MMRBM initiative.

But while these initiatives were stimulated by specific European concerns, they also ran the risk of increasing pressure for unilateral proliferation. Would host countries for Thor and Jupiter missiles long be satisfied with dual-key control arrangements that gave the United States an effective veto over launch? Having come so close to acquiring strategic nuclear forces of their own, would Italy and Turkey eventually press for full control over these missiles? If so, how would the United States resist this pressure? Furthermore, would the provision of Thors and Jupiters, over time, stimulate the interest of other European allies—particularly West Germany—in acquiring similar, or even more independent, capabilities? These questions illustrate one of the central dilemmas that faced U.S. planners throughout this period: how to reassure the allies over the American strategic guarantee without at the same time encouraging nuclear proliferation.

Certainly Norstad was motivated in part by a desire to help resolve European doubts and fears over sputnik. During his years as SACEUR, Norstad came to be known as a particularly sensitive spokesman for the views of European members of the alliance. In his discussions with European officers and political leaders, he no doubt received many of the signals that led him to believe the allies wanted a greater share of control over the strategic arsenals of the alliance.

But Norstad's motivations for leading negotiations to create an MMRBM force for NATO extended beyond the desire to resolve these doubts. Norstad was concerned about the many technical problems associated with the IRBM deployments and believed that if NATO was to have its own nuclear force, that force would have to be the most up-to-date one available to the alliance. Since Thors and Jupiters did not meet this requirement, he sought a more modern mobile missile, finally settling on a land-based deployment of Polaris.

The Europeans resisted the IRBM deployments largely because they recognized they were in a more exposed strategic position than the United States vis-à-vis the retaliatory force of the Soviet Union. They felt that such deployments would entail an unequal sharing of risk. Each of the governments, except that of Turkey, also faced extensive domestic opposition. The specific reaction of France reflected the beginning of a long negative chapter in U.S.-French relations, with de Gaulle's rejection of the IRBM offer and his insistence that any MMRBM production consortium be permitted to produce extra missiles for French national forces.

European public reactions to the IRBM proposals were somewhat muted because of the secrecy of the negotiations taking place at SHAPE. Norstad's proposal never provoked serious controversy in public, except when the general made one of his occasional speeches outlining his vision of NATO as a fourth nuclear power. These speeches raised some comment, but no evidence suggests that opposition to the Norstad initiative in Europe ever blocked the negotiations.

Both the Thor-Jupiter initiative and the MMRBM proposal were examples of hardware solutions to NATO's nuclear dilemmas. As such, they began to reveal some of the generic weaknesses of the hardware approach. Attention became focused on the political visibility of the weapons and their potential for provocation. They quickly became lightning rods for political opposition. Arguments were generated over the technical adequacy of the systems to perform their missions. Questions about control of the systems were raised, although these questions were, by and large, resolved to everyone's satisfaction.

The IRBM offer was obviously a success, though a mixed one, with only three of the six potential host countries ultimately agreeing to deploy the missiles on their territory. In the process of negotiation, however, intra-alliance tensions that were to plague NATO for a decade arose for the first time. The story of the multilateral force follows naturally from this episode, since that force represented an alternative to the Norstad plan that was consciously pursued by the U.S. government for the next three years.

CHAPTER FIVE

The Multilateral Force

HOWEVER one views the controversial American proposal to create a multilateral nuclear force for NATO—and it inevitably arouses strong passions in proponents and detractors alike—it merits a central place in this study. For more than three years the multilateral force (MLF) was the U.S. response to NATO's doubts about the strategic guarantee. It dominated discussions with the allies for a long time and nearly came into being.[1]

The Origins of the MLF

At the NATO ministerial meeting held in Paris in December 1960, outgoing Secretary of State Christian A. Herter made a proposal that marks the formal birth of the MLF. Allegedly responding to European desires for greater control over the strategic deterrent of the alliance, and to SACEUR General Lauris Norstad's stated requirement for a NATO medium-range ballistic missile force, Herter noted America's willingness to assign to NATO five Polaris missile submarines, soon to be built as the initial phase of the U.S. Polaris program. He also suggested that Washington would look favorably on a European request to put 100 U.S.-built MRBMs out to sea in addition to the five Polaris submarines,

1. Much of this chapter is based on Steinbruner's detailed account of the internal American political and bureaucratic dynamics behind the MLF proposal. John D. Steinbruner, *The Cybernetic Theory of Decision,* pp. 153–342. Other important accounts are found in J. W. Boulton, "NATO and the MLF," pp. 275–94; Alastair Buchan, "The Multilateral Force," pp. 619–37; Catherine McArdle Kelleher, *Germany and the Politics of Nuclear Weapons,* pp. 228–69; and Andrew J. Pierre, *Nuclear Politics,* pp. 217–74. Primary source material has been drawn from the *New York Times.*

as the centerpiece of a NATO nuclear force. He made these two offers conditional on agreement by the European members of NATO on how to control the launch of this force.[2]

Coming as it did in the final weeks of the Eisenhower administration, the proposal received a noncommittal response. For one thing, it was reasonable to expect that the incoming Kennedy administration would not feel committed to a tentative offer put forth so late in its predecessor's tenure. For another, Herter's claim that the proposal was intended to satisfy Norstad's requirement probably seemed hollow; Norstad was known to have favored a land-based mobile MRBM system and had gone to considerable lengths to negotiate the creation of such a force.

The Herter offer would have been more explicable to the Europeans, if not more attractive, had they been privy to the bureaucratic origins of the offer. Norstad's efforts to create his land-based MRBM force caused concern within the State Department.[3] Many officials feared that such a force would grant West Germany too much access to long-range nuclear weapons, which would in turn aggravate U.S.-Soviet relations and U.S.-French relations. Furthermore—so these officials reasoned—it would provide additional impetus for German political insecurities, already stimulated by France's decision to build its own nuclear forces.

Concerned that the Norstad initiative might succeed, the director of the State Department Policy Planning Staff, Gerard Smith, persuaded Herter to call on Robert Bowie of Harvard, an old friend of Smith's and a former Policy Planning Staff director, to study serious alternatives to Norstad's proposals in the context of a broad examination of the tasks facing the Atlantic community in the 1960s. In the summer of 1960 Bowie and his staff, which included members of both the bureaucracy and the academic community, produced a paper that outlined the basis for the MLF. The section relating to NATO defense was in two parts.[4] The first was a sustained argument in favor of improving NATO's conventional capabilities, which reflected a growing awareness both inside and outside the government that a strong conventional shield was both necessary

2. The details of this proposal can be found in *New York Times*, December 17 and 19, 1960.

3. Steinbruner, *Cybernetic Theory of Decision*, pp. 188–89.

4. The text of the Bowie Report has recently been declassified under the Freedom of Information Act and is available in the National Archives. See also Steinbruner, *Cybernetic Theory of Decision;* and *Nominations of Robert R. Bowie and U. Alexis Johnson,* Senate Hearings, pp. 9–10, 36, in which Bowie gives his recollection of the report.

and feasible. The second part argued for the creation of a multilateral NATO strategic nuclear force, which would combine elements of participation in and control by many NATO nations into an integrated NATO force. The creation of such a force would be conditional on the achievement of conventional force improvements and on an expressed European desire for a more active participation in the strategic nuclear posture of the alliance.

Bowie proposed the creation of the MLF in two phases. The first phase would consist of assigning some number of American strategic missile submarines to SACEUR, who would be granted authority in advance to launch the force under certain specific circumstances. To launch the force otherwise, he would need the approval of the North Atlantic Council, with the understanding that the United States would concur in the judgment of the council.

The second phase would entail creating a truly multilateral sea-based strategic nuclear force. This force would differ from the Polaris force largely in the way the crews for the vessels were formed. Each unit of the new force would be manned by a multinational crew from at least three countries; this would make for a truly multilateral force, each unit of which would be invulnerable to commandeering by any of the participating national crews. The participants would have to agree in advance on some arrangement for authorizing launch; Bowie suggested an arrangement like the one in the first phase. He insisted that the United States would have to maintain formal custody of the nuclear warheads to maintain security on warhead design; however, the United States would undertake to release the warheads under the prearranged procedures. He evidently believed that under this formal arrangement continued U.S. custody of warheads would not be construed as a veto. Finally, Bowie stipulated that to move from the first to the second phase would require the further improvement of NATO's conventional capabilities.

Bowie argued that the MLF would undermine national aspirations for independent nuclear forces in nonnuclear NATO countries, thus stopping what was seen as an otherwise inevitable trend toward nuclear proliferation. To the opponents of nuclear proliferation, the spread of independent national nuclear arsenals within the alliance would be dangerously destabilizing, at best complicating alliance coordination in wartime, at worst heightening tensions and provoking crises that could lead to nuclear war. By granting nonnuclear NATO partners some degree of control over the launch of strategic weaponry, the MLF was supposed to meet their nuclear aspirations halfway, allowing them to help determine the circumstances under which these weapons would be used while seriously constraining use without the full agreement of NATO members.

To Bowie and his State Department colleagues, it was probably apparent that neither Britain nor France could be induced to give up its independent nuclear capability in exchange for participation in the MLF, though their participation would be sought to provide incentives for NATO's nonnuclear members to join the project. By the same token, however, Bowie opposed U.S. acquiescence in any arrangements that would enhance these independent capabilities.

At bottom, proponents of the multilateral nuclear force were largely concerned about West German objectives. The assumption behind Bowie's original MLF plan seems to have been that Bonn's political insecurities, stimulated by the examples of Britain and France, were on the rise; hence West Germany's unseemly eagerness for access to U.S. tactical nuclear weapons and its interest in Norstad's initiatives. Furthermore, basic West German policy strove to reduce whatever discrimination existed in NATO against Bonn; the growing French nuclear program and the continuing Anglo-American special relationship, it was felt, would lead Bonn to rectify its "second class" status within the alliance, perhaps by pursuing more intimate nuclear cooperation with France. The MLF was seen as a clever way of forestalling such an action without running the risks Norstad seemed to be taking.

The Philosophic Context: European Integration

A second, related theme, taken up in the final sections of the Bowie paper, was the need to promote European unity.[5] For many years State Department and other U.S. officials had been influenced by the thinking and efforts of Europeans like Jean Monnet and Paul-Henri Spaak, who favored creating institutions and policies that would promote the unification of Europe and a trans-Atlantic partnership between a united Europe and the United States. These efforts were the natural result of

5. Steinbruner, *Cybernetic Theory of Decision*, pp. 190–91. The volume of literature on the European unity and integration movement is staggering. Some interesting introductory treatments are found in Ben T. Moore, *NATO and the Future of Europe;* Mary Margaret Ball, *NATO and the European Union Movement;* and Max Beloff, *The United States and the Unity of Europe.*

the experience of two European conflagrations in the previous half-century. To such people, the prime culprit in the tragedy of modern European history was rampant, virulent nationalism. When competing nationalisms gripped the highly industrialized, closely crowded nations of Europe, war was the inevitable result. Moreover, these wars always involved the United States. This dilemma seemed especially tragic to those who were convinced of the strong cultural heritage shared by the European nations. Many Europeans and Americans could thus agree that postwar Europe would have to rid itself of its divisive and destructive nationalisms.

But how to do this? While some European visionaries pursued the quixotic goal of a totally integrated Europe operating as one social, political, and economic entity, others sought to solve specific, narrow, manageable problems on a cooperative basis. Through institutions like the European Coal and Steel Community, the European Economic Community, and NATO, patterns of European cooperation and integration began to form and flourish. The most ardent proponents of integration tried to make sure that these modest, initial steps would have tangible effects that would further reduce old nationalistic divisions and enmities. For them, NATO was far more than a military organization; in it were the seeds of a supranational European state.

Even the most skeptical American observers of these efforts could agree that a strong, conflict-free Europe was in America's best interest. As a result, the United States had never blocked these integrative efforts. In fact, Washington usually encouraged them, even if some officials doubted the inevitability of a unified Europe. So when the alliance began to reflect the stress brought about by the crisis of confidence over America's nuclear guarantee to Western Europe, the natural reaction in Washington was to try to reverse the trend, to preserve what progress had already been achieved, and to eliminate the strains that threatened to undo the process of European integration.

For Bowie, and increasingly for high officials in the State Department, the MLF provided a unique opportunity to eliminate tensions created within the alliance in the previous few years, and at the same time to create a new, vital institution to promote further European integration. Thus the stakes that rested on the success of the MLF proposal were perceived at the outset to be extraordinarily high. The Bowie report was presented to Secretary Herter; at the same time, Livingston Merchant, a State Department official, arranged for Bowie to brief President

Eisenhower on its conclusions. The report was apparently circulated to many high-level officials, including SACEUR General Norstad and General Andrew Goodpaster. It formed the basis of Herter's December 1960 presentation to the NATO ministers. According to Herter, "a firm proposal could not be made since [the NATO] meeting was held after election day and before the newly elected administration had taken over." As he further stated:

The concept was that the United States would commit to NATO five submarines carrying a total of eighty Polaris missiles. If our allies provided additional missiles on a multilaterally manned, owned, and controlled basis, deployed either in submarines, in surface vessels, or on land, the United States would then combine its five submarines with the contribution made by our allies into a NATO deterrent force under NATO command. How the NATO command should be constituted was left for subsequent consideration.[6]

Also left for subsequent consideration was how the allies would provide these missiles, whether by their own production or, more likely, by acquisition from U.S. manufacturers.

President Kennedy in Ottawa, May 1961

When John F. Kennedy assumed office in January, he had no elaborate preconceived notion of how to restructure alliance relations.[7] He understood the complexities of the strains besetting the alliance but was skeptical about the dangers these strains allegedly posed to NATO. He had some well-formulated doubts about the wisdom of NATO's primary reliance on strategic nuclear capabilities to deter all forms of Warsaw Pact aggression, doubts that his secretary of defense, Robert McNamara, shared. As time passed and de Gaulle's challenge to American leadership of the alliance grew in scope and intensity, Kennedy evolved his own "Grand Design" for Western political relations, stressing European integration and partnership with the United States. But when he took office, all this lay in the future, and he seemed willing to entertain a variety of possible, and not always compatible, American policies toward Western Europe.

6. Christian A. Herter, *Toward an Atlantic Community*, pp. 41–42.

7. This is the general impression one derives from Arthur M. Schlesinger, Jr., *A Thousand Days*, pp. 842–66; Theodore C. Sorensen, *Kennedy*, pp. 562ff; and Joseph Kraft, *The Grand Design*.

Thus one would not expect Herter's MLF offer to have had a high priority for Kennedy, and indeed it did not. What the president might have done if the Europeans had responded more positively to that offer is impossible to know. As it was, they took a wait-and-see attitude; in this environment Kennedy felt no need to kill rumors that he and his secretary of defense favored shelving the proposal. In fact, Kennedy and McNamara immediately began to review U.S. strategic policy and were rapidly concluding that devolution of U.S. control over the strategic deterrent was undesirable.

At the same time, however, Kennedy seemed willing to entertain the MLF concept as one of many possible ways to resolve the strategic nuclear problems of the alliance. This noncommittal stance gave planning officials in the State Department, who still favored the MLF, an opportunity to lobby for the Herter concept. They eventually succeeded in persuading Kennedy to reaffirm the December 1960 offer.

In a speech before the Canadian Parliament in May, Kennedy emphasized the need for a strong and prosperous Atlantic community and essentially reiterated Herter's offer:

We must make certain that nuclear weapons will continue to be available for the defense of the entire Treaty area, and that these weapons are at all times under close and flexible political control that meets the needs of all the NATO countries. We are prepared to join our Allies in working out suitable arrangements for this purpose.

To make clear our own intentions and commitments to the defense of Western Europe, the United States will commit to the NATO command five—and subsequently still more—Polaris atomic-missile submarines, which are defensive weapons, subject to any agreed NATO guidelines on their control and use, and responsive to the needs of all members but still credible in an emergency. Beyond this, we look to the possibility of establishing a NATO sea-borne force, which would be truly multi-lateral in ownership and control, if this should be desired and found feasible by our Allies, once NATO's non-nuclear goals have been achieved.[8]

The careful wording of this offer falls far short of an unequivocal endorsement of the multilateral force. Kennedy had set forth stringent preconditions for American support of the MLF, which indicate the tentative nature of Kennedy's proposal:

— NATO would have to agree on guidelines for control and use of the force.

8. *Public Papers of the Presidents: John F. Kennedy, 1961*, p. 385.

— These guidelines, once established, would have to be responsive to the needs of all members of the alliance.

— The control arrangements would further have to demonstrate credibility in an emergency.

— American support for the MLF would depend critically on positive European assessments of the desirability and feasibility of the force.

— The MLF would be pursued only after NATO's nonnuclear goals had been achieved.

These preconditions were stiff, and in May 1961 most observers would have agreed that it would be difficult to meet any of them. Perhaps Kennedy believed this difficulty would prevent him from having to make good on his offer. Perhaps he was more concerned with placating State Department officials eager to see the MLF reemerge as an American proposal than he was with actually creating a NATO nuclear force. As time passed, however, each precondition was abandoned in the effort to press the MLF on the Europeans.

Exploratory or not, the Ottawa pledge elicited little reaction from European governments, who were sensitive to the stiff preconditions and increasingly preoccupied with other matters, including the Berlin crisis and the Kennedy administration's attempts to bolster NATO's conventional forces.

The Lavaud Visit and Its Aftermath

The first opportunity after the May 1961 NATO meeting for the MLF advocates to resurrect their idea came in March 1962, when French General Gaston Lavaud visited Washington with a list of items France wanted to buy from the United States. Most of the items related to France's ongoing nuclear weapons program and totaled some $250 million.[9] The request set off a major debate within the U.S. government. From his post as U.S. ambassador to France, General James Gavin actively lobbied for State Department approval of the request. So did many other American officials who viewed the Lavaud mission as an opportunity to improve Franco-American relations.

9. The account of the Lavaud mission presented here relies on Steinbruner, *Cybernetic Theory of Decision*, pp. 216–20; and Wilfrid L. Kohl, *French Nuclear Diplomacy*, pp. 217–22.

Equally vociferous were those who opposed granting aid to the maverick French program. Officials in the Pentagon had been carefully developing a coherent strategic policy that viewed the evolution of independent national nuclear arsenals as a planner's nightmare and were preparing to present the new policy to NATO at the May ministerial meeting in Athens. There McNamara would present a surprisingly blunt critique of small, independent nuclear forces. In the State Department, as already noted, many officials were also worried about the French program, which they felt set a tempting example for Bonn. In their view, too, the French request could not be granted.

Seizing this opportunity, planners in the State Department advanced the MLF as an alternative to the French request.[10] The deputy director of the Policy Planning Staff, Henry Owen, had helped to formulate the Bowie proposal; in April, Owen prepared a paper arguing that Kennedy's Ottawa pledge provided a basis for a creative response to Lavaud.

Owen's paper remains classified, but informed accounts reported that it recommended offering help to France as a potential participant in the multilateral force as conceived by Bowie and put forth by Herter and Kennedy. The force, as proposed by Owen, would consist of 200 sea-based MRBMs, placed on vessels manned by crews of mixed nationalities, to minimize the possibility of one nation commandeering strategic nuclear forces for its own purposes. Participation in the force would be as broad as possible; the cost of the force would be shared fairly by the participants. The United States would maintain an effective veto over launch of the missiles, but would make clear its willingness to review this arrangement later if the Europeans showed greater progress toward political unification. While this force was in the process of being negotiated, the United States should immediately assign five Polaris submarines to NATO under NATO command structures.

When Kennedy, McNamara, Secretary of State Dean Rusk, and the president's national security adviser, McGeorge Bundy, met later in April to review the Lavaud request and to work out a response, the Owen paper apparently formed the basis for their discussions. Given State's aversion to nuclear proliferation and McNamara's impending flexible response proposal in Athens, it was relatively easy for Kennedy's group to decide to reject the French request. With the Owen version of the MLF in front of him as an alternative, Kennedy agreed to internal

10. See Steinbruner, *Cybernetic Theory of Decision*, pp. 225–34.

exploratory studies and tentative discussions among the allies on the MLF scheme, endorsing the Owen plan but refusing to relinquish U.S. control over the Polaris submarines to be assigned to NATO, in compliance with the strongly held position of the Joint Chiefs of Staff. Kennedy also reiterated his opposition to giving up a U.S. veto over launch of any future MLF, but agreed that the possibility of a future U.S. change of position on this issue could be raised with European officials if it would enhance European interest in the proposal.

With this decision, the U.S. bureaucracy moved into high gear. On the home front the navy examined the feasibility of the MLF. Under the supervision of Admiral Frederick Michaelis and his deputy, Admiral Claude V. Ricketts, studies began to appear in the summer of 1962 that identified a surface-fleet configuration, as opposed to a subsurface configuration, as the desirable and feasible direction for the MLF project to take. The studies also examined the problems associated with the vulnerability of a surface fleet to conventional enemy attack and concluded that certain measures could be taken to minimize this vulnerability.

On the civilian side of the Pentagon the International Security Affairs (ISA) staff spent the summer working out in detail plans for the proposed MLF, including design specifications, possible command arrangements, missile control procedures, and language training. By the end of the summer, with the Michaelis studies and staff work at ISA complete, the proposal had gained "serious organizational stature."[11]

Even before the studies had been finished, however, the State Department had begun to sound out European reactions to the Owen plan. In April, Under Secretary of State George Ball, well-known to be sympathetic to the cause of European integration and an activist when it came to the MLF, traveled to Bonn and talked up the plan before Chancellor Adenauer and Defense Minister Strauss, who were becoming more and more interested in it. When Secretary Rusk went to Europe in late June to calm European fears over the McNamara speech in Ann Arbor, he brought with him the MLF scheme as evidence of American commitment not to decouple its nuclear forces from the NATO deterrent. In London and Bonn he stressed American opposition to the much discussed idea of an integrated European nuclear force independent of Washington, but indicated that the United States would support the

11. Ibid., pp. 229–32.

creation of a NATO-wide integrated nuclear force along the lines of the MLF. Rusk received a positive response from his West German counterpart Gerhard Schroeder. In London, Prime Minister Harold Macmillan was decidedly cooler, reserving judgment on whether Britain would be interested in participating in the MLF. Adenauer was apparently so enthusiastic about the proposal that he went to Paris to try, unsuccessfully, to convince de Gaulle to support the plan.

All this activity succeeded in signaling to the Europeans that the United States was indeed interested in pursuing the MLF scheme. But until the summer studies had been completed, the details were vague. This vagueness was rectified in October, when, armed with the voluminous Pentagon studies, U.S. officials, led by Gerard Smith and Admiral John Lee of the ISA staff, created a briefing on the MLF for European capitals.

The Smith-Lee briefing described a fleet of twenty-five surface vessels armed with eight Polaris MRBMs apiece. This fleet would be jointly owned and operated and would be controlled by a governing board composed of representatives from the participating countries. Each vessel would be manned by crews from at least three nations. Regarding control over the launch, the United States would retain a veto, but the possibility of devolving control to the Europeans at some unspecified future date was raised.

From the European perspective the Smith-Lee mission must have been somewhat confusing. First, the proposal now seemed to call for a surface configuration, but had not the United States pledged to provide NATO with Polaris submarines? Was this a shift? Second, a few months earlier the allies had been treated to rather blunt lectures by McNamara, at Athens and Ann Arbor, emphasizing the adequacy of present strategic nuclear arrangements. The MLF proposal, by McNamara's logic, seemed at best superfluous; at worst, if control was eventually devolved or decentralized, the proposal violated central canons of the new McNamara strategy.

As might be expected, these briefings received a mixed reaction in several countries.[12] In Bonn the interest that had been aroused by prior visits from Ball and Rusk was enhanced. The foreign ministry agreed

---

12. For the German reaction to the briefing, see Kelleher, *Germany and the Politics of Nuclear Weapons*, pp. 190–91; for the reactions of the other countries, see Schlesinger, *A Thousand Days*, p. 885.

with the chancellor and his defense minister that the proposed MLF would grant the Federal Republic fully equal status within the alliance and tie down the American nuclear commitment to NATO. Strauss even hinted that failure of the MLF initiative would force West Germany to reconsider its original nonproliferation pledge.

The German military leaders, on the other hand, had doubts about the details of the Smith-Lee briefing. They were quick to recognize that a continuing American veto over launch would not fundamentally alter the basis for West German insecurity over the U.S. nuclear guarantee. They were also concerned about the vulnerability of the surface vessel configuration, doubting whether the measures proposed by ISA for minimizing this problem—such as designing ship hulls to resemble merchant vessels—would really suffice. These doubts, however, were apparently stifled by the West German political leadership, which gave Smith and Lee positive assurances of interest and support, though falling short of a formal commitment to participate.

Reports of the reaction in Brussels are less detailed, but it appears that the Belgian leadership was generally favorable to the scheme. One might speculate that appeals to the goal of European integration, which inevitably became associated with the MLF, given the circumstances of its birth, fell on particularly receptive ears within a political elite that had spawned one of the most ardent advocates of European integration, Paul-Henri Spaak, at that time secretary general of NATO.

The Italian reaction was more reserved. Although top political leaders seemed interested, they were constrained by their chronic domestic political instability from actively supporting a proposal that would draw heavy criticism from anti-American elements on the right and on the left. Nevertheless, Italian officials had generally supported the creation of a NATO nuclear force in the previous few months. Smith and Lee probably left Rome believing that the Italians would eventually give their full support.

Reaction in London was the most skeptical. The Foreign Office, while sensitive to the potential challenge implicit in the MLF scheme to the special relationship between Britain and the United States, calculated that it was worthwhile giving the proposal "a fair wind." The Defense Ministry, however, had strong reservations. Not only did it place a higher priority on preserving the uniqueness of the special relationship; the Royal Navy positively scoffed at the notion of mixed-manned vessels, in spite of Britain's historical success in mixed-manned fleets (Lord

Nelson's flagship at Trafalgar, for example).[13] Lord Montgomery derided the scheme as "utter and complete poppycock."[14] Other British officials, notably the chief science adviser, Sir Solly Zuckerman, also questioned the feasibility of and necessity for the MLF.[15] Macmillan, faced with this ambivalence among his advisers, apparently saw no need to change his stand of the previous summer and did not offer a British commitment to participate in the force.[16]

Significantly, France was not included on the briefing itinerary. De Gaulle and his prime minister, Maurice Couve de Murville, had repeatedly emphasized French plans to proceed with an independent nuclear deterrent.[17] They had shown intermittent interest in the creation of a European nuclear deterrent independent of the United States, as an alternative to the U.S.-sponsored MLF, and even suggested integrating France's future deterrent into the NATO framework, but these proposals remained vague. These considerations may have prompted Smith and Lee to bypass Paris, as they had undoubtedly prompted Rusk some months earlier, when he stopped in Paris on his post–Ann Arbor mission, to avoid discussing the MLF proposal with de Gaulle and his aides.

In any case, even the mixed reception accorded to Smith and Lee made McNamara question whether the two emissaries had overstepped their mandate. He had profound misgivings about the need for an MLF; to him, the American nuclear guarantee was a political and technical fact, dictated by the growing size of the superpower arsenals, the revolution in delivery systems, and the requirements of counterforce strategy and flexible control. The proposed force would add little to the programmed nuclear capability of the West; furthermore, it threatened to violate the requirement for a centrally controllable, unified strategic nuclear arsenal, which became the hallmark of the McNamara approach to strategic planning. Finally, McNamara was convinced that when the Europeans, who were supposedly clamoring for the MLF, realized that the United States would not relinquish a veto over launch and that the financial burden of creating, operating, and maintaining the force would

13. Wilfrid L. Kohl makes this point in his early study of the MLF, "Nuclear Sharing in NATO and the Multilateral Force," p. 96.

14. Cited in Boulton, "NATO and the MLF," p. 289.

15. Pierre, *Nuclear Politics*, p. 246.

16. Schlesinger, *A Thousand Days*, p. 855.

17. A thorough discussion of the development of French strategy, which will help to place these statements in their appropriate context, is found in the next chapter.

be shared among all the participants, they would quickly lose their enthusiasm. That this was not the immediate outcome of the Smith-Lee mission led McNamara to suspect that the authorized message had not been accurately transmitted. In a subsequent meeting with Smith, Lee, Rusk, and McGeorge Bundy, he voiced these suspicions.[18] Rusk and Bundy came to their colleagues' defense and apparently persuaded McNamara that Smith and Lee had not exceeded their instructions, though Rusk expressed personal doubts about whether the Europeans would ultimately agree to participate in the MLF. At this meeting McNamara apparently discovered that the State Department planned to propose a "mini-MLF" for the Mediterranean, as a replacement for Thor missiles in Italy and Turkey to be dismantled in the wake of the Cuban missile crisis, to serve as a first phase in the creation of a NATO-wide MLF.[19] McNamara quickly killed this proposal and got the Italians and Turks to agree to accept the Polaris submarines pledged to NATO, but under American control, as a replacement for the dismantled missiles.[20]

This setback notwithstanding, by the beginning of December 1962 the MLF proponents in the United States could review the events of the previous eight months with a sense of accomplishment. In April the proposal had existed mainly as a passing reference in a few speeches by American officials. By December the proposal had been staffed out in some detail and presented in a preliminary fashion to four of the allies. The reactions had been mixed, of course; and France seemed to continue in its determination to remain outside the MLF. But in West Germany the enthusiasm of Ball, Smith, and Lee had been infectious. Other events, notably the debate over McNamara's flexible response doctrine,

18. Steinbruner, *Cybernetic Theory of Decision,* pp. 233–34.
19. The relation between the missiles in Cuba and the Jupiter missiles in Turkey has long been the subject of controversy. Specifically, it is claimed that Kennedy thought about, and decided against, offering to remove the aging Jupiters from Turkey in return for Soviet withdrawal of MRBMs from Cuba. Others claim that Robert Kennedy suggested such a sub-rosa trade-off in his secret meeting with Antonin Dobrynin, a claim supported obliquely by the late senator's memoirs of the crisis. (Robert F. Kennedy, *Thirteen Days,* pp. 108–09.) For a revealing account of the Cuban crisis and the missiles in Turkey, see the article by Barton J. Bernstein based on extensively declassified minutes of the so-called ExComm: "The Cuban Missile Crisis," pp. 97–125.
20. For evidence that Polaris submarines under sole control of the United States were offered—and accepted—as replacement for Thor missiles in Italy and Turkey, see *New York Times,* January 18 and 21, 1963.

had intensified this enthusiasm. The energy and dedication of the MLF "theologians"—as they were quickly coming to be known—had paid off in substantive terms. They had had help from many sources, including the Action Committee for a United Europe, headed by Jean Monnet, which was active in lobbying for the MLF in European capitals.[21] Along the way, the various preconditions for American support of the proposal, expressed clearly in Kennedy's Ottawa speech, had conveniently been forgotten.

Skybolt, Nassau, and de Gaulle

Still, the success of the MLF was not assured. McNamara was known to be skeptical, and the president had yet to come down firmly one way or the other. At this point, however, several critical events turned the tide in favor of the MLF, neutralizing much of the remaining opposition to it.[22]

The Origins of the Crisis

The crisis in Anglo-American relations over the cancellation of the Skybolt air-to-surface missile, which affected the fortunes of the MLF decisively, began in April 1960, when for technical and financial reasons the British government scrapped its three-year-old program to develop a silo-based ballistic missile force known as Blue Streak.[23] The decision, it was recognized, left Britain with only an aging Vulcan bomber (V-bomber) fleet increasingly incapable of high-confidence penetration of Soviet air defense networks. Looking for a way to keep the V-bombers

21. Buchan, *Multilateral Force,* pp. 623–26; and Boulton, "NATO and the MLF," p. 280.

22. Many sources detail these fascinating two months in alliance relations. Among the most useful are Robert Kleiman, *Atlantic Crisis;* Nora Beloff, *The General Says No;* John Newhouse, *De Gaulle and the Anglo-Saxons;* and Richard E. Neustadt, *Alliance Politics.* Neustadt's book is especially valuable for its account of the Skybolt crisis, which is based on a more detailed, recently declassified—though heavily sanitized—report that Neustadt wrote for President Kennedy at the latter's request: "Report to the President: Skybolt and Nassau, American Policy-making and Anglo-American Relations."

23. Pierre, *Nuclear Politics,* pp. 196–201, has an excellent account of the Blue Streak cancellation.

as the backbone of the independent British deterrent, the British discovered an American project, already in the development stage, to create an air-to-surface missile named Skybolt for deployment on B-52s for defense-suppression missions against enemy airfields and early-warning radars. To the British, Skybolt could be used for another purpose: to give the V-bombers stand-off capability to strike strategic targets deep within Soviet territory without having to perform the increasingly risky operation of penetrating Soviet air defenses. Accordingly, Britain asked to buy Skybolt missiles from the United States. At the March 1960 Camp David meeting between Eisenhower and Macmillan, the United States agreed, but there were enough technical uncertainties associated with the missile at this early stage of its development to warrant an escape clause for both parties should the development process run into problems. The United States agreed, however, not to cancel development or production of Skybolt without prior consultation with Britain.

At the same meeting the British agreed to make available docking and support facilities for U.S. Polaris submarines at Holy Loch, Scotland. Although the two agreements were not formally related, the British were later to argue, with some justification, that the Holy Loch arrangement was an implicit quid pro quo for Skybolt.

The Decision to Cancel Skybolt

As work on Skybolt in the United States progressed, however, it became apparent that the new missile would have no appreciable advantage over existing U.S. defense-suppression missiles; that it was plagued by technical problems, most important, its guidance system; and that program costs would be much higher than originally anticipated. Eisenhower's last secretary of defense, Thomas Gates, was ready to recommend cancellation of the missile by the time he left office; his successor, Robert McNamara, decided to stick with the program for a while longer. But by August 1962 McNamara had concluded, from repeated recommendations by Charles Hitch, Pentagon comptroller, and Harold Brown, director of defense research and evaluation, that Skybolt would not meet the standards of cost-effectiveness that would allow a positive production decision.

British officials were occasionally briefed on Skybolt's many development problems; in addition, British liaison staff was assigned to the Skybolt program. But apparently the British discounted the repeated

American warnings that Skybolt would be produced only if it turned out to be technically and economically feasible.

Right after the resolution of the Cuban missile crisis, in early November 1962, McNamara brought his recommendation for canceling the project to the White House. The president agreed. McNamara warned British officials, including Minister of Defense Peter Thorneycroft, of the impending cancellation, which would be made final at a previously scheduled budget meeting at Hyannis Port over Thanksgiving.

Macmillan was apparently informed of these contacts, but chose to do nothing for the moment, having more pressing matters on his mind— specifically the arduous British negotiations for entry into the European Community that were reaching a crucial stage. He seemed to believe that Kennedy, with whom he had established a surprisingly friendly rapport, would understand the difficult position cancellation would create for Britain and overrule McNamara.

For his part, McNamara fully expected Thorneycroft to push for Polaris as a substitute. With this in mind, he asked his staff to study possible alternative substitute arrangements for the British, including:

1. continuation of Skybolt development and production, with greater financial participation by Britain, solely for British deployment;

2. purchase of the shorter-range Hound Dog air-to-surface missile from the United States;

3. purchase of Polaris missiles and submarines from the United States;

4. purchase of Polaris as part of the MLF.[24]

Initially the ISA staff favored the third alternative, but they checked with Henry Owen, J. Robert Schaetzel, and other State Department officials, suspecting State opposition to any continuation of a bilateral nuclear relationship with Britain.

As can be imagined, State officials were adamantly opposed to providing Polaris submarines to Britain on a strictly bilateral basis. The whole rationale for their efforts to create the MLF rested on the presumed dangers of allowing the British and French nuclear programs to flourish outside an integrated NATO framework. The MLF was supposed to ease the tensions within NATO created by the existence of growing national nuclear arsenals, to remove incentives for West Germany to adopt a national nuclear arsenal on the French model, to deemphasize

24. Neustadt, "Report to the President," pp. 23–32.

the special Anglo-American relationship—especially in nuclear matters—and to substitute an Atlantic partnership between the United
States and a united Europe that included Britain. While pleased with
McNamara's decision to kill Skybolt, since doing so would threaten the
imminent demise of British nuclear independence, State officials could
not tolerate the notion of replacing the Skybolt offer with another, even
more extensive bilateral arrangement with no strings attached. Such an
alternative would remove whatever incentives existed for Britain to
participate in the MLF. They also expressed fears that, by angering de
Gaulle with yet another flagrant example of "Anglo-Saxon collusion,"
a deal of this sort would ruin British chances for entry into the European
Community.

As the ISA staff studied the issue further, it recognized that the offer
of Polaris to the British national arsenal went against the widely promulgated American policy to oppose the development of small, independent nuclear forces within the alliance. Thus such an offer would
require a review of basic NATO policy. But the staff expressed no strong
preference among the other alternatives—a redefined Skybolt deal,
Hound Dog, or MLF. This advice was passed to McNamara.

In the meantime the State Department, warned of the deliberations
across the Potomac, sent McNamara a letter outlining its position on
acceptable alternatives to Skybolt:

> In any discussion with the UK we should mention these possibilities:
> 1. British continuation of a Skybolt program . . .
> 2. Use of Hound Dog on at least some British aircraft . . .
> 3. Participation in a sea-based MRBM force under multilateral manning and
> ownership, such as NATO is now discussing . . .
> It seems essential that we make quite clear to the British that there is no
> possibility of our helping them set up a nationally manned and owned MRBM
> force . . . the difficulties of bringing EEC negotiations to a successful conclusion
> might be significantly enhanced . . . the political costs of our continuing to deny
> MRBM aid to France would be significantly increased.[25]

During this period Kennedy met in Hyannis Port with his top advisers
on the budget and formally canceled production plans for Skybolt. This
decision leaked to the press on December 7. At nearly the same time
former Secretary of State Dean Acheson delivered a speech in which he
remarked on Britain's reluctance to accept its reduced status in world
affairs. By the time McNamara arrived in London on December 11 to

25. Ibid., p. 32.

discuss alternatives with Thorneycroft, the British press and public were in an uproar. To them, it seemed that Kennedy had reneged on a firm commitment to its staunchest ally *before* consultations in London; the unfortunate timing of the Acheson speech had made difficult matters even worse.

The McNamara-Thorneycroft Meeting

Under these circumstances, the discussion between the two defense ministers got off to a troubled start. Constrained by the State Department and by the advice of his own staff from offering Polaris on his own initiative, McNamara fully expected the request for Polaris to come from Thorneycroft. This would allow McNamara to return to Washington to consider the formal British request. For his part, Thorneycroft was angered by McNamara's reluctance to offer the submarines on his own. The other alternatives discussed seemed unattractive to Thorneycroft. McNamara had made disparaging remarks about Skybolt at his airport press conference, thus undermining Thorneycroft's enthusiasm for the troubled missile. Hound Dog, apparently, was too absurd a name for the British public to accept, and anyway the system was rapidly growing obsolete and would not give the V-bombers stand-off capability comparable to that provided by Skybolt. And finally, strong elements within the British Defense Ministry considered the MLF a foolish enterprise. Apparently exceeding his mandate, McNamara suggested that the United States would be willing to make Polaris submarines available to Britain provided that Britain pledged them to NATO, much as the United States was planning to do. For Thorneycroft, this was unacceptable; Skybolt had been offered with no strings attached, and any replacement for it would have to be so offered too.

The two parted company without reaching any agreement: McNamara was frustrated that Thorneycroft had not asked for Polaris outright; Thorneycroft was equally frustrated that McNamara had not offered Polaris outright. McNamara headed for Paris, where he reaffirmed American interest in the creation of a European nuclear force with some form of American control—an imprecise formulation—but he was considerably less enthusiastic than Owen and his colleagues had been in previous talks with NATO members. By default, a decision on a replacement for Skybolt was left to Kennedy and Macmillan, who had previously been scheduled to meet at Nassau in the Bahamas for their semiannual *tour d'horizon* on December 19; intended to be an engaging, relaxing encounter between fast friends, Nassau would now become a setting for some difficult decisions.

Kennedy and Macmillan at Nassau

Kennedy and Macmillan had planned to spend considerable time discussing the status of negotiations for Britain's membership in the European Community. For Macmillan these negotiations were becoming something of a personal crusade; on December 17 he had met with de Gaulle to feel out the French president's assessment of the status of negotiations. Conflicting accounts of this meeting exist, but Macmillan arrived at Nassau expecting that, whatever the immediate obstacles, these drawn-out negotiations over membership in the Community would eventually succeed.

Rusk and McNamara had briefed Kennedy on the Skybolt problem before he left for Nassau, but the president was unaware of the gravity of the problem he faced until he discussed it with the distressed British ambassador, Sir David Ormsby Gore, on board Air Force One on the way to the conference. Otherwise he might not have been so critical of the Skybolt in defending his cancellation of it at a press conference the day before he left. Ormsby Gore, a close friend of Kennedy's, filled him in on the serious political problems that the Skybolt cancellation was causing the Macmillan government. Together with Ormsby Gore, Kennedy drew up a proposal to share the cost of future development and production of Skybolt equally with Britain, even though Britain would be the only one to deploy the missile.

By the time the president arrived in Nassau, however, this scheme had been fatally compromised. Arriving a few hours earlier, Macmillan had been presented by a reporter with a transcript of Kennedy's press conference comments casting doubt on the value of the Skybolt program. For Macmillan this indiscretion amounted to "compromising the lady in public"; he could no longer accept Skybolt under any circumstances.

In this inauspicious atmosphere the two leaders sat down to discuss Skybolt.[26] Kennedy opened discussions by putting forth the production

---

26. Henry Brandon, cited in Pierre, *Nuclear Politics*, p. 232, found in the British delegation "a resentment and suspicion of American intentions such as I have never experienced in all the Anglo-American conferences I have covered over the past twenty years."

formula he and the British ambassador had worked out on the plane trip. For Macmillan the proposal was unacceptable, irretrievably compromised by Kennedy's disparaging press conference remarks. Why should the British prime minister be satisfied with a missile system so clearly inadequate in the eyes of the president of the United States?

Somewhat surprised by Macmillan's position, Kennedy presented a substitute: would Macmillan be willing to accept Hound Dog as an alternative? Macmillan again demurred. The British press had already been ridiculing the unfortunate name of the system, which was in any case obsolete and incapable of giving the V-bombers an adequate stand-off capability.

Was Macmillan willing to postpone a final decision, pending the findings of a joint U.S.-British study team to be formed to examine alternatives? Again Macmillan said no; he would need an immediate deal, and Polaris submarines were the only acceptable alternative. In fact, Macmillan had extracted cabinet authority to ask for Polaris should the situation call for it. The recalcitrants at his Defense Ministry, when faced with the virtual certainty of Skybolt cancellation, had come to see the attractiveness of subsurface strategic vessels and had given their support to such a request.

It was now Kennedy's turn to balk; fully aware of the resistance within both the State and Defense departments to a Polaris arrangement with no strings attached, he told Macmillan that any Polaris submarines provided to Britain would have to be pledged to a NATO-wide nuclear force.

In response, Macmillan launched into what, by inside accounts, seems to have been an eloquent, moving plea for Anglo-American cooperation.[27] He reviewed the whole history of Anglo-American cooperative undertakings from 1939 onward, highlighting the advantages each country had enjoyed when the relationship was close and noting how quickly breaches in the special relationship—for example, the Suez crisis—had been repaired time and again to everyone's benefit. What he was asking for was that the United States follow through on its commitment to maintain the independence of the British deterrent. If the president felt he could not do this, then let the two countries part with

27. The declassified version of Neustadt's "Report to the President" is heavily sanitized in this part. But a detailed account of Macmillan's speech can be found in Pierre, *Nuclear Politics*, pp. 235–36.

honor; Macmillan would not cancel the Holy Loch arrangement. But if Polaris was to be the basis of American aid, then commitment to a NATO force could in no way be irrevocable; the United States and NATO would have to recognize Britain's sovereign right to withdraw the force if "supreme national interests" were at stake.

Ever the Anglophile, Kennedy was not about to cause permanent damage to Anglo-American relations over insistence on a particular hardware arrangement. He knew and liked Macmillan and fully understood the desperate political situation Macmillan would face should he return from Nassau empty-handed. Macmillan had braved considerable domestic opposition when he struck the original Skybolt agreement with Eisenhower. Without compensation for Skybolt, his return to London would be greeted with derision and might even cause his government to fall. Kennedy later recalled, "If you were in that kind of trouble, you would want a friend."[28] Kennedy was looking for a way to save Macmillan without undermining *both* basic NATO policy, as defined by the Defense Department, *and* the MLF favored by the State Department. Macmillan's offer to pledge British Polaris submarines to NATO subject to withdrawal under emergency conditions seemed to provide a basis for compromise. The two readily agreed on this formula and instructed their respective staffs—unprepared for this surprise turn of events—to work out a joint communiqué to reflect the formula.

The Nassau Agreement

That communiqué, which came to be known as the Nassau Agreement, has an ambiguity that was perhaps the inevitable result of inadequate preparatory staff work, tight deadline pressures, and the inherent difficulty of reconciling British strategic independence with an integrated multilateral force concept. The subsequent confusion over interpretation of the agreement stems from the wording of paragraphs 6, 7, and 8:

(6) The Prime Minister suggested and the President agreed, that for the immediate future a start could be made by subscribing to NATO some part of the forces already in existence. This could include allocations from United States Strategic Forces, from the United Kingdom Bomber Command, and from tactical nuclear forces now held in Europe. Such forces would be assigned as part of a NATO nuclear force and targeted in accordance with NATO plans.

(7) Returning to Polaris the President and the Prime Minister agreed that

28. Cited in ibid., p. 241.

the purpose of their two governments with respect to the provision of the Polaris missile must be the development of a multilateral NATO nuclear force in the closest consultation with the other NATO allies. They will use their best endeavors to this end.

(8) Accordingly, the President and the Prime Minister agreed that the U.S. will make available on a continuing basis Polaris missiles (less warheads) for British submarines. The U.S. will also study the feasibility of making available certain support facilities for such submarines. The U.K. Government will construct the submarines in which these weapons will be placed and they will also provide the nuclear warheads for the Polaris missiles. British forces developed under this plan will be assigned and targeted in the same way as the forces described in paragraph 6.

These forces, and at least equal U.S. forces, would be made available for inclusion in a NATO multilateral nuclear force. The Prime Minister made it clear that except where Her Majesty's Government may decide that supreme national interests are at stake, these British forces will be used for the purposes of international defense of the Western Alliance in all circumstances.[29]

Paragraphs 6 and 8 are somewhat contradictory. Paragraph 6 makes no reference to assigning strategic forces to NATO under *multilateral* arrangements. In fact, it implicitly refers to the prior U.S. offer of five Polaris submarines, which would remain under American control. These forces were to be assigned to NATO under national contingents as part of a *multinational* NATO force. Paragraph 8 seems to suggest that Britain's Polaris fleet will be assigned in a similar manner, though it also states that they will be made available to a future mulilateral force. It is probably incorrect to suggest, as does Andrew J. Pierre, that the British assumed that the term *multilateral* was synonymous with the term *multinational;*[30] after all, they had been exposed to the Smith-Lee briefing on the MLF. More plausible is the assumption that the British believed— correctly, as events were to show—that the prospects of the MLF ever coming into being were remote enough to permit them to agree to assign their Polaris submarines to the MLF without ever having to make good on the pledge. In this belief they were bolstered by Kennedy's acknowledgment, shortly after Nassau, that any circumstances in which the use of nuclear weapons might be contemplated by the alliance would by definition place Britain's "supreme national interests" at stake.

29. The text of the Nassau Agreement can be found in ibid., pp. 346–47.

30. Ibid., p. 236, in which Pierre claims that "the British were under the impression that the future NATO force was to be organized on the basis of existing forces plus the projected Polaris submarines, and that the 'multilateral' commitment of Paragraph Eight referred to a force based on national contingents"—an odd claim considering the detailed MLF briefing given to British officials in October 1962.

At the State Department, the Nassau Agreement drew a mixed reaction.[31] On the one hand, the president had clearly agreed to help Britain maintain its independent nuclear status and its special relationship with Washington, however temporary such an arrangement might be, given the "imminence" of the MLF. To those at State concerned with assuring British entry into the European Community, the fact that Kennedy had authorized the same offer to be made to de Gaulle did not seem likely to undo the damage already done by "Anglo-Saxon collusion" at Nassau.

On the other hand, the Nassau Agreement had allowed the MLF to regain the momentum it might otherwise have lost. MLF advocates quickly seized the opportunity afforded by paragraphs 7 and 8 of the agreement to bring their proposal to the negotiating table. Ball immediately went to Bonn to brief Adenauer on Nassau; in spite of Adenauer's interest in concluding a treaty of friendship and cooperation between West Germany and France, where suspicions about Nassau and the MLF were increasingly bitter, the chancellor could not conceal his enthusiasm for the proposal. At the same time Henry Owen wrote yet another MLF paper, worked it through the State Department hierarchy, and finally obtained Kennedy's approval to begin negotiations with interested NATO partners to bring the MLF into existence.

De Gaulle's Salvo

These efforts were considerably helped by de Gaulle's dramatic press conference on January 14, 1963, in which he vetoed British entry into the Community, rejected the American Polaris offer, and refused to participate in any NATO nuclear force. One week later he administered his *coup de grace:* the Treaty of Friendship and Cooperation between France and the Federal Republic of Germany.

31. Robert Bowie's reaction to Nassau can be taken as representative of the State Department's ambivalence. See *Nominations of Bowie and Johnson, Hearings,* p. 9. An interesting aside on the relation between the State Department and the Nassau outcome is the fact that Dean Rusk was not present at Nassau, allegedly owing to prior commitments. As Steinbruner notes in *Cybernetic Theory of Decision* (p. 235), why the prior commitments could not be rescheduled so that the secretary of state could attend a major summit conference has not been satisfactorily explained. Perhaps whatever the outcome, Rusk had no intention of being made the scapegoat for Nassau. George Ball was the highest-ranking State official at Nassau; one needs little imagination to comprehend his frustration at the outcome of Nassau and his subsequent determination to have Nassau become the first step toward a multilateral force.

To this day it is not possible to determine how much the Nassau meeting prompted this frontal assault on U.S. policy in Europe. A strong case can be made that de Gaulle would have come to those decisions anyway, motivated as he was by a commitment to leading Europe away from Anglo-Saxon domination. Nevertheless, the spectacle of Nassau must have angered him. Macmillan took just forty-eight hours to come to a rather far-reaching strategic agreement with the Americans, yet he had dragged out the European Community negotiations over technicalities for more than eighteen months. Furthermore, Macmillan had not warned de Gaulle about what might emerge at Nassau; apparently de Gaulle was informed only after the fact through press reports. If de Gaulle had already decided to block Britain's bid for membership in the Community, Nassau gave him a convenient excuse to be dramatic about it; if he was undecided, Nassau might have tipped the scales decisively in favor of the veto.

Whatever de Gaulle's rationale, his press conference is widely and correctly seen as a turning point in alliance relations. With one blow de Gaulle had shattered the European unity movement. At the same time he raised again the specter of Franco-German nuclear cooperation and foreclosed French participation in an integrated NATO nuclear force.

In the eyes of MLF proponents, all this lent a new sense of urgency to their project. De Gaulle's actions had deeply angered American officials. The MLF took on a new, more critical purpose—to undo the damage done to the cause by de Gaulle. Fears of West German national nuclear aspirations were now even more acute; the MLF was seen as the only way to bring West Germany back into the fold and to renew the sense of purpose in the European unification movement so suddenly shattered on January 14. At the same time the MLF could be used in political retaliation against de Gaulle—though this motivation, of course, could never be acknowledged.

The Merchant Mission

In the weeks after the January 14 press conference, MLF proponents at the State Department set up a special office in the department to coordinate MLF activity with interested European parties. Livingston Merchant, a career diplomat long known for his enthusiasm for the

European unity movement and a former close associate of Robert Bowie during the latter's tenure at State, was selected to head the office and to conduct the negotiations.[32] In February 1963 Merchant met with President Kennedy to receive instructions on how to proceed with the negotiations. Both State and Defense proposed authorizing Merchant to negotiate an agreement based on the Smith-Lee briefings of the previous October. Kennedy, fearing British and Italian rejection, was reluctant to do so.

Intervening British actions had indicated that country's firm reluctance to participate in the MLF. After Nassau, U.S. officials had gone to London to work out the details of the Polaris deal for Britain. During these negotiations it became clear to them that the British were preparing to initiate a counterproposal, an Atlantic nuclear force, to consist of *national* nuclear contingents assigned to NATO but controlled by the donating countries. Macmillan was preparing to announce the assignment of part of the V-bomber force, as well as the Polaris force, to NATO with a certain amount of pomp and fanfare at the upcoming NATO ministerial meeting in May and would also put forth the proposal for the Atlantic force as an alternative to the multilateral force.

But though Kennedy was not eager to approve Merchant's proposed instructions, he finally did so under arguments that the MLF was the only practical response to the de Gaulle offensive against Kennedy's Grand Design; that the Nassau Agreement, if not followed by quick progress on the MLF, would serve only to reinforce West German sensitivity to discrimination within the alliance and thus to enhance Bonn's nuclear aspirations; and that the long-term political organization of Europe was now at stake, and only with an MLF could Washington hope to lead the allies. Responding to these arguments, Kennedy authorized Merchant to proceed with negotiations toward creating an MLF along the lines established in the first Smith-Lee briefing, and further directed his envoy to stand by the control formula requiring a unanimous vote for launch, giving each participant, including the United States, an effective veto. He agreed, however, that future review of this arrangement should not be explicitly excluded.

But before Merchant left for Europe, the U.S. Joint Atomic Energy

32. Steinbruner, *Cybernetic Theory of Decision*, pp. 269–75; and Schlesinger, *A Thousand Days*, pp. 872–74.

Committee had begun to explore the implications of the MLF and did not like what it saw. In closed session the committee grilled Merchant about the details of his upcoming trip; its members were skeptical about the desirability and feasibility of the MLF and made it clear that any arrangement along the lines of the Smith-Lee plan would require revising current legislation restricting the degree of access of foreign nationals to U.S. atomic secrets.

At the same time, William Tyler, another high State Department official, tried to persuade the British to table the Atlantic nuclear force so as not to jeopardize the Merchant mission. He succeeded; the communiqué of the May NATO meeting, while noting Britain's assignment of V-bombers and Polaris to NATO, made no reference to an overarching Atlantic force.

Deputy Secretary of Defense Roswell Gilpatric also conferred in Rome with top political leaders, to seal the replacement of Jupiter missiles with U.S. Polaris boats; at the same time he obtained Italian support for the MLF.

The Merchant mission, which included MLF stalwarts Smith and Lee, left Washington in late February for a tour of European capitals. To recapitulate, the plan they brought with them called for the creation of a fleet of twenty-five surface vessels, each armed with eight Polaris A-3 MRBMs with a range of 2,500 miles and armed with one-megaton nuclear warheads. The accuracy of the missiles would permit strikes against certain types of counterforce targets, such as airfields. Each ship would be manned by a crew consisting of at least three national contingents, with no nation contributing more than 40 percent of the total crew on each ship, to prevent any single national contingent from commandeering a unit of the fleet for its own purposes. To avoid easy detection, the hulls were to be designed to look like merchant vessels, although to go one step farther and mark them noncombatants would contravene international law of the seas. The whole project would carry a price tag of $500 million a year over the next decade; the force would become operational midway through that decade. This cost would be shared by the participants in the force. Finally, the force would be controlled by SACEUR (not SACLANT [Supreme Allied Commander Atlantic] as some Europeans had feared) during peacetime; during a crisis a committee of MLF participants would make the decision to launch, which would require unanimity of approval. However, "the possibility of an eventual elimination of the [implicit] U.S. veto, should the Europeans desire it and should they develop common political mechanisms, was to be held out as an incentive."[33]

In West Germany, Adenauer, the Foreign Ministry, and elements of the Defense Ministry once again gave the proposal an enthusiastic reception.[34] Aside from the reasons previously noted, which were still important to the German leadership, the MLF now represented a concrete way to minimize friction with Washington over the new treaty between Paris and Bonn. So far, de Gaulle was not forcing Adenauer to choose between France and the United States, and Adenauer had no intention of allowing the events of January to create such an obviously difficult choice. The Foreign Ministry, under Gerhard Schroeder, was also intent on salvaging the American connection and thus was eager to cooperate.

Within the Defense Ministry there had been a change of leadership. Defense Minister Strauss had been forced to resign because of the *Spiegel* affair, in which he authorized the illegal search and seizure of material from the offices of Germany's largest newsweekly after its publication of sensitive defense-related material. His replacement, Kai-Uwe von Hassel, shared Strauss's interest in, if not enthusiasm for, gaining operational access to strategic weaponry.

But once again West German military leaders made known their serious reservations about the plan. For them, the surface fleet configuration, strongly supported by President Kennedy in public statements in February, was too vulnerable to conventional naval attack. Traditional German military fascination with submarine capabilities reinforced their interest in a subsurface MLF based on Polaris. They also had doubts about the control mechanism; feasibility aside, they could not see the advantages for West Germany in an MLF subject to American or other European vetoes. In response, Merchant could only remind them that modifications of the control formula at some later date would not in principle be excluded by the United States. Adenauer, however, was politically strong enough to override these objections, and a joint communiqué on the Merchant visit noted West German support of the MLF. Adenauer and Merchant had reportedly agreed to have the United States and West Germany together absorb 75 percent of the total cost

33. Steinbruner, *Cybernetic Theory of Decision*, p. 256.
34. For a general discussion of West German interest, and reservations, stimulated by the Merchant mission, see Kelleher, *Germany and the Politics of Nuclear Weapons*, pp. 234–40.

and manpower of the force and to have West Germany take on some 40 percent of the manpower burden.[35]

In Brussels the Merchant mission was met with a polite but unenthusiastic response. In Rome the Italian government, again unable to make a firm commitment to participate in the MLF, nevertheless stressed that it considered the initiative important. Some Italian officials shared the West German military's suspicion that a surface fleet configuration would be too vulnerable to Soviet attack.

It was in London that Merchant received the coolest reception. As has been mentioned, Macmillan had just been gearing up for a proposal to create a multinational Atlantic nuclear force. Although Tyler had succeeded in getting British officials not to put the proposal forward at the May NATO meeting, he certainly was unable to shift British preference for this proposal. The Royal Navy had just come around, under the pressure of the Skybolt cancellation, to accepting an underwater extension of the life of the British independent deterrent. In doing so, and in subsequent negotiations to work out the details, the navy was quick to appreciate that Polaris represented the most advanced technology the United States had to offer. A surface fleet configuration naturally held less attraction. Nor had the navy reconciled itself to the workability of mulitnational crews. On top of this, the Macmillan government, expected to shoulder some 10 percent of the cost of the fleet, was beginning to doubt its ability to pay for the MLF, especially after the costly Polaris deal.

What resulted from Merchant's talks in London, therefore, was a restrained British endorsement of the multilateral nuclear force; the communiqué noted that Britain hoped eventually to participate in the force. As a sort of quid pro quo, Merchant endorsed the British concept of a multinational nuclear force.

Merchant also met with the NATO ministers in Paris and presented the proposal. As a result of the presentation, Turkey, Greece, and the Netherlands apparently expressed willingness to endorse the American proposal, though it was recognized that domestic political considerations precluded any of these countries from committing themselves to participate at that time.

Merchant returned to Washington in mid-March, having failed to elicit firm commitments of participation from most of the governments

35. *New York Times*, March 9, 1963.

he visited. Bonn was the most enthusiastic, but problems with the control formula still persisted. Other nations showed interest but no firm commitment, whereas Britain remained markedly cool to the proposal. Von Hassel soon went to London to lobby for the proposal but was only able to get Thorneycroft to restate the position Britain had taken in its communiqué during the Merchant mission. The French, not directly consulted by Merchant, remained aloof.

Kennedy's European Tour, June 1963

Nevertheless, Merchant returned to press Kennedy into authorizing speedy negotiations to conclude the MLF plan. He apparently believed, with others in the State Department, that a draft treaty creating the MLF could be readied for presidential signature during Kennedy's already scheduled European tour in June, which was in any case intended to reaffirm American commitment to European security and prosperity.[36]

But Kennedy once again refused to give the MLF the final go-ahead. Still smarting from de Gaulle's January offensive, he was reluctant to put himself in a position to be undercut by the French president so soon after the January events. Furthermore, he and his top advisers, including Rusk, still considered the MLF an exploratory plan.[37] This may have been because the MLF initiative was giving the administration problems elsewhere, most notably in the U.S.-Soviet negotiations to conclude a Limited Nuclear Test Ban Treaty. The Soviet Union had declared that the MLF was incompatible with progress in these negotiations, alleging that it violated the nonproliferation concerns that largely motivated the treaty. The administration denied that the MLF did anything of the kind, but negotiations continued to be hampered by the Soviet attitude.[38] Kennedy's reluctance to push the MLF may also have been in part caused by the suspicion that West German and Italian support was not as firm as it seemed. To test this suspicion, Kennedy sent letters to

36. Steinbruner, *Cybernetic Theory of Decision,* p. 275.

37. See Kennedy's press conference, reported in *New York Times,* March 7, 1963; and Dean Rusk's comments shortly after: "Secretary Rusk's News Conference of March 8," p. 434.

38. See, for example, *New York Times,* April 10, 1963. For the American response, see a speech by the U.S. representative to the UN disarmament conference, Jacob Beam, "A Nuclear Test Ban and Arms Control," pp. 489–93.

Adenauer and Prime Minister Amintore Fanfani reiterating the American proposal in essential details, though hinting that the control formula, while preserving the American veto, could be based on something other than the unanimity principle, thus eliminating other vetoes. He made further MLF initiatives contingent on a positive response from Adenauer.[39]

This move sent the MLF advocates into an even greater lobbying effort to get the president to agree to negotiate a preliminary draft treaty by the time of his June trip. Walt W. Rostow and Schaetzel at State produced more MLF papers, arguing for "resolve and commitment to the cause of integration during a period of drift."[40] Tyler left for Bonn and Rome, presumably to press the two governments into a timely response to the Kennedy letters. At the same time, a cable from the U.S. embassy in Bonn to Washington noted that an unnamed high German official had warned that if the MLF initiative failed, West Germany might be forced to seek parity with Britain and France. Finally, Admiral Ricketts was sent to Bonn to persuade his German counterparts of the merits of the surface fleet configuration, which they finally acceded to under some political pressure from Adenauer.

In May these forces tried once again to get Kennedy to agree to an MLF commitment during his June trip. Under Secretary Ball urged the president to permit full congressional consultations on the initiative. Again Kennedy demurred, even though he had received a positive response from Adenauer in which the German chancellor agreed to the Merchant version of the MLF but noted his desire for a promise to leave issues such as the control formula open for future renegotiation. Now Kennedy wanted a commitment from Macmillan. He wrote a letter to Macmillan urging British participation, but sticking to the 10 percent figure for Britain's financial contribution to the force. In a response that was by now becoming predictable, Ball and Ricketts went to London to persuade the Macmillan government to respond positively to the Kennedy letter. In a somewhat unusual move State Department officials persuaded German Social Democratic party leaders to make contact with leaders of the British opposition Labour party to persuade Harold Wilson and his colleagues to cease their incessant harangue against the MLF.

All these efforts were doomed to failure. During April and May the

---

39. Steinbruner, *Cybernetic Theory of Decision*, pp. 275–79.
40. Ibid., pp. 275–76.

British government had stepped up its campaign for the multinational force, in a less grandiose form than had been contemplated in January. These efforts were beginning to pay off; Dirk Stikker, secretary general of NATO, was giving the British government his diplomatic support, and even France had been somewhat receptive to the scaled-down version of the Atlantic nuclear force, which would now not be controlled by a separate command but would remain under the control of the individual nations donating to the force. The possibility of French participation attracted the interest of Kennedy, McNamara, Rusk, Chairman of the Joint Chiefs Maxwell Taylor, and SACEUR Lyman Lemnitzer. The May NATO meeting came to a provisional agreement on these multinational assignments of strategic nuclear forces.

This complex diplomatic activity must have confused NATO allies about who was pursuing exactly what NATO nuclear force arrangements; it is easy to understand British reluctance to commit itself to participate in the MLF under these circumstances. Further elements intervened to make British interest even more difficult to obtain. The Profumo scandal, which called the discretion and integrity of a member of the Conservative government into question, had rocked the British government, making it difficult for Macmillan to focus on the MLF issue; furthermore, the Royal Navy remained unpersuaded. Domestic political factors also continued to prevent the Italian government, in the midst of a leadership transition, from committing itself to participate.

Thus Kennedy refused to make the MLF a centerpiece of the June European tour. At each capital he visited, he raised the proposal and urged participation but was clearly more concerned with broader issues of alliance solidarity. He was able to gain British commitment to participation in future MLF discussions "without prejudice to question of British participation in the force."[41] In West Germany he reviewed the current obstacles in the way of progress on MLF in talks with Adenauer, and Adenauer apparently agreed with him that because of the difficulties facing the initiative, alternatives to the MLF should also be pursued.

The MLF at the Negotiating Table

With these results, Kennedy apparently decided it was time to see just how far the initiative could progress. If it were to succeed, all the

41. *New York Times*, July 1, 1963.

better; yet if it were to fail, he had not placed the full weight of American prestige on the proposal. He authorized Merchant to return to Europe to proceed with negotiations with interested European nations to see if an agreement could be reached. By September, Merchant had won agreement from West Germany, Italy, Belgium, Greece, and Turkey to participate in MLF negotiations. Britain held off agreement until Macmillan had been assured in late September, according to the terms of the June meeting with Kennedy, that London's participation in the negotiations did not necessarily imply a commitment to participate in the force itself. The Netherlands followed suit in December, after similar assurances from Washington. By October, then, negotiations were under way. In Paris, Merchant and the U.S. ambassador to NATO, Thomas Finletter, led the political discussions; in Washington, Rear Admiral Norvell G. Ward led talks on the military aspects of the MLF.

At the same time Finletter and Merchant announced that the United States would make available to NATO the USS *Biddle*, soon renamed the USS *Claude V. Ricketts*, to serve as a pilot project to test out the workability of a multinationally manned surface vessel. This was apparently Kennedy's brainchild, designed to convince skeptics in London and Washington that the MLF was, in principle, feasible. By the spring of 1964 this pilot project was in operation, participating in NATO maneuvers and calling on friendly ports.

Almost immediately, however, the issue of the control formula again became a political obstacle. The Western European Union, a political organization of European parliamentarians, began to deliberate about whether to endorse the initiative. Its military committee reportedly opposed the creation of a control mechanism providing for a veto by any participant. This opposition may well have been motivated by fears of a U.S. veto; at one point a study committee of the union had proposed bringing part of the U.S. Minuteman force under multilateral control, to demonstrate a full NATO role in the strategic deterrent of the alliance. When the Assembly of the Western European Union met to discuss the issue in December, it withheld its endorsement of the MLF plan, despite vigorous urging by West German Foreign Minister Schroeder.

At about the same time a NATO parliamentarians' conference rejected the MLF proposal as militarily superfluous, while stressing the need for greater European participation in the planning for use of the U.S. strategic forces. The French began a diplomatic campaign to sidetrack the talks. The Soviet Union also mounted a vigorous campaign to kill the talks, claiming the MLF was a clever device to give West Germany strategic nuclear weapons.

Late 1963 also saw two political transitions that, while not necessarily detrimental to the cause of the MLF, forced the issue into the background. In October Adenauer stepped down from his decade-long tenure as chancellor. He was replaced by Ludwig Erhard, who, though favorable to the MLF and somewhat distrustful of de Gaulle, had to deal with a growing number of party stalwarts who saw increasing merits in closer Franco-German collaboration.[42] And in late November President Kennedy was assassinated; his successor, Lyndon B. Johnson, came to office largely ignorant of the complex diplomatic activity surrounding the MLF issue.

Johnson's Deadline

For all these reasons the MLF negotiations in Paris and Washington recorded little substantive progress. Fearing a potentially fatal loss of momentum, the MLF advocates in the State Department began to search for ways to reinvigorate the negotiations. They first tried to set up a series of briefings for congressional committees, already skeptical of the supposed European desire for the proposal. But Congress had other issues of higher priority with which to contend. Furthermore, Rusk and McNamara did not seem eager to bring the case for the MLF to Capitol Hill. As a result, scheduled briefings were postponed and then canceled.

Failing to stimulate congressional interest, the MLF advocates now turned to another tactic that had been tried unsuccessfully before, to use an upcoming presidential trip to Europe to force the president to commit himself to a timetable for negotiating the MLF treaty. Here they apparently had greater success. Meeting with Johnson in April 1964, Ball, Finletter, and Gerard Smith impressed on the president the need to set a timetable for negotiations in order to get the stalled talks moving again. Johnson had not been exposed to the issue in detail before; he now viewed it with some favor and authorized an end-of-the-year

42. An excellent discussion of the Atlanticist-Gaullist split in German politics at this time can be found in Kelleher, *Germany and the Politics of Nuclear Weapons*, pp. 248–50.

deadline.[43] Cables were sent to European capitals informing the parties to the negotiations of Johnson's decision; moreover, Smith now took charge of the negotiations, replacing Merchant. In June the president met with Erhard and renewed the U.S. commitment to reach a final agreement by the end of the year.

All these efforts were hampered by events that were unfolding in Geneva. After the Limited Test Ban Treaty had been agreed to in August 1963, the Geneva Committee on Disarmament turned to the negotiation of a treaty banning the spread of nuclear weapons. Washington placed a high value on these negotiations. But now the Soviet Union renewed its criticism of the MLF, stating that the force would undermine any such treaty by giving nuclear weapons to West Germany. The United States resisted this charge, noting repeatedly that under the plan the United States would retain ultimate control over weapons placed at the disposal of nonnuclear allies. One of the most strident Soviet statements on this subject came as the USS *Biddle* was making a port call in New York City, prompting disarmament groups in the United States to demonstrate at the New York City pier where the *Biddle* was docked. Nevertheless, the United States held firm in its support for the MLF and continued to reject the Soviet and East European contentions that the MLF would violate a future nonproliferation treaty.

Still, progress in the Paris-Washington negotiations remained slow. In late June the British threw the negotiations into confusion by proposing an alternate MLF scheme based on a force of land-based aircraft. What prompted this new British scheme is unclear, but it may have been intended to distract the mounting, and rather vocal, opposition of the British Labour party to the MLF. It may also have been intended to undercut the Royal Navy's continued opposition to the surface fleet configuration. Finally, it may have been an attempt to further sidetrack already unproductive talks.

Whatever the reason for the British proposal, it signaled that the United States was unlikely to obtain Britain's participation in the sea-based MLF by the end of the year. Furthermore, Italian commitment was still elusive. So Ball and others in the State Department began to lobby for a decision to seek only West German participation by December, through the vehicle of a draft treaty that would allow for broader

43. Steinbruner, *Cybernetic Theory of Decision*, pp. 288–89. The description of the final months of the MLF is based largely on Philip Geyelin, *Lyndon B. Johnson and the World*, pp. 159–80.

participation at a later date. But Chancellor Erhard unwittingly undercut this effort. The West German leader, fearful of the growing influence of pro-French forces in his party, sent a letter to Johnson arguing that agreement by December was essential for Bonn; after December the Gaullists in his party would make closer Franco-German cooperation a major issue in the 1965 elections, a campaign that would make support for the MLF even more difficult for Erhard. Furthermore, the nonproliferation treaty negotiations would increasingly become an issue in West German politics, and it would be easier for Erhard to obtain Bonn's accession to the treaty if he had the MLF agreement behind him. Would it not be possible, he wrote, for the United States and West Germany to come to an MLF agreement in December, if necessary without other participants?[44]

Unfortunately Erhard aired this suggestion publicly before Johnson had a chance to reply. Rusk, wary of undermining the slow and delicate multilateral negotiations in Paris and Washington, immediately came out with a statement precluding a bilateral agreement by December. To add to these troubles, French Prime Minister Georges Pompidou announced in early November that West German participation in the MLF would be incompatible with the Franco-German Cooperation Treaty of 1963.

The French then launched an active diplomatic effort to woo West Germany, and other European nations, away from the MLF. Two themes were constantly stressed: any system that relied on a U.S. veto would suffer from the lack of U.S. credibility, and progress toward European unity could come only from abandoning the MLF as an instrument of U.S. hegemony and domination. De Gaulle was now supported by none other than the retired Adenauer, who, after visiting de Gaulle and coming away convinced that the MLF would mean a complete Franco-German political rupture, was able to persuade the Christian Democratic party caucus to vote a resolution delaying West German participation.

So by the end of the fall, while reaffirming support for the concept, West German officials, particularly von Hassel, let it be known that Bonn's eagerness for a quick agreement, so great in October, had considerably diminished.

The final blow—and in retrospect the decisive turn—in the fall of 1964

44. Steinbruner, *Cybernetic Theory of Decision*, pp. 289–91.

was the victory of the British Labour party in the October elections. Britain's new prime minister, Harold Wilson, had spent the better part of the past year attacking the government's policy of maintaining an independent deterrent, the multinational nuclear force, and the American multilateral nuclear force. While in opposition, he and his Labour followers had evinced almost total faith in the American nuclear guarantee and therefore considered European, or NATO, nuclear aspirations unnecessary and wasteful.

Yet soon after his election, for reasons that remain unclear, Wilson and his closest colleagues were reported to be studying yet another British alternative to the MLF, this time a force, to be cosponsored with West Germany, in which mixed-manned MRBM ships would be only one element; other elements would include American and British strategic bombers, Polaris submarines, and most of the tactical nuclear weapons deployed by the United States in Europe. Some of these components would be nationally manned; a committee would be responsible for overall control of the force, with the United States exercising a veto over launch and the European members together exercising another veto. The West Germans were reportedly cool about such a complex proposal, but it did provide Erhard and von Hassel with another excellent excuse for not coming to an agreement with the United States by the end of the year.

Johnson's Decision

In the meantime, with Johnson's landslide November 1964 victory, thoughts in the White House naturally turned to salvaging the MLF: after all, the president had gone on record on many occasions in support of the proposal. Nevertheless, the diplomacy of October and November was not only increasing Britain's reluctance to participate but was adding to West Germany's (and others') hesitancy as well. Agreement by the end of the year seemed increasingly remote; in fact, steps had to be taken soon if the initiative was to be salvaged at all.

The president's national security adviser, McGeorge Bundy, had become sensitive to the negative effect of the pressure being put on European leaders by Ball and others in what was now being called the MLF cabal. As early as June, when Bundy detailed his old friend Richard E. Neustadt, a Harvard professor, to London to canvas Labour leaders' attitudes toward the MLF, Neustadt had returned with a report not only recording in detail the various sources of MLF opposition in the party hierarchy (the potential defense minister, Denis Healey, was judged to be particularly hostile to the whole scheme) but advising Bundy to avoid sending cabal members to a Labour government to lobby for the MLF: "a 'cabal' member (would be) fatal."[45] With the elections in both countries now over, Prime Minister Wilson wanted to come to Washington to touch base with Johnson. The date was set for December 6. For Bundy in the White House, the question became: how strongly should the president try to force the MLF, or some sort of compromise, onto Wilson?

To get at this problem, an interagency committee headed by Bundy and Ball set out to study what Johnson's strategy with Wilson should be. Bundy hired Neustadt to oversee the staff work of the committee, apparently to prevent the MLF advocates from dominating and to direct more detailed study of the various sub-issues raised by the MLF, such as MLF and France and MLF and disarmament. As part of this effort to give the president some way of salvaging the MLF, Ball and Neustadt went to Bonn and London to identify the main sticking points. Their conclusions were as follows:

—If Britain was allowed to participate with a national contingent only, the MLF would be too discriminatory for West Germany to join. Bonn required London's participation in the mixed-manned fleet.

—There now appeared to be an irreconcilable split over the issue of control: Britain, true to Wilson's preelection position supporting the U.S. guarantee, was loath to see the United States give up its veto; von Hassel had all along insisted that a future reformulation of the control arrangement devolve U.S. control so as to eliminate the U.S. veto.

—Somewhat less crucially, Britain favored a separate command for the MLF, whereas West Germany favored placing the MLF directly under SACEUR.[46]

Both Ball and Neustadt saw Wilson as the one who would have to compromise. Ball wrote a detailed report, with Neustadt's help, to present to the president. Essentially, the memo suggested that Johnson insist on British participation in the MLF, though the number of ships

45. Richard E. Neustadt, "Memorandum on the British Labour Party and the MLF," pp. 11–21, especially p. 18.

46. Steinbruner, *Cybernetic Theory of Decision*, pp. 302–03.

could be reduced if Britain contributed three Polaris submarines to the force. This would ease London's financial concern about participating. As long as Britain participated in the multimanned surface fleet, the memo said, Johnson should not discourage the contribution of national nuclear contingents to the force, provided that such contributions were acceptable to Bonn. The United States should remain absolutely firm on retaining veto over launch of the force, stopping just short of precluding further discussions of the control issue should a single all-European executive authority evolve. Any draft treaty would have to include statements favoring the speedy conclusion of a nonproliferation treaty. The issue of SACEUR's role should be left open for the moment, though the United States should favor placing the MLF under SACEUR. Finally, if Wilson and Erhard remained above any compromise, the president should be in a position to let the whole issue fade away.[47]

On December 5 Ball, Rusk, McNamara, and Bundy met with Johnson to consider the Ball memo and to come to a decision on how to handle Wilson. While Ball was clearly the most enthusiastic MLF supporter, he was not alone; all the advisers present, aware of the president's previous statements supporting the initiative and of the lack of workable alternatives, were generally supportive. In any case, Ball presented the memo to Johnson, noting that without some sort of collective nuclear force West Germany would now probably go nuclear on its own. Johnson apparently agreed and also agreed that Wilson would have to be the one to compromise to save the MLF.

But Johnson was clearly having his own doubts about the MLF. It was doing damage to negotiations on the nonproliferation treaty, since Soviet officials were increasingly tying progress on the negotiations to a NATO decision to drop the whole initiative. British and German reluctance to move on the issue, and rather vocal French opposition, made it difficult to sustain the argument that the United States was acceding to European demands. Even the once-enthusiastic Paul-Henri Spaak was now cool to the project, announcing that Belgium, while continuing to participate in the now thoroughly stalled Paris talks, would not participate in the creation of the force.[48] Generalized European coolness to the proposal was growing because of clear indications that the MLF would

47. Ibid., pp. 303–04.
48. New York Times, November 27, 1964.

create a serious rift between France and the rest of the alliance. Johnson needed no State Department briefing to see the problems the MLF was causing in Europe. In late November 1964 he stated that the United States would not be adamant about pushing the MLF; in a speech at Georgetown University on December 3, he had noted that though the United States would continue to urge participation in the MLF, he was determined to find a "common way" to solve the alliance's defense problems.[49]

At the December 5 meeting Johnson also expressed reservations about getting an MLF treaty through Congress, especially because of the Joint Committee on Atomic Energy, which had never ceased to oppose the concept. Ball and the others argued that congressional opposition could be overcome; Johnson, the master of congressional politics, was not so sure. He postponed a final decision for a day.

The president spent the next day looking into the matter for himself. His national security adviser, Bundy, conceded that Johnson had not been exposed to the case against the MLF and agreed to write a memo summarizing the negative viewpoint, although insisting that he personally still favored the proposal. Along with this negative memo, Bundy presented Johnson with a copy of a June 1963 memo he had written detailing Kennedy's reluctance to make the MLF the centerpiece of his trip to Europe. For Johnson this memo came as a surprise; he had assumed that Kennedy had been fully committed to the project. Now he recognized the importance Kennedy had placed on the precondition that the Europeans must want the MLF before the United States would be willing to push it.

He also put out feelers in Congress and found support for the MLF weak-to-nonexistent. Senator J. William Fulbright, chairman of the Senate Foreign Relations Committee, which would have to vote on any MLF treaty, reported that he had just attended a NATO parliamentarians' meeting and encountered vocal opposition to the MLF. If the Europeans did not want it, the Senate would be hard pressed to support it. Johnson agreed.[50]

The president called his advisers together on December 6 and in-

49. Ibid., November 29, 1964, and December 4, 1964.

50. Johnson personally leaked this directive to James Reston of the *New York Times*. See *New York Times*, December 21, 1964.

formed them of his decision: he would not try to get Wilson to participate in the MLF. The Europeans did not seem to want it any more; Congress was unlikely to support an MLF draft treaty; and the whole issue was creating more friction than it was worth. He would need a fallback.

Over the strenuous objections of Ball, Bundy, and even McNamara, who argued that too much U.S. prestige rested on the MLF for the president to move away from it, Johnson held firm. He would not press Wilson to commit Britain to the MLF. Instead, he would listen politely to the proposals Wilson was bringing with him, inform Wilson that much of what Wilson proposed would be unacceptable to Bonn, and direct Wilson to confer with his European colleagues to arrive at some sort of common position that Johnson could then support.

This, to Ball and the MLF community's collective dismay, was exactly what Johnson proceeded to do. To clarify his intentions further, he also promulgated a new decision document that forbade any more U.S. pressure until the Europeans had a chance to formulate a common position, and noted that any future agreement on a joint nuclear defense would have to have the strong backing of both Britain and West Germany, as well as be at least acceptable to France. Furthermore, Johnson said, any future arrangement would have to be compatible with European unity. These requirements effectively killed the MLF.

As could be expected, discussions between European nations and the United States on nuclear sharing arrangements continued through 1965. Many different schemes were examined, but none was able to develop the momentum that the MLF had had throughout most of 1963 and 1964. By early July 1965 a special administration panel had concluded that the United States should drop the whole notion of nuclear sharing if it jeopardized progress on nonproliferation.[51] By August it was a poorly kept secret that the MLF was a dead issue, though not surprisingly the State Department continued to deny it, even though Ball had resigned and the MLF office in State had disbanded soon after the Wilson visit. At the end of 1965 a meeting between Erhard and Johnson in Washington publicly acknowledged the final demise of the MLF. By that time U.S. national security policymakers were devoting their efforts to a new scheme: a forum within NATO for discussion and consultation on American strategic planning, the Nuclear Planning Group.

51. Ibid., July 1, 1965.

Conclusions

It would be tempting to draw the following conclusions from this complex and somewhat perplexing episode: that the multilateral nuclear force was an idea pushed with determination and energy by a small group of State Department officials who were convinced—wrongly, as it turned out—that European desire for a greater share of responsibility in the strategic posture of the alliance could be met by a mixed-manned, multilaterally controlled fleet of MRBM-carrying vessels subject to an American veto over launch; that the energetic lobbying of those officials for the MLF was as much the cause as the result of whatever European interest existed in the force; that they were able to move the proposal so far in such a short time because of accidental circumstances like the Skybolt cancellation and the de Gaulle offensive of January 1963; that high-level U.S. officials in a position to block the initiative were either too ambivalent or too distracted to do so, thus giving the effort tacit support; that the problems of the control formula and of the mixed-manned crew prevented any real progress in negotiations throughout 1964; and that when faced with a real deadline, Europeans made their reservations so clear that Johnson decided not to press the initiative, which in any case was now facing growing skepticism from Congress. Such an interpretation, though simplistic, does have an important element of truth. But it also ignores the deeper issues involved, which in turn explain why the United States pursued the proposal in the first place; why the Europeans found the proposal attractive enough to listen to, but not attractive enough to act on; and why the MLF eventually failed.

The Deeper Rationale

The reasons behind the determination of the MLF advocates to bring about the creation of the force, though touched on throughout the chapter, are important to review.[52] In the early 1960s men like Robert R. Bowie, who was in many ways the intellectual father of the MLF, felt

52. The main arguments here are taken from Robert R. Bowie, "Strategy and the Atlantic Alliance," pp. 709–32.

that a crisis was stirring NATO debates over strategy and policy and threatening to destroy NATO along with the products of U.S. postwar policy in Europe. Bowie traced this crisis to two causes: a shift in the "strategic environment" of the United States and the West as the Soviet Union developed a large stockpile of advanced nuclear weapons and delivery systems; and a shift in the political environment within NATO, in which Europe, once "stagnant, weak, and fragmented," had now been restored in strength and self-confidence by the phenomenal postwar economic revival and the birth of the European Community, which together had "nourished the sense of a common European destiny."[53] The first trend had eroded the credibility of the nuclear arsenals of the West to deter a wide range of potential aggression; the second had created an increasing gap between aspirations and capabilities in Europe. Bowie and most of those who favored the MLF endorsed the need for an improved conventional capability for NATO to enhance the alliance's overall deterrent. But they also believed that the two trends had created the political, if not the military, need to reevaluate the way the alliance controlled its strategic nuclear deterrent.

Bowie himself was quick to deny that these trends had in any way undermined the essential credibility of the American nuclear commitment to NATO's defense:

The idea that the United States would not be prepared to use its nuclear weapons to defend Europe under appropriate conditions is hardly tenable. The interests of the United States are so deeply involved in Europe and its integrity that it must treat any effort to conquer the NATO area in Europe as an attack on itself. If Europe were under Soviet control, the United States would clearly be at the mercy of the Soviet Union. Hence, it would have to treat any Soviet move to destroy or control Europe as a direct threat to its own survival.[54]

Bowie even went one step further to concede that, militarily, the requirements of a strategy for conducting a nuclear war would be best served by a continued U.S. monopoly, and centralized control, over the strategic arsenal of the West. Yet, he argued, it was not politically feasible to maintain the status quo, even if the United States were to grant a larger share of planning responsibilities to the European allies. France and Britain had long committed themselves to courses of nuclear independence, thus permanently ending the American monopoly within the alliance. But more important:

53. Ibid., pp. 709, 711.
54. Ibid., pp. 721–722.

With their enhanced confidence and revived strength, many European members *inevitably* desire a larger part in the planning of NATO strategy and in the control over the forces for its defense, especially nuclear. Thus, many Europeans now feel that a virtual monopoly in United States hands is no longer appropriate or acceptable over the long term. *This feeling is mainly political,* but it must be recognized and treated as real.[55]

As Bowie noted, one European reaction to this problem had been the development of national nuclear arsenals in Britain and France. To Bowie and others, this trend was anathema. Bowie agreed with McNamara's contention (examined in the next chapter) that such forces were intolerably expensive, seriously divisive, and problematic to the requirements of a unified NATO defense. Of particular concern to Bowie was the divisive and provocative effect of the British and French rationale for maintaining their own independent deterrent, which placed in doubt the credibility of the American nuclear guarantee—a guarantee that Bowie held to be strong:

According to this theory, since no nation will risk suicide to defend another, the French or British forces could hardly be expected to protect other European nations. Thus the Germans and others are bound to be faced sooner or later with the question of whether they should have such forces.[56]

American aid to these national nuclear forces—requested time and again by France and Britain—would serve only to underscore the second-class status of West Germany within the alliance. It might be decisive in stimulating German review of its 1954 pledge to forgo its own nuclear forces; if the United States remained firm in its aversion to a German national nuclear force under these circumstances, aid to the British and French would create "tensions and cleavages within the alliance which the Soviets would certainly seek to exploit."[57] Moreover, aid to the French nuclear program would be seen as an endorsement of de Gaulle's own design for a Europe led by France, not by the United States. Even the merging of the French and British nuclear forces as the cornerstone of a European deterrent would "hardly satisfy a German aspiration for equality. Germany and other European nations would certainly not be content with merely taking part in a 'control group' for French and British national forces."[58]

A fully integrated NATO nuclear force—the MLF—would solve the

55. Ibid., p. 722. Emphasis added.
56. Ibid., p. 724.
57. Ibid.
58. Ibid., p. 727.

dilemma of Germany's equal status in nuclear matters, offer an instrument for creating greater alliance cohesion, grant the increasingly strong and self-confident European nations meaningful participation in nuclear defense matters without stimulating proliferation, and foster the twin goals of European unity and Atlantic partnership. Bowie saw the mixed-manning aspect of the MLF as crucial:

The full force could be counted on for performing a specified strategic function. In the absence of national units, no member could threaten to undertake withdrawal as a lever or pressure on the others. Moreover, no one nationality would have unimpeded access to missiles or equipment aboard ship. Beyond this, unlike divisive national forces, the joint force with mixed manning would be a striking symbol of the cohesion of the alliance and of the mutual dependence of its members for their security.[59]

The control over the use of the force, Bowie admitted, presented "the hardest problem," the "ultimate dilemma." But for the time being, he argued, the issue need not become a sticking point:

In the long run Europeans are not likely to be satisfied with a solution which leaves all decisions to a President elected by only one portion of NATO. Yet, in practice the issue seems more theoretical than real. It is extremely hard to envisage a case where Europeans would wish to use strategic nuclear weapons when the United States would not be ready to do so. What is involved is more a matter of self-respect. Many Europeans want to feel that they have a genuine participation in the nuclear deterrent. And if they are to be treated as partners in the nuclear field, some way must be devised to provide for greater equality, at least for a unified Europe, in the matter of nuclear control.[60]

Thus, although for the moment the United States could retain an effective veto over the force, this control formula should be revised as the European political situation evolved toward true political, economic, and social unity. The final control formula might provide for U.S. participation in the MLF without a veto, or for close coordination between U.S. strategic forces and a purely European MLF. "Either form has its disadvantages. But either would be far better than the continuance and spread of national nuclear forces, which involve serious problems in more intractable forms."[61] Further, Bowie noted that West Germany and other European nations expected a revision of the control formula in the future.

Would Britain or France eventually participate in the MLF and

59. Ibid.
60. Ibid., pp. 727–28.
61. Ibid., p. 728.

renounce its national nuclear arsenal? Bowie thought that Britain would in time reappraise its national position and that "pressures to merge the British force into the joint force are likely to grow."[62] As for France, Bowie held out no similar hope, at least while de Gaulle was in power. He did, however, view eventual French participation as a possibility and rejected the notion that progress toward an MLF would isolate France and rupture European unity. He could not disguise his contempt for de Gaulle's current policies:

The objection that a multilateral force will tend to divide the alliance by isolating France is hardly valid. Actually, France has isolated herself by her insistence on a wholly independent national nuclear force. To refrain from action in which France may not join would give her a veto and paralyze the alliance.[63]

In summary, then, the Bowie argument for the MLF—which was echoed and shared by most of the other MLF advocates over the duration of the episode[64]—saw multiple opportunities and benefits to be had in the creation of an MLF:

A multilateral force avoids or resolves many of the problems posed by national forces in Europe, whether or not grouped together. Unlike national forces, a multilateral force would not fragment the alliance, but would tend to pull it together. Such a force would also enable the Federal Republic and Italy to have a proper part in nuclear defense without raising the specter of a separate German strategic force. The question of discrimination against the Germans or other nations would not arise. The cost of such a force would be materially less for the members. By combining their efforts, they could create a respectable nuclear force without unduly diverting resources from more adequate conventional forces. The multilateral force should foster European integration by bringing together the Five and the British into an integrated nuclear effort, open to France when she is ready to join. By initially involving the United States, the multilateral force would offer the best prospect. Even if it developed into a European force, it would still have close ties with the United States.[65]

To these broad arguments in favor of the force were added many others when the occasion was suitable. The MLF was seen variously as a way to fulfill Norstad's requirement for medium-range missiles (ironically, since it was in part intended to undercut the Norstad land-based

62. Ibid., p. 729.

63. Ibid.

64. See, for example, George W. Ball, "The Nuclear Deterrent and the Atlantic Alliance," pp. 736–39; Robert R. Bowie, "Tensions within the Alliance," pp. 49–69; Henry Owen, "What the Multilateral Force Could Achieve," pp. 12 ff; Claude V. Ricketts, "Multilateral Force," pp. 9 ff; and W. W. Rostow, "The Atlantic Agenda," pp. 578–87.

65. Bowie, "Strategy and the Atlantic Alliance," p. 730.

MRBM initiative); as a counterforce weapon against the growing number of Soviet MRBMs and IRBMs aimed at Western Europe; and as a safer arrangement, from the command and control perspective, than dual-key arrangements between the United States and NATO national armies provided with American tactical nuclear weapons. Others were quick to point to the benefits of a sea-based force as opposed to a land-based force: it was less vulnerable to preemption, less visible and hence less politically provocative, and more palatable to governments sensitive to the political problems of placing nuclear missiles on the densely populated plains of central Europe.[66]

The MLF was attractive even to some skeptics of European trends toward unity. On the whole they took a more pragmatic, accepting view of the French national nuclear program, but argued, as did Robert Osgood, that de Gaulle's *force de frappe* need not be incompatible with the MLF:

America's interest lies in consolidating the kind of nuclear ties with the German Federal Republic that the MLF promises to strengthen, but . . . these ties are not incompatible with France's interest in having an independent nuclear force for whatever margin of security it may provide. For the disadvantage of France's nuclear effort to American interests lies not so much in the prospect of France triggering the United States into a nuclear war, preventing a controlled nuclear response, impeding European unity, or wasting money that might otherwise go into conventional forces as in the danger that the *force de frappe*, combined with de Gaulle's European political strategy, might undermine the security of Western Europe by foreclosing a nationally acceptable but internationally safe role for Germany in the alliance and eroding the necessary engagement of American power in Europe. If the function of the MLF is conceived to be the limited one of fostering a constructive place for Germany in Europe through a multilateral nuclear association with the United States and other major participants, a better case can be made for it than if it is conceived to be an alternative to French and British nuclear forces.[67]

Such thoughtful and moderate support, however, was unusual. In their vigorous campaign of persuasion the MLF advocates often sounded more like Robert J. Manning, assistant secretary of state for public affairs, who made these remarks in a characteristic speech:

[The] trend to increasing military, diplomatic, and economic cohesion between the Western Europeans, the North Americans, and Japan is the Atlantic wave of the future. . . . it is important that . . . squalls of choppy water not be mistaken

66. For variants of these arguments, see Boulton, "NATO and the MLF," pp. 282–83; and Robert E. Osgood, *The Case for the MLF*.
67. Osgood, *Case for the MLF*, pp. 52–53.

for the big wave which, in the opinion of many who shape policy here and across the Atlantic, is the inexorable one. . . . There will be long and complicated ruminations as we attempt to work out, in a manner acceptable for the allies and ourselves, an answer to the Europeans' desire to have a greater share in the control of the nuclear power that now rests so largely with us. . . . In some ways, this most complex of problems, bristly with conflicting national prides and ambitions, may yet prove the most beneficial because it dramatizes more clearly the D'Artagnan indivisibility of the free world's position—in a nuclear showdown it is quite simply "all for one and one for all."[68]

The Lines of Criticism

It was, of course, possible to take issue with any one of the claims made by MLF supporters. Some preferred, like the Royal Navy, to challenge the operational feasibility of a mixed-manned fleet, stressing, in Osgood's words, "the difficulties of recruiting, training, and administering an efficient multi-national military organization in the face of national differences of language, pay, discipline, career structures, skills, food, religion and social customs"[69]

Others believed that the strong opposition of the MLF supporters to the continuation of French and British nuclear independence was short-sighted, unrealistic, and potentially even more divisive than the nuclear forces themselves. Some believed that the United States should take a more benign view of these forces and try to help them, to bind them closer to the American deterrent and to the alliance as a whole. And they saw American pressure on Europe to deploy an MLF as driving a wedge between de Gaulle and the rest of the alliance. Some of these analysts were sympathetic toward France's often repeated doubts about the credibility of the U.S. nuclear guarantee. Many simply did not share one of the root assumptions motivating the MLF proponents, that is, the inevitability of West German nuclear aspirations if the discriminatory nature of Bonn's nonnuclear status within the alliance was not rectified. Given the nature of postwar Europe, they did not believe West Germany would ever contemplate an act that would create deep anxiety not only among its friends and neighbors but within the United States, upon which German security and independence heavily depended, and within the Soviet Union, still haunted by the legacy of German aggression in

68. Robert J. Manning, "U.S. Foreign Policy," p. 142.
69. Osgood, *Case for the MLF*, p. 11.

the Second World War. Defense Minister Strauss's warnings aside, no decision would isolate West Germany so quickly and so completely in the world political arena as the development of an independent nuclear deterrent.

And finally, the issue of control worried many opponents of the MLF. Although the MLF advocates were convinced that the control formula need not be an obstacle to the creation of the force, the formula was in many ways the essence of the MLF. Through the control formula nations that felt discriminated against in the nuclear affairs of the alliance would be able to overcome that feeling. Europeans interested in gaining a greater share of control over alliance nuclear weapons would hardly be satisfied—even temporarily—with a system in which the United States retained an ultimate veto. But a reformulation to end the American veto, while welcomed in Bonn, would have been feared in other European countries that were wary of letting West Germany gain too great a share in the control of strategic nuclear weapons. A majority voting system, perhaps weighted according to the amount of each participant's contribution, would have been even more attractive to Bonn, and even less attractive elsewhere, because clearly West Germany would be providing the lion's share of manpower and finance to the MLF.

The control problem raised military issues never far from the minds of McNamara and his colleagues at the Pentagon. How credible a deterrent would the MLF be if, with a unanimity formula, any single participant could veto NATO's use of the force? Assertions to the contrary, it *was* conceivable that some members of the MLF—not necessarily the United States—would be reluctant to authorize launch of the force, especially those members not directly exposed to conflict on the central front or those susceptible to Soviet political or military inducements. Under a control formula requiring a unanimous vote, how sure would an enemy be that the force would ever be used against it? And wouldn't that enemy seek to exploit national differences to assure a veto—in ways simply not possible against strategic forces held by one country under a centralized, unified command authority?

If the unanimity principle was abandoned so as to eliminate an American veto, would there be circumstances in which the European members of the alliance could commit the West to a nuclear war against the wishes of the United States? Though such an event was possible, it was heavily discounted by those familiar with strategic and political realities. If the president of the United States was unwilling to launch

American strategic forces, the allies, it was believed, would be even less eager to launch their own forces.

But if the United States did not retain control over launch or targeting of the MLF, some serious planning problems might arise. To oversimplify somewhat, the European and American strategic arsenals might work at cross-purposes in the prosecution of a nuclear engagement, especially if the European force was targeted against cities while the American force was targeted against enemy military forces. An uncoordinated attack of that sort might ensure that no one's objectives would be achieved. This potential problem was resolvable in principle if the strategic planners on both sides of the Atlantic were to develop strong, pervasive systems of cooperative planning.

Another military problem, however, seemed less amenable to solution. The responsiveness of a force dependent on a voting mechanism of any kind—much less one that required unanimity—could not be counted on to be speedy enough for efficient execution of military plans. In the emotion-laden, desperate hours of a true nuclear confrontation, discussions among a control committee could easily deadlock; even if they went smoothly, they might take too long in a world where intercontinental ballistic missiles are capable of arriving at their targets from launch in less than half an hour. One way out of this dilemma would have been to delegate authority to SACEUR to launch the force under certain specifically prescribed circumstances, and otherwise to await orders from the control group. But such a system, while providing for swifter execution of retaliation under the prescribed circumstances, would also have removed whatever flexibility nations might have wanted to retain in those circumstances and at the same time would have resulted in equally long, arduous, and agonized deliberations in unforeseen circumstances.

The irony of the situation was that for all the effort involved, the MLF would not have appreciably added to the strategic arsenals of the West. The United States was in the process of procuring its 1,700-odd strategic land-based and sea-based missiles, besides its enormous strategic bomber force, at an annual cost of some $15 billion. A force of some 200 missiles would add little to the striking power of this vast arsenal, which, to those who planned the force dispositions and even to MLF advocates, was irrevocably committed anyway to the defense of the alliance. As is seen in the next chapter, McNamara and his colleagues at the Defense Department were at the time revising U.S. strategic policy to make the U.S. guarantee even *more* credible. From this perspective, even if the control problems could have been worked out to everyone's satisfaction, and even if coordination of targeting and use between the MLF and the rest of the American strategic arsenal could have been effected, the imposing U.S. strategic forces available for defense of the alliance would have made the MLF superfluous. That McNamara did not act decisively after December 1962 to kill the MLF may have been due to several factors, including a desire to keep a low profile on the whole issue of nuclear sharing in the wake of the Nassau debacle and a belief that the Europeans could be counted on to kill the proposal in the end.

And kill it they did. The obstacles that the French put in the way of West German participation, and British delaying tactics that made clear that no prime minister—neither Macmillan, Sir Alec Douglas-Home, nor Wilson—wanted to see the MLF come into existence, had worked decisively by November 1964 to cool general European enthusiasm for the American proposal. Even Paul-Henri Spaak, the Belgian leader who at first was one of the loyal proponents of the scheme, lost interest in the project when it became apparent that it was working to divide rather than to unite the great European powers. If de Gaulle was finding it difficult to follow through constructively on his challenge to the Atlantic partnership posed at the January 1963 press conference, he was more effective in using his leverage on Erhard and others to prevent the American Grand Design from bearing fruit in the form of the MLF. While making the MLF an issue of choice for Bonn between Paris and Washington—a choice that no West German leader would have been eager to make—de Gaulle also continued to emphasize the lack of credibility of the American guarantee, which served to reinforce European doubts about the adequacy of a control system in which the United States retained a veto over use of the force.

For the British the issue was somewhat different. At various times the Macmillan government and the succeeding Conservative government, led by Douglas-Home, used a more sophisticated version of the French criticism of American credibility to justify its independent nuclear arsenal, an argument that once again placed American insistence on retaining a veto over launch in an ominous light. At the same time it is clear that the British valued the uniqueness of the relationship that had developed between Washington and London on nuclear matters since 1958, a relationship unabashedly pursued by Macmillan in his 1960 decision to accept Skybolt from the United States and his 1962 decision to rely on American submarine technology when Skybolt was canceled. Any arrangements the United States might pursue with other European powers that would reduce the uniqueness of this relationship were to be looked on with jealousy and suspicion. Macmillan's Atlantic nuclear force, and its variants put forward under succeeding British leaders, had the two qualities of preserving whatever strategic independence Britain had and of making it impossible for West Germany and other nonnuclear countries to have their own special relationships with Washington. When Wilson came into office, he was openly skeptical of the Conservative party's rationale for an independent deterrent and quite willing to accept McNamara's logic regarding the credibility of the U.S. nuclear guarantee. He and his Labour colleagues were to find it politically expedient, however, to retain the Conservative government's independent arsenal. Yet this did not change Wilson's skepticism about the need for greater European control over the strategic weapons of the alliance. And historical Labour suspicion of West German military aspirations argued against acquiescence in a strategic nuclear role for Bonn, especially since such a role would lead to East-West tensions that Labour was not eager to aggravate. Those in the United States who put a high priority on the successful conclusion of a nonproliferation treaty had forceful allies in Wilson's government. As long as the Russians insisted that the MLF would block the conclusion of that treaty, these arms-control advocates in Washington and London saw no harm in allowing the MLF to be delayed indefinitely. The powerful Royal Navy's opposition on grounds of feasibility made it even easier for Conservative and Labour alike to place many obstacles in the way of the successful completion of the MLF negotiations.

Although this whole complex of military and political phenomena was an essential part of the failure of the MLF, one can make a strong case, as did Alastair Buchan, that the originators of the MLF misperceived the underlying desires of most European governments. At several times during the episode, Buchan argued that what was needed to calm European insecurities about the strategic deterrent of the alliance was *not* some new arrangement to give Europeans greater *control* over specific weapons systems that they could launch more or less independently of the American deterrent. What the Europeans needed was to recognize (1) that some persuasive thought lay behind American claims that the nuclear umbrella really covered them too, and (2) that the United

States was willing to consider the attitudes and interests of its European partners as an essential part of the operational planning and disposition of the American strategic forces. In 1962 Buchan wrote the following:

The controversy which the idea [of a NATO deterrent] has created in recent years has illuminated a profound confusion of thought that exists within the alliance, as in disarmament negotiations, between the French concept of *contrôle* which means examination, verification, the right to criticize, and the English word *control* which in this context means the physical grasp of buttons and levers. If one analyzes European fears, or examines the reasons why first Britain, then France, embarked on an independent nuclear capability, it becomes clear that the basic European desire is not so much for operational control of bombers or missiles as *pour contrôler* American strategic policy, to gain some measure of control over the context of peace and war. . . . If the United States could present a clear and continuous picture of its strategic policy . . . and accept informed criticism of its plans, then not only would European governments at last have a clear picture of the considerations which must govern their own defense policies and diplomacy, but their main motive for wishing to acquire operational control of nuclear weapons would disappear. The United States would not then have to consider devolving operational control of nuclear weapons; by bringing NATO within the American policy *planning* process, the President's *operational* freedom of action in an emergency would thus be enhanced. . . . It is not unreasonable, in these circumstances, to assume that if it were clear in London and Paris that the civil-military machine of NATO provided a better channel of *contrôle* than the independent maintenance of increasingly expensive national nuclear strategic forces, these could be replanned within NATO as tactical forces and in the end very probably dispensed with.[70]

And in October 1964 Buchan looked back over two years of active intra-alliance negotiations over the MLF and concluded, with impressive prescience, that

it may well be, therefore, that the MLF will in the end prove to have been nothing but an expensive and time consuming *détour* on the road to a more effective system of political and strategic planning among the Western allies, centered perhaps in Washington rather than in Paris: a solution which became blocked by means of French chauvinism, British hesitations and a series of false American judgments about the nature of Europe and about the strength of her own position there, during the earlier years of this decade.[71]

Buchan may have been altogether too sanguine about the possibility of persuading Britain and France to forgo independent nuclear capabilities. And he may have understated the damage done by the MLF effort. Catherine Kelleher reported the comment of one high-ranking German

70. Alastair Buchan, "The Reform of NATO," pp. 179–80.
71. Buchan, "Multilateral Force," p. 637.

official that eloquently summarizes the consequences of moving so far on an initiative, only to cancel it abruptly: "The United States and Germany climbed up the mountain and then they—we—climbed back down again. In terms of time, money, personnel, and prestige, neither of us can afford that again."[72]

Still, the United States had been preparing, simultaneously with the MLF initiative, a package of proposals that were designed to challenge directly the perceived need for Europeans to have a "physical grasp" of the "buttons and levers" of NATO's strategic forces, to convince them that they could play a crucial role in improving the broad deterrent posture of the alliance, and to open the process of U.S. strategic planning to greater NATO-wide participation.

72. Cited in Kelleher, *Germany and the Politics of Nuclear Weapons*, p. 255.

CHAPTER SIX

Flexible Response and the Nuclear Planning Group

THE United States next tried to address NATO's nuclear dilemmas by focusing not on any particular weapon, or on a new way to share strategic weapons, but on a new broad strategy for NATO that eventually became known as flexible response.

What was this new strategy? To simplify, it started from the premise that the best deterrent resided in the threat to respond *appropriately* to whatever aggression the enemy mounted. The threat to launch a strategic nuclear attack would be an appropriate and reasonably believable threat against a massive Soviet nuclear attack on the West, but it would hardly be believable, much less appropriate, as a response to a small-scale border incident or to stepped-up political and military pressure against West Berlin. NATO would thus have to develop a strong nonnuclear (or conventional) posture to deal with such threats. If deterrence failed and NATO proved incapable of halting and reversing Warsaw Pact aggression by conventional means, options would still be open for the West to escalate its military response to include the use of nuclear weapons.

The strategy of flexible response extended this search for options to the strategic nuclear level.[1] It was assumed that the president should have the option of executing a strategic retaliation against enemy military forces (counterforce), holding enough strategic reserve to threaten enemy urban-industrial centers (countervalue). Sparing enemy cities would create incentives for the Soviets to spare Western cities; holding enemy cities hostage in this way would also give the West political

1. The term *search for options* is taken from William W. Kaufmann, *The McNamara Strategy.*

leverage to bring the enemy to favorable terms. Underlying these ideas was the assumption, suggested by studies made in the late 1950s and early 1960s, that counterforce targeting by both sides could, under certain circumstances, lead to substantially fewer casualties on both sides.

The Origins of Flexible Response, 1957–60

Chapter 3 reviewed some critiques of the doctrine of massive retaliation as propounded by the Eisenhower administration from 1954 to 1957. The origins of flexible response lie in those studies and in the search to define a workable alternative to massive retaliation.

American Roots

The main objection to Dulles's doctrine was its lack of credibility. Criticism focused attention on how to improve the strategic deterrent to make its use against some forms of aggression more credible and on how to improve the other forces of the West—the conventional forces—to give NATO a sound, reliable, and credible deterrent against a broad range of possible aggression.

Regarding U.S. strategic nuclear posture, many studies between 1957 and 1960 found that the U.S. strategic deployment had problems, such as vulnerability of the aging bomber forces, lack of progress on ballistic missile technology, weaknesses in command and control, and lack of appropriate civil defense measures. Some studies, like the so-called Gaither Report, remained secret but were leaked to the press; others, like the so-called Rockefeller Report, were public and attracted much attention. And Henry Kissinger, as the rapporteur for a Council on Foreign Relations study group, wrote a popular book on the subject.[2]

Whether because of these studies or for other reasons, the Eisenhower administration gradually moved away from its position on massive retaliation; in 1957 John Foster Dulles suggested that the defense of Europe might be possible on a local basis with the help of new, "small"

---

2. *Deterrence and Survival in the Nuclear Age (The "Gaither Report" of 1957)*, Committee Print. See also Rockefeller Brothers Fund, *Prospects for America*, pp. 93–155; and Henry A. Kissinger, *Nuclear Weapons and Foreign Policy*.

nuclear weapons to compensate for conventional inferiority.[3] While satisfactory to some, to others this shift was not enough. Debates in public and private focused on the need for improved conventional forces so that NATO would not be forced to meet Warsaw Pact conventional aggression with nuclear weapons.

Several studies done at the Rand Corporation in 1959 and 1960 dealt with improving the strategic deterrent.[4] For years Albert Wohlstetter had been arguing, on the basis of studies he and others at Rand had conducted in the early 1950s, that U.S. strategic forces should be made invulnerable to preemptive attack and be sufficiently reliable to hit their targets. For the bomber force this would mean increasing alert rates and bringing strategic bombers back to the continental United States and dispersing them; for new ballistic missiles this would largely mean underground basing in silos hardened against the effects of nuclear blast. In 1959 Wohlstetter summarized this work in an influential article for *Foreign Affairs,* in which he argued that (1) the deterrent capability of a strategic force was intimately linked with its survivability for a second-strike retaliation; (2) such survivability was difficult to achieve; and (3) such a capability must nevertheless be pursued because any posture falling short of it would be inherently destabilizing, with potentially disastrous consequences.[5]

Meanwhile others at Rand were beginning to examine ways in which U.S. strategic employment strategies could be improved. They discovered, after a complex series of analyses of general war between the United States and the Soviet Union, that the choice of employment strategy had radical consequences for both sides. Specifically, targeting strategies that avoided cities but that aimed at enemy military forces—primarily enemy strategic forces—could result in dramatically lower casualties for both sides. By September 1960 they were able to derive a table that related targeting strategies, war contingencies, and deaths on both sides. A declassified version of the table is presented here:[6]

3. John Foster Dulles, "Challenge and Response in United States Policy," pp. 25–43.

4. The discussion of the effect of the Rand studies on the subsequent adoption of flexible response draws heavily on Desmond J. Ball, *Politics and Force Levels.* See also Ball, *Déjà Vu: The Return to Counterforce in the Nixon Administration,* pp. 10–17.

5. Albert Wohlstetter, "The Delicate Balance of Terror," pp. 211–34.

6. The table comes from Desmond J. Ball, "The Strategic Missile Programme of the Kennedy Administration, 1961–63" (Ph.D. dissertation), p. 49.

| | | Deaths in millions | |
Contingency	Target strategy	U.S.	Soviet
Soviets strike first	Indiscriminate	150	40
United States strikes first	Indiscriminate	110	75
Soviets strike first	Avoid cities	10	8
United States strikes first	Avoid cities	3	5

The Rand analyses suggested that there might be important incentives for both sides to avoid cities in the first rounds of a strategic exchange. By avoiding cities, but retaining a sufficient reserve to target them later, the United States could, in effect, hold the enemy's society hostage, thus providing powerful bargaining leverage to end the war quickly on terms favorable to the West. Of course, these analyses depended critically on a set of restrictive assumptions made in the face of many uncertainties. But the dramatic difference in results argued for taking the *possibility* of damage limitation through counterforce targeting seriously.

At the same time, various groups within the air force were showing an active interest in a "no-cities" strategy. Air Force Chief of Staff General Thomas D. White, who had been aware of the Rand work early on, lobbied for the idea within his service. On his air staff, Brigadier General Noel Parrish and Colonel Donald Martin had been working in parallel with the Rand counterforce studies; in mid-1960 they coordinated with the Rand project. By the end of 1960, a no-cities strategy existed on paper at Rand and within certain air force offices; however, resistance from the Strategic Air Command made its adoption as an official targeting policy difficult.

Rand's civilian analysts were not the only ones who were running into SAC resistance to the adoption of flexible response. General Maxwell Taylor, army chief of staff, recounts in vivid detail his frustrations as the air force effectively blocked all army efforts to improve its conventional ground warfare capabilities to deal more effectively with the contingencies in which strategic air power alone would not be an adequate deterrent. In fact, so frustrated was General Taylor over these obstacles that he resigned and published a revealing memoir and critique of the Eisenhower administration's defense policy.[7]

Nevertheless, General Taylor's vocal concerns led the Joint Chiefs of Staff in 1959 to begin to reexamine the feasibility of conventional

7. General Maxwell D. Taylor, *The Uncertain Trumpet.*

defense efforts. Throughout 1959 and 1960 Colonel (later General) Edward L. Rowny conducted studies for the Joint Chiefs and gradually concluded that conventional defense against a Warsaw Pact conventional attack was more feasible than generally assumed at the time.[8]

NATO Roots

Some important studies along these lines had already been taking place at SHAPE. In early 1957 Colonel (later General) Richard G. Stilwell, director of the strategic studies group under the Plans and Policy Division at SHAPE, began to evaluate the requirements for NATO's basic strategy and concluded that the credibility of the threat of general nuclear war in response to any Warsaw Pact aggression was seriously eroding, for the reasons suggested above. As a recent leader of the strategy course at the U.S. Army War College, Stilwell had been exposed to the intense academic debate over massive retaliation and limited war. With members of his staff, he produced a study paper that presented an elaborate rationale for shifting NATO's basic strategy to a version of flexible response.[9] According to Edward Rowny,

the study envisaged a forward defense concept whereby the use of conventional land, sea, and air forces would be used. Should these forces-in-being be judged to be incapable of countering Warsaw Pact aggression, then tactical nuclear weapons would be used and additional forces would be rapidly transported to Western Europe.

Stilwell's study used the term "direct defense" as the concept for countering aggression on the level at which the enemy might choose to fight. It also introduced into NATO, for the first time, the notion of "deliberate escalation" whereby aggression would be countered by deliberately raising the scope and intensity of combat so as to make the threat of nuclear response more imminent. This would be done by intensifying the non-nuclear engagement, by taking offensive action on another front, or by using tactical nuclear weapons. This failing, strategic nuclear weapons released to SACEUR's control would be used initially against military targets.[10]

The Stilwell study worked its way up through the chain of command of SHAPE, to General Norstad, who then invited Stilwell to present a briefing on the study to him and to the entire SHAPE staff. Norstad took

8. Private correspondence with author.
9. The details of this episode are recounted in Edward L. Rowny, "Decision-Making Process in NATO" (Ph.D. dissertation), pp. 178–90.
10. Ibid., pp. 178–79.

a keen interest in the proposal; it tended to support his pause concept, discussed in chapter 3, though to what degree Norstad believed that lower-level responses to Warsaw Pact aggression would require tactical nuclear components remains unclear. In his statements to Congress Norstad repeatedly insisted that his shield forces were *not* conventional and that any alliance effort to defeat the Warsaw Pact on the central front would require the application of tactical nuclear firepower. At the same time, however, he pushed strongly in NATO for his five-year defense plan, MC 70, to create 30 active and 30 reserve divisions for the central front—a force so strong that, given adequate warning time, it would have a chance of mounting a successful nonnuclear defense against a conventional Warsaw Pact attack.

In any case, Norstad organized a lobbying campaign for the report in Europe and the United States, appealing to military men, government leaders, and influential private citizens to support the recommendations of the Stilwell study. He also had his staff prepare a briefing on the report for the December 1957 meeting of the NATO Military Committee. Norstad presented the briefing himself, and according to Rowny, "most of the members of the Military Committee were convinced of the correctness of the suggested new strategy, even though few dared, because of domestic pressures at home, to publicly espouse a change in basic strategy for NATO."[11]

Faced with inaction by the committee, Norstad passed the report along to Washington and the Joint Chiefs of Staff. There, the Joint Chiefs, except for General Taylor, gave it the same resistance they had given all previous attempts to draw resources away from strategic nuclear forces into building up conventional capabilities. General Taylor prevailed upon the Joint Chiefs to pass the report along to Secretary of Defense Charles E. Wilson, who not surprisingly also rejected the findings. But the report had, after all, come from a key U.S. and alliance military commander—presumably this was in Wilson's mind when he decided to pass the report along to President Eisenhower for final decision. Eisenhower showed no more sympathy for the report than had Wilson or the Joint Chiefs. He sent the report back to the Pentagon for further study, thereby effectively shelving it. Thus General Norstad's attempt to have NATO adopt a version of flexible response was set aside indefinitely.

11. Ibid., pp. 187–88.

Eisenhower's Response

All these reports, studies, and debates had begun to advance a coherent, comprehensive defense strategy as an alternative to the one then pursued by the United States and NATO. Eisenhower and his advisers showed little interest. The president had, admittedly, presided over an increase in the NATO tactical nuclear stockpile, though the strategy behind this increase was never fully elaborated, if indeed it ever existed. He had also initiated the U.S. strategic ballistic missile program and the Polaris submarine program. In time these programs would constitute the most survivable portion of American strategic forces.

But still the conventional forces of the United States and NATO Europe were below the requirements set in MC 70, and the Eisenhower administration was in no rush to rectify the problem. This lack of interest had many causes; in particular, economic and budgetary concerns, reliance on the nuclear guarantee, and rather bitter interservice rivalry.

Kennedy's Challenge

During the 1960 presidential campaign, Senator John F. Kennedy showed sympathy with the views of General Taylor and other critics of the Eisenhower defense policy.[12] He believed that U.S. strategic forces had to be placed on a sounder basis; whatever its merits, the alleged missile gap between the United States and the Soviet Union had become a hot campaign issue, and Kennedy entered office committed to plugging this gap. Furthermore, he brought into his campaign, in advisory capacities, many of the people responsible for those broad critiques of Eisenhower defense policy, the Gaither and Rockefeller reports: Paul H. Nitze, Roswell Gilpatric, Jerome Wiesner, Walt W. Rostow, Maxwell Taylor, and Dean Rusk, to name but a few. As early as 1958, Kennedy was aware of Wohlstetter's work; he apparently used a preliminary draft of "The Delicate Balance of Terror" as the basis for his August 14, 1958, speech on the missile gap.[13] By the time Kennedy came to the White House in January 1961, he had developed a strong desire to undertake a comprehensive review of U.S. defense policy and had put together a

12. See Ball, *Politics and Force Levels*, pp. 15–22; Kaufmann, *McNamara Strategy*, pp. 40–44; and Harland B. Moulton, *From Superiority to Parity*, pp. 36–41.
13. See Ball, *Politics and Force Levels*, pp. 39–40.

strong team of advisers, formal and informal, to help him achieve this objective.

A Strategy for the United States

In the first months of 1961, that review took place in both the Pentagon and the White House. In the Pentagon, McNamara issued his now famous "ninety-six trombones," a memorandum consisting of ninety-six questions designed to prod the Pentagon bureaucracy into reexamining old assumptions and policies. One of these called for the development of a flexible response doctrine for the strategic forces. McNamara had become a quick convert to the no-cities strategy emerging from the air force–Rand studies; he had been briefed on this work within a week of installment as secretary and by March 1961 had directed Paul Nitze, his new assistant secretary for international security affairs, to revise the U.S. strategic posture. Nitze and his staff drafted a revised version of the "basic national security policy" papers of the Eisenhower administration, emphasizing the critical importance of conventional forces and flexible options for nuclear war. Rather than promulgate this as a new, formal policy paper, Kennedy and McNamara directed that it be used to revise the employment plans for the strategic nuclear forces, including the single integrated operational plan (SIOP), which assigned weapons to targets in an integrated fashion.[14]

What the new administration had inherited from the old one, in the SIOP and its supporting plans, consisted of one massive, "spasm" option in which the United States would launch *all* its nuclear weapons, leaving little or no reserves, against an indiscriminate list of cities and military targets. The new targeting package, according to Desmond Ball, set the following policy lines:

1. Soviet strategic forces were separated from Soviet cities on U.S. target lists.

14. Ball, *Déjà Vu*, pp. 11–12. Relatively little has been published about this plan, about what it is, and how it is generated. One brief but informative discussion is in Captain Mark D. Mariska, "The Single Integrated Operational Plan," pp. 32–39. A more authoritative account, though less directly to the point, can be found in Henry S. Rowen, "Formulating Strategic Doctrine," in *Commission on the Organization of the Government for the Conduct of Foreign Policy (Murphy Commission)*, pt. 3 of vol. 4 appendixes, pp. 219–34.

2. Strategic reserves were to be held by the United States in accordance with the concept of intrawar deterrence.

3. American command and control systems were to be protected, to allow controlled response.

4. Soviet command and control was to be preserved, at least in the initial stages of any nuclear exchange.

In accordance with these new guidelines, a new SIOP was devised, grouping target categories into options:

1. Soviet strategic retaliatory forces;
2. Soviet air defense away from cities;
3. Soviet air defense near cities;
4. Soviet command and control centers;
5. an all-out spasm against military and urban-industrial targets.[15]

Henry S. Rowen, who was closely involved with this revision, later wrote:

The new guidance distinguished more clearly among . . . attack on (1) nuclear threat targets, (2) other military forces, and (3) urban-industrial targets. It also provided options for withholding attack by country and for withholding direct attack on cities. However, the tasks all involved large attacks, and civilian damage, at least from radioactive fallout, would have been very heavy. And there was not a clear distinction between "urban" and "industrial" targets, a distinction that had almost disappeared in the 1950s with the advent of high-yield weapons.[16]

These guidelines were forwarded to the Joint Chiefs in late 1961; they approved the changes, and the final general war plan options were formally adopted over the next few months.

These guidelines generated specific implementation efforts. A study group within the National Security Council, the Net Evaluation Subcommittee, chaired by General Thomas F. Hickey, tried to derive the required strategic force levels for implementing the new strategy. An interagency study chaired by General Earle E. Partridge looked into the characteristics of the command and control system required for the revised SIOP. At about the same time, the air force directed Dr. James C. Fletcher, a prominent defense science specialist, to put together a group of technical experts from inside and outside the government to recommend changes in the Minuteman ICBM program to fit the new flexible response policy. As a result, the program underwent "changes in the command and

---

15. Ball, *Politics and Force Levels*, p. 191.
16. Rowen, "Formulating Strategic Doctrine," p. 230.

control electronics so that the operational concept of the Minuteman force would enforce that national policy. Force improvement, such as selective launch and stop launch, increased target selection capability, lighter guidance and control packages, safety, refinements in propulsion, and a new re-entry system (Mark-II) were developed."[17] These changes added some $840 million, or 15 percent, to the 1961 estimates of the program costs for an 800-missile Minuteman force.

While this work on reassessing strategic nuclear policy continued, planners in the Pentagon were beginning to examine the requirements for improving the conventional forces.[18] Emphasis on improved conventional forces was a direct result of the belief held by McNamara and his colleagues that, while crucial in deterring massive nuclear attacks against the West, the U.S. strategic nuclear arsenal was not a suitable means for deterring less catastrophic attacks, especially those that came from limited conventional operations arising from political crisis or accident. NATO's flexible response strategy would have to permit the alliance to rely on nonstrategic threats to deter less than all-out attacks and to defend against such attacks should deterrence break down.

For analysts brought into the Pentagon under McNamara, past arguments about the value of a tactical nuclear defense were unconvincing. They took issue with the proponents of a tactical nuclear posture for many by now familiar reasons:

—Virtually every war game and analysis that had studied the problems of tactical nuclear warfare had concluded that, far from rectifying conventional manpower imbalances, tactical nuclear war would exacerbate those imbalances without reducing the importance of conventional manpower to the outcome of the conflict.

—For various technical reasons—the immense destructiveness of these weapons, the uncertainties associated with accuracy of delivery, the fact that the central front was heavily congested with urban population centers, the high tempo of nuclear operations using fast delivery systems—warfare begun with the intention of limiting tactical nuclear warfare to discrete military objectives would quickly devastate civilian

17. Testimony of General Schultz before the House Appropriations Committee, 1970, cited in Ball, *Politics and Force Levels*, p. 194.

18. Perhaps the most authoritative account of the review of the conventional option for NATO under McNamara appears in Alain C. Enthoven and K. Wayne Smith, *How Much Is Enough?* pp. 117–64. See also Kaufmann, *McNamara Strategy*, pp. 79–87; and Timothy W. Stanley, *NATO in Transition*, pp. 243–305.

societies in the process and would probably escalate quickly into an uncontrolled and unrestrained use of nuclear weapons on the Continent, which in turn would probably escalate quickly into central strategic nuclear war.

—The inherent vulnerability of forward-based nuclear systems would create significant instabilities, since pressure would mount, during a crisis or during a conventional attack, to use the weapons before they were destroyed or fell into enemy hands.

—Even if NATO's tactical nuclear posture could be improved to minimize these weaknesses, there would be no guarantee that the Soviets would follow suit. As one analyst has pointed out, "Limited nuclear wars with one side using discrete-fire techniques and the other using terrain-fire are likely to be notoriously one-sided in favor of the latter."[19]

From this theoretical criticism emerged an argument for maintaining "firebreak" between nuclear and conventional operations in NATO strategy. Conventional operations were a known quantity; one understood, within limits, how to control them to achieve political objectives with relatively few casualties. Once the firebreak between conventional and nuclear operations had been crossed, however, one entered a conflict about which little was known, but which seemed to hold fewer prospects for control and greater likelihood of rapid escalation to levels of unprecedented destruction. One might be able to achieve traditional political-military objectives through a tactical nuclear campaign. But the prospects of doing so were at best uncertain, and the consequences of failure were potentially apocalyptic.

All this being recognized, it was still possible, the argument ran, to assign the tactical nuclear weapons deployed in NATO Europe a deterrent role. The very presence of the weapons on European territory implied that they might be used against a Warsaw Pact invasion. This uncertainty would weigh heavily on Warsaw Pact leaders contemplating even a limited attack on NATO territory. The probability that they might be used might outweigh the potential gains to be had from an attack and so help to dissuade the Warsaw Pact from initiating one. But for NATO to rely solely on a tactical nuclear response if deterrence failed—as NATO had explicitly done for the previous six years—seemed unwise in light of the uncertainties and potential consequences.

19. Enthoven and Smith, *How Much Is Enough?* pp. 124–29. Quotation is from p. 127.

But, the proponents of a tactical nuclear posture for NATO replied, what was the alternative? The Soviet Union had 175 divisions on the ground, facing some 25 undermanned and poorly equipped and trained NATO divisions; so overwhelming was the disparity, in fact, that few bothered to add in the 31 divisions in Eastern Europe provided by the other Warsaw Pact members. Even the most optimistic assessments concluded that to counter this threat, NATO would need more than 50 divisions on the central front alone and more than 100 divisions for the whole of NATO. This kind of buildup would, it was supposed, require at least a 20 percent increase in spending. The allocation of scarce resources would be politically impossible to obtain from allies who believed that conventional forces were no more than a trip wire to launch the U.S. strategic nuclear arsenal and that nothing could be worse than a replay of World War II.[20]

It was upon this assessment of the conventional balance, which imputed a superiority to the Warsaw Pact so great as to be unchallenge-able by the West at acceptable political cost, that the case for a tactical nuclear posture finally rested. If NATO was to be pushed away from heavy reliance on tactical nuclear weapons toward establishing a work-able conventional posture, it would be necessary to show flaws in this assessment of the balance.

During the first year of McNamara's tenure in office, analysts at the Defense Department's Office of Systems Analysis, headed by Alain Enthoven, in close conjunction with the ISA staff headed by Paul Nitze and his deputy Henry Rowen, set about to reexamine this assessment. The direction of their work had been foreshadowed by General Taylor, who had pointed to the superiority of the alliance over the Warsaw Pact in gross population and economic indicators, concluding that it would be surprising if the Warsaw Pact could actually build a conventional force as superior to NATO's as was usually claimed.[21] General Rowny, as mentioned above, had also done work in this area.

Enthoven and Nitze picked up where Taylor and Rowny had left off, and examined raw economic and demographic data that would indicate the total resources available to both East and West for building conven-tional military forces. Comparisons of aggregate population, gross national product, basic military-related resources, levels of technology,

20. Ibid., p. 132.
21. Taylor, *Uncertain Trumpet*, p. 138.

and the specific composition of national economies suggested that some rethinking was in order. As Enthoven and K. Wayne Smith put it, "If anything, it appeared that it would be much harder for the Soviets than for NATO to support a large army."[22]

Next the staffs under Enthoven and Nitze compared the total number of people under arms in the two blocs. Their conclusion reinforced their instincts: NATO, with some 6 million people under arms, outnumbered the Warsaw Pact by some 1.5 million people.[23] Granted, gross manpower comparisons could tell only part of the story; still, it was reasonable to wonder why, if NATO had such economic and manpower advantages, the Warsaw Pact could maintain such clear-cut conventional superiority over the alliance.

By 1962 Pentagon officials began to suspect that the problem in reconciling division counts with basic economic, manpower, and military resources lay in the way these divisions were being counted. Simple inductive reasoning partly led to this conclusion. For example, Enthoven and his colleagues became aware of what they called the PEMA (procurement of equipment and missiles, army) paradox. For the full complement of active army, National Guard, and Reserve divisions, some 22 divisions total, the United States was spending $2.2 billion a year on procurement of equipment and missiles. The Soviets had 175 divisions. Was it possible they were spending the equivalent of $17.5 billion a year on procurement? Even half that amount would have been incredible. And there was another manpower paradox: with 16 active-duty divisions the United States had some 960,000 people in active duty strength; with more than ten times the number of divisions, the Soviets had 2 million people, a little more than twice the U.S. total.[24] Clearly a difference existed between a Soviet division and an American division.

Defense Department officials had already become sensitive to the difference between NATO's combat-ready and less-ready units after the Berlin crisis. Now they asked the same question of the Soviet order of battle: to what degree were Soviet divisions combat-ready? The results of their study were little short of astonishing. Careful review of intelligence showed that at least *half* of Soviet divisions were in low states of

22. Enthoven and Smith, *How Much Is Enough?* p. 134.
23. Ibid.
24. Ibid., pp. 134–36. Kaufmann, while differing slightly in numbers, makes a similar analysis in *McNamara Strategy*, pp. 84–85.

readiness in both manpower and equipment. A new division balance devised to compare commensurables on a rough basis came to a new ratio, 80:25, still in the Pact's favor. Pentagon analysts then began to examine the combat effectiveness of Soviet divisions compared with U.S. divisions; by the end of 1962 they had concluded that, using admittedly rough measures, the ratio of combat effectiveness of U.S. divisions to Soviet divisions was between 1.1:1.0 and 1.3:1.0.[25] The Sino-Soviet dispute was also now coming into the open; no longer could it be taken for granted that the Soviets would be able to allocate all 80 of their combat-ready divisions to the European theater; some would probably have to remain on the border with China. What had seemed a 10:1 advantage in 1960 now took on the relatively manageable proportions of a 2:1–3:1 advantage.

These analyses, and others that examined the balance in tactical air forces, continued throughout the early-to-middle 1960s. They all pointed in one direction: the magnitude of the Warsaw Pact conventional superiority had been grossly exaggerated. In fact,

eliminating paper divisions, using cost and firepower indexes, counts of combat personnel in available divisions, and numbers of artillery pieces, trucks, tanks, and the like, we ended up with the same conclusion: NATO and the Warsaw Pact had approximate equality on the ground. Where four years earlier it had appeared that a conventional option was impossible, it now began to appear that perhaps NATO could have had one all along.[26]

Such conclusions, however, met with stiff resistance from the army, which saw in them the potential for undermining the by now cherished claims about the need to maintain a strong tactical nuclear posture. Belief in the inevitability of the Warsaw Pact's conventional superiority made the difficult task of examining conventional force requirements less relevant. Destined to lose if the battle remained conventional, NATO would have no alternative but to cross the nuclear firebreak early in any military confrontation with the Eastern bloc. Those who were comfortable with this view were not eager to accept the implications of the Pentagon studies of 1961 and 1962.

Civilian Pentagon leaders were more receptive to the message that the conventional option was possible. In 1963, for example, Nitze and Cyrus Vance, then secretary of the army, made several speeches endorsing the conclusions drawn in 1962. McNamara used the Pentagon

25. Enthoven and Smith, *How Much Is Enough?* pp. 136–37.
26. Ibid., pp. 140–41.

studies as one justification for his decisions to bring the active unit strength of the army from 11 to 16 divisions; to increase tactical fighter strength from 16 to 21 wings; to improve the combat readiness of active duty units; to improve the army's logistical networks; to improve the reserve structure to permit rapid mobilization in times of crisis; to increase the airlift capacity of the United States so as to be able to rapidly reinforce the central front with American troops; and to pre-position two U.S. division equipment sets in Europe to aid in rapid reinforcement.[27] McNamara took these measures in part because he had quickly seen the importance of enhancing U.S. conventional capabilities, and in part because revised estimates of the NATO–Warsaw Pact balance showed that efforts to build a serious conventional capability were not futile.

A Strategy for NATO?

Unilateral U.S. conventional force improvements alone, however, would not solve NATO's problems. The allies were contributing to the expensive and crucial conventional forces at NATO's disposal, but the results of this contribution were some 20 nominal divisions, undermanned and underequipped, that were backed up by poor logistics and small reserves. Compared with SACEUR's revised requirements of 30 active and 30 reserve divisions, this was disappointing, to say the least. NATO's lack of conventional preparedness in January 1961 was probably the result of three interrelated factors:

—The cost of conventional forces was viewed as politically prohibitive.

—The Warsaw Pact was alleged to be so superior that conventional efforts seemed futile.

—Serious efforts to build up nonnuclear capabilities would be tantamount to admitting that the U.S. strategic nuclear capability lacked credibility in some circumstances.

The administration set out to challenge these notions in order to reinforce the credibility of the strategic deterrent and at the same time to prod the European allies to join the United States in improving active and reserve conventional capabilities. The basis for this effort emerged

27. Kaufmann, *McNamara Strategy*, pp. 78–80.

from a study directed by former Secretary of State Dean Acheson at President Kennedy's request. The results of the study coincided with the work already described, which was rapidly leading the United States to revise its strategic nuclear policy and to reemphasize conventional capabilities.

The report Acheson submitted in March 1961 readily accepted the critique of U.S. strategic policy as developed at Rand and elsewhere.[28] Specifically, it advocated adopting counterforce options in the strategic plans of the United States. Such options would undermine arguments raised by the French—and by some Americans—that the threat of strategic retaliation in response to attacks on allies was not credible, since the United States would never "risk Chicago for Hamburg." With strategic counterforce options, the president would have options that would not necessarily put American cities at risk. But NATO would need to improve its options too. Conventional forces would have to be improved so that NATO would have an effective and credible response to Warsaw Pact aggression that began on the conventional level. Norstad's requirement of 30 active and 30 reserve divisions should be taken seriously. The nuclear option should not be abandoned. Having nuclear weapons in Western Europe would confront any Soviet planner with the awesome possibility that they might be used in response to a Warsaw Pact invasion; hence they would enhance the deterrent of the alliance. But a serious conventional option would also have a deterrent effect, by demonstrating that NATO could impose heavy costs on a Warsaw Pact conventional effort without necessarily having to make the difficult decision to initiate nuclear war.

Besides advocating the adoption of counterforce options, the report noted the need for centralized command and control over the strategic response of the alliance should deterrence fail and nuclear war become necessary. For military and strategic purposes, it was simply not acceptable for one part of NATO's strategic arsenal to pursue missions against Soviet cities that the United States would be striving to avoid, in order to hold them hostage. Independent strategic nuclear forces within the alliance—specifically, the British and French forces—were likely to create just such problems for the alliance in the conduct of a centralized, coordinated strategic nuclear campaign. The conclusion: the United

28. Acheson Report, "A Review of North Atlantic Problems for the Future," now declassified under the Freedom of Information Act.

States should work to gain an effective veto over the British and French nuclear forces and to encourage these allies to abandon their efforts to maintain their independent strategic deterrents. If Skybolt proved inadequate for U.S. strategic objectives, it should be canceled. The Herter proposal for a multilateral nuclear force could be raised again if deemed politically necessary, but it should be made clear that the United States would not devolve control over these or any of its central strategic systems and that a precondition for serious consideration of a collective nuclear force for NATO would be the fulfilling of NATO's conventional force requirements.

Because the report coincided with the ideas Kennedy had entertained during his campaign and with the efforts of McNamara and his colleagues in the Pentagon, the Acheson report was quickly adopted as official U.S. policy toward NATO. At the same time, however, the report set forth strategic concepts at variance with those of the multilateralists at the State Department, who had a different approach to shoring up the U.S. strategic nuclear guarantee. As has been seen, Robert Bowie, Henry Owen, Walt Rostow, Gerard Smith, and others did not object to improving NATO's conventional capabilities; in fact, they were as eager as Kennedy, McNamara, Acheson, and, increasingly, the rest of the U.S. defense community to build up these capabilities. Where they parted company was over the direction of American strategic nuclear policy. The multilateralists felt that as long as the United States pursued a policy of strategic nuclear monopoly, as the Acheson report recommended, European doubts about the credibility of the U.S. nuclear guarantee would remain, doubts that, if not met, would eventually stimulate West German desires for an independent strategic deterrent. This conflict of perspectives among Kennedy's top advisers was never resolved. As a result, until 1965, when the multilateral force was formally interred, the United States pursued two somewhat incompatible policies. One must keep this fact in mind when considering allied responses to the efforts of McNamara and others to gain NATO's support for flexible response.

Persuasion and Education

The Acheson report had now been accepted by the president as the basis for U.S. policy toward NATO. Supported by the Pentagon studies that were examining the feasibility of a conventional option for NATO, various administration officials began to mount a concerted effort at home and abroad to elaborate the new policies, to justify the American actions that resulted from the adoption of flexible response, and to persuade the allies to increase their contribution to NATO's conventional capabilities.

Phase I: Initial Attempts

The president took an active role in this effort to educate and persuade. Before a meeting of the NATO Military Committee in April 1961, Kennedy urged the alliance to improve its nonnuclear forces. As seen in chapter 5, he renewed this plea in his speech in Ottawa in May, making conventional force improvements a prerequisite for U.S. support of the MLF. In a note to allied leaders in July, he once again urged conventional force improvements.

Kennedy's aides in the Pentagon were just as active, energetically taking up the challenge to explain the new American strategy to the American public and to allied governments. McNamara paid special attention to the conventional requirements of the alliance in his speech to the NATO ministers in December. Earlier his deputy, Roswell Gilpatric, had elaborated on the policy in a June 1961 press conference, when he took the occasion to deny rumors that the United States had abandoned the nuclear option for European defense but to emphasize the importance of achieving a broadly based, flexible NATO deterrent. After the Berlin crisis in the summer of 1961, Gilpatric and Assistant Secretary Nitze took the stump again, this time pointing to the Berlin experience as reinforcing the need for a strong and flexible conventional war capability.[29] In all their speeches they recognized the important deterrent effect of Western strategic nuclear superiority. But time and again they argued that this superiority, while crucial, was not sufficient. For example, Nitze stated:

If a strong nuclear force were all we had to meet Communist challenges, a situation of superior local Communist strength might force on us the alternatives of either national humiliation or all-out war. For this reason, the second goal of the Administration is to strengthen and expand the intermediate options in terms

29. Paul H. Nitze, "The World Situation: Strengthening of the United States Armed Forces," speech delivered at the annual meeting of the Association of the United States Army, Washington, D.C., September 7, 1961, pp. 26–28.

of military force. In these intermediate options the U.S. Army plays a vital role. Our ability to respond to challenges with increased levels of force short of all-out war has been neglected in the past. We are doing our best to make the necessary adjustments.[30]

Nitze made the same point in a slightly different way in a speech at the International Institute for Strategic Studies in London in December 1961. Foreshadowing the presentation by McNamara in Athens the following May, he said:

Let us assume two hypothetical situations [with respect to Berlin]. In the first situation the central NATO front is very lightly covered. It is subject to the risk of deep penetration by Soviet non-nuclear forces starting from a standing start. The only option which the West has, to demonstrate its determination to have its vital interests respected, is to initiate the action with the use of nuclear weapons. In the second situation, the NATO front is firmly held on a continuous line. There are enough reserve forces to mount a really serious non-nuclear probe in the air corridors or along the autobahn. That probe can be thrown back by a full application of Soviet non-nuclear power, but only by involving Soviet and NATO in a major fight.

If you were sitting in the Kremlin, which situation would be considered most likely to bring you face to face with nuclear war if you persisted in a train of actions violating what the West considers to be its vital interests? To me, the answer is clear. If I were in the Kremlin I would be much more concerned in the second situation; I would consider it much more likely that the West would find it politically possible to initiate action in defense of the Berlin access routes from the second posture than from the first.[31]

In Europe, this campaign was not well received. All the old arguments that had so far held the Europeans back from improving their conventional capabilities continued to hold sway: the expense of conventional forces, the supposedly insurmountable Warsaw Pact superiority in conventional forces, the by now almost unalterable reliance on nuclear weapons to compensate for the inadequacy of NATO's conventional forces, and the notion that conventional capabilities would undermine the credibility of a nuclear response.

For the West Germans, the renewed emphasis on conventional forces signaled a new American unwillingness to use nuclear weapons in defense of NATO, whether they be tactical nuclear weapons on the battlefield or strategic nuclear weapons against targets deep within the Soviet Union. Adenauer's trip to Washington to confer with the new president in April 1961, in the wake of Kennedy's speech to the NATO Military

30. Ibid., p. 27.
31. Cited in Kaufmann, McNamara Strategy, p. 110.

Committee, had left the aging chancellor with a bitter impression that Kennedy either would not or could not appreciate the Federal Republic's perspective. Further doubts about America's new policy were raised when the United States canceled the German 1957 order of Mace missiles—which, it may be recalled, had aroused a passionate debate in the Bundestag—and offered the shorter-range Pershing missile as a replacement.[32] But the greatest source of friction between Bonn and Washington during this period was over Western reaction to the Berlin crisis. While the Americans moved ahead with its call-up of reservists and its other conventional responses and urged a broad conventional buildup on the European allies, Bonn remained publicly supportive but privately doubtful.

In private . . . apparently almost all of the German political and military leaders questioned the need for and consequences of the American push for improved conventional capabilities. In NATO as in the Four Power Ambassadorial Working Group, Bonn's basic position remained that of Norstad, namely, any non-nuclear military phase would of necessity be limited in scope and duration. Of what value would a non-nuclear response be if a convoy's start toward Berlin met a firm, substantial Soviet trap, or at several points precipitated popular uprisings of the size that had occurred in 1953, or set off a rush of East Germans toward the major crossings into the Federal Republic? Moreover, despite the president's firm words, a major conventional effort still would suggest irresolution regarding early use of nuclear weapons, the basis of any threat of escalation.[33]

Defense Minister Strauss explicitly expressed his doubts about the emerging American doctrine, describing concepts like *pause* and *flexible response* as "conceptual aids for the precalculation of the inconceivable and incalculable nature of the specific."[34] Tension increased even more when the United States came up with a plan calling for Germany to bring its armed forces up to full strength, and to add 6 more brigades, at a cost of some 30 billion deutsche marks (10 billion more than the Finance Ministry was willing to spend).[35]

Among other European nations, reaction was generally cool. Strauss's verbal assaults on the new doctrine were not matched in Britain. But Britain made no attempt to increase its manpower for nonnuclear ground warfare. In fact, of the some 78,000 military personnel cut from the

32. Catherine McArdle Kelleher, *Germany and the Politics of Nuclear Weapons*, pp. 161–62.
33. Ibid., p. 165.
34. Ibid.
35. Ibid., p. 171.

British armed forces between 1960 and 1962, about 59,000 were taken from army rolls.[36] The French continued their nuclear programs, essentially oblivious to Washington's new urgings. Elsewhere, silence and inaction met this first American effort at strategic persuasion.

Still, NATO made a few conventional improvements between early 1961 and May 1962. Through the concerted efforts of General Norstad and Secretary McNamara, SACEUR's ready division equivalents on the central front had increased from about 16 to about 25 by January 1962. But more was needed, and the reactions in Europe, which ranged from disinterest to outright hostility, gave little hope that more would be forthcoming.

Phase II: The Athens Speech of May 1962

McNamara forcefully took matters into his own hands. He decided that the upcoming NATO ministerial meeting, scheduled to be held in Athens in early May, would be the appropriate forum for an extensive briefing on the rationale for the new American strategic nuclear policy; for driving home the dangers of NATO's excessive reliance on nuclear weapons for deterrence; for demonstrating the problems caused by small, independent nuclear forces within the alliance; and for arguing once again for the need to build up NATO's nonnuclear capabilities. This was a tall order, admittedly; one of McNamara's advisers closely involved with the drafting of the speech later wrote, "The task [McNamara] had set for himself was a burdensome one, perhaps too heavy for a single speech to bear."[37] Nevertheless, the Athens speech stands as one of the most remarkable *tours de force* ever presented by an American official to the North Atlantic Council. It was unprecedented in its candor, unusually blunt in its argument, and coldly logical in its structure. It set the agenda for alliance deliberations that resulted in the adoption of flexible response by the alliance in 1967. Because it was such a landmark as well as a remarkably clear expression of the rationale for flexible response, it merits close examination.[38]

After some brief introductory remarks, McNamara presented the

36. R. N. Rosecrance, *Defense of the Realm,* app. table 2.
37. Kaufmann, *McNamara Strategy,* p. 114.
38. The quotations that follow come from "Remarks by Secretary McNamara, NATO Ministerial Meeting, 5 May 1962, Restricted Session." The speech was declassified on August 17, 1979.

conclusion of the Kennedy administration's year-long review of strategic policy:

Nuclear technology has revolutionized warfare over the past seventeen years. The unprecedented destructiveness of these arms has radically changed ways of thinking about conflict among nations. It has properly focused great attention and efforts by the Alliance on the prevention of conflict. Nevertheless, the U.S. has come to the conclusion that to the extent feasible basic military strategy in general nuclear war should be approached in much the same way that more conventional military operations have been regarded in the past. That is to say, our principal military objectives, in the event of a nuclear war stemming from a major attack on the Alliance, should be the destruction of the enemy's military forces while attempting to preserve the fabric as well as the integrity of allied society. Specifically, our studies indicate that a strategy which targets nuclear forces only against cities or a mixture of civil and military targets has serious limitations for the purpose of deterrence and for the conduct of general nuclear war.

McNamara went on to give two justifications for pursuing a new strategy. First, he noted that it could reduce the damage to allied societies substantially:

If both sides were to confine their attacks to important military targets, damage, while high, would nevertheless be significantly lower than if urban-industrial targets were also attacked. As an example, our studies of a hypothetical general nuclear war occurring in 1966 show that, with the conflict starting under one particular set of circumstances, and with the Soviets confining their attacks to military targets, the United States under present civil defense plans might suffer 25 million deaths and Europe might suffer somewhat fewer. On the other hand, were the Soviets to attack urban-industrial as well as military targets, the United States might incur 75 million deaths and Europe would have to face the prospect of losing 115 million people. While both sets of figures make grim reading, the first set is preferable to the second. There are others like them.

In light of these findings the United States has developed its plans in order to permit a variety of strategic choices. We have also instituted a number of programs which will enable the Alliance to engage in a controlled and flexible nuclear response in the event that deterrence should fail.

Second, the nature of nuclear warfare would give the Soviet Union a strong incentive to confine its nuclear attacks to military targets. In a hypothetical 1966 counterforce exchange, McNamara noted, the Soviet Union would suffer about 25 million deaths, while if the alliance retaliated against the Soviet urban-industrial base, it would suffer at least 100 million deaths.

To support these contentions McNamara noted some technical elements that could be tailored to a counterforce strike designed to minimize collateral damage: yields could be reduced, accuracy of missiles could be improved, the height of the nuclear detonation could be set to minimize fallout, and civil defenses could be strengthened. "Depending on these and other factors," he said, "the number of deaths could vary over a wide range—by four times or more. The more discriminating the attacks, the less the damage."

With these important considerations in mind, he then turned to a broad assessment of the general war posture of the alliance. He began by noting, "Perhaps the most important implication of these observations is that nuclear superiority has important meanings." Outlining the strategic nuclear superiority the West would hold over the Soviets at least through 1965, he then described the relation between internal U.S. planning and SACEUR planning:

More than [deleted] weapons are scheduled against SACEUR's nuclear threat list. SACEUR plans to assure the destruction of [deleted] targets on the list with his forces alone. Approximately [deleted] targets are scheduled for attack and destruction solely with external forces. SACEUR schedules sorties against another [deleted] or more targets with his own forces, but the assurance that he will be able to destroy them is not enough to warrant reliance on his attacks alone. Therefore, with respect to these [deleted] targets additional sorties are assigned to forces external to his theater. The entire threat list is covered and approximately [deleted] of it is scheduled for attack by external forces. Of the weapons now assigned to this task, about [deleted] will be delivered by the U.S. Strategic Air Command.

Even without the numbers the point McNamara was making is clear; SACEUR could not rely only on forces assigned to him to strike all his targets, but would require considerable support from U.S. central strategic forces and would receive it: "The United States has made clear that it places the major Soviet nuclear forces threatening Europe in the same high priority category as those also able to reach North America. In short, we have undertaken the nuclear defense of NATO on a global basis." The operational planning thus illuminated was meant to show the degree to which the U.S. nuclear guarantee had actually been written into the operational plans of the alliance.

McNamara then observed that size alone would not be sufficient to carry out the strategy of flexible response on the nuclear level. Also required were high survivability and reliable and secure command and control networks. "For this purpose, distance, dispersal, mobility, hardness, and alertness represent the most effective measures at our disposal. All are being exploited in current bomber and missile programs.

. . . the bulk of the nuclear forces of the Alliance . . . is . . . designed to function as a single instrument to accomplish a single indivisible task." Against such force, "the Soviets could not win such a war in any meaningful military sense and they might lose their country in the course of the conflict."

Next he focused on the requirement for indivisibility of control, to refute the rationale for independent national nuclear arsenals within the alliance. Because this argument is so important, his remarks are cited in full:

The efficient use of our resources implies that the Alliance deterrence system have three vital attributes: unity of planning, executive authority, and central direction—for in a major nuclear war there are no theaters, or rather, the theater is world-wide. Specific missions and the most efficient way to perform them should determine the weapons that we acquire, where we deploy them, and who should command them.

It is even more important that the Alliance have unity of planning, decision-making, and direction with respect to responses to enemy actions and especially to retaliatory attacks against him. There must not be competing and conflicting strategies in the conduct of nuclear war. We are convinced that a general nuclear war target system is indivisible and if nuclear war should occur, our best hope lies in conducting a centrally controlled campaign against all of the enemy's vital nuclear capabilities. Doing this means carefully choosing targets, pre-planning strikes, coordinating attacks, and assessing results, as well as allocating and directing follow-on attacks from the center. These call, in our view, for a greater degree of Alliance participation in formulating nuclear policies and consulting on the appropriate occasions for using these weapons. Beyond this, it is essential that we centralize the decision to use our nuclear weapons to the greatest extent possible. We would all find it intolerable to contemplate having only a part of the strategic force launched in isolation from our main striking power.

If a portion of the Alliance nuclear force, acting by itself, were to initiate a retaliatory attack by destroying only a small part of the Soviet nuclear force, our enemy would be left free to reallocate other weapons to cover the targets originally assigned to the destroyed part. Thus, aside from endangering all of us, a strike aimed at destroying the Soviet MRBM's aimed at Country A, which left the others standing, would be of little value to Country A. It would merely oblige the Soviets to shift other missiles to cover the Country A targets. We would all find it equally intolerable to have one segment of the Alliance force attacking urban-industrial areas while, with the bulk of our forces, we were succeeding in destroying most of the enemies' nuclear capabilities. Such a failure in coordination might lead to the destruction of our hostages—the Soviet cities—just at a time at which our strategy of coercing the Soviets into stopping their aggression was on the verge of success. Failure to achieve central control of NATO nuclear forces would mean running a risk of bringing down on us the catastrophe which we most urgently wish to avoid.

In this connection, our analyses suggest rather strongly that relatively weak nuclear forces with enemy cities as their targets are not likely to be adequate to perform the function of deterrence. In a world of threats, crises, and possibly even accidents, such a posture appears more likely to deter its owner from standing firm under pressure than to inhibit a potential aggressor. If it is small, and perhaps vulnerable on the ground or in the air, or inaccurate, it enables a major antagonist to take a variety of measures to counter it. Indeed, if a major antagonist came to believe there was substantial likelihood of its being used independently, this force would be inviting a pre-emptive first strike against it. In the event of war, the use of such a force against the cities of a major nuclear power would be tantamount to suicide, whereas its employment against significant military targets would have a negligible effect on the outcome of the conflict. In short, then, weak nuclear capabilities, operating independently, are expensive, prone to obsolescence, and lacking in credibility as a deterrent.

But a coherent strategic nuclear posture would not be enough, according to McNamara. Although the current strategic balance in favor of the West and the adoption of flexible response by the United States had given the alliance a considerable measure of diplomatic freedom in the face of Soviet nuclear threats, the decision to use nuclear weapons would inevitably be awesome in its consequences. Even though "the United States is prepared to respond immediately with nuclear weapons to the use of nuclear weapons against one or more of the members of the Alliance," and even though "the United States is also prepared to counter with nuclear weapons any Soviet conventional attack so strong that it cannot be dealt with by conventional means," NATO's conventional deficiencies would be likely to place the burden of a decision to use nuclear weapons arising out of a more probable "ambiguous situation," like the recent Berlin crisis, on the shoulders of the West.

Faced with the more likely contingencies, NATO, not the Soviets, would have to make the momentous decision to use nuclear weapons, and we would do so in the knowledge that the consequences might be catastrophic for all of us.

We in the United States are prepared to accept our share of this responsibility. And we believe that the combination of our nuclear superiority and a strategy of controlled response gives us some hope of minimizing damage in the event that we have to fulfill our pledge. But I would be less than candid if I pretended to you that the United States regards this as a desirable prospect or believes that the Alliance should depend solely on our nuclear power to deter the Soviet Union from actions not involving a massive commitment of Soviet force. Surely an Alliance with the wealth, talent, and experience that we possess can find a better way than this to meet our common threat.

We shall continue to maintain powerful nuclear forces for the Alliance as a whole. They will continue to provide the Alliance a strong sanction against Soviet first use of nuclear weapons. Under some circumstances they may be the only instrument with which we can counter Soviet non-nuclear aggression, in which case we shall use them. But, in our view, the threat of general war should constitute only one of several weapons in our arsenal and one to be used with prudence. On this question I can see no valid reason for a fundamental difference of view on the two sides of the Atlantic.

Would tactical nuclear weapons be able to make a significant contribution? He did not totally dismiss their potential utility: "To be sure, a very limited use of nuclear weapons, primarily for purposes of demonstrating our will and intent to employ such weapons, might bring Soviet aggression to a halt without substantial retaliation, and without escalation. This is a next-to-last option we cannot dismiss. . . . But we do not rate these prospects very highly." Noting that "it could rapidly lead to general nuclear war," he pointed out the following:

Highly dispersed nuclear weapons in the hands of troops would be difficult to control centrally. Accidents and unauthorized acts could well occur on both sides. Furthermore, the pressures on the Soviets to respond in kind, the great flexibility of nuclear systems, the enormous firepower contained in a single weapon, the ease and accuracy with which that firepower can be called in from unattacked and hence undamaged distant bases, the crucial importance of air superiority in nuclear operations—all these considerations suggest to us that local nuclear war would be a transient but highly destructive phenomenon.

Here he found it appropriate to interject his answer to those who feared that the new American policy would permit the superpowers to fight a nuclear war in Europe without sustaining damage to each other's homeland. Such a fear, he argued, "ignores the basic facts of nuclear warfare I have described; it contemplates geographical limits unrelated to the actualities of target locations and of the varied sources from which attacks would come. Any substantial nuclear operation in Europe inevitably would involve both forces and targets in the U.S. and U.S.S.R."

Admitting again the remote possibility that such escalation might be contained or limited, he nevertheless concluded that "there is likely to be no effective operational boundary, or set of mutual restraints, which could restrict large-scale nuclear war to NATO Europe and the satellites. As we understand the dynamics of nuclear warfare, we believe that a local nuclear engagement would do grave damage to Europe, be militarily ineffective, and would probably expand very rapidly into general nuclear war."

Now McNamara drove home the point that each preceding level of argument had prepared: the need for improved conventional forces for

NATO. To bring the point across, he posed a hypothetical choice confronting a Soviet decisionmaker, virtually identical to the choice Nitze had posed in December:

Let us assume two situations:

In the first, the NATO front is lightly covered by our forces. In the event of deep penetration by Soviet non-nuclear forces which our forces cannot prevent, the only military options open to Alliance forces are immediate nuclear response or defeat. This might be true even for a minor Soviet challenge.

In the second, we assume the NATO front firmly held under a concept of forward strategy. Ready and able to deal with any Soviet non-nuclear attack less than all-out, NATO forces guard positively from the frontier against any quick strike or ambiguous aggression. The NATO front can be broken only by massive application of Soviet power. In such a major fight, if Western forces were thrown back, Alliance nuclear action would follow.

If you were on the other side, which situation would you consider more laden with a real risk of nuclear war with all its consequences? Which would make you more inclined to refrain from a series of actions designed, step by step, to erode NATO's interests? To us the answer is clear.

In the first situation, it is simply not credible that NATO, or anyone else, would respond to a given small step—the first slice of salami—with immediate use of nuclear weapons. Nor is it credible that a chain of small actions, no one of which is catastrophic, would evoke a response of general nuclear war. We regard it as much more evident that NATO would find it politically possible to act in effective defense of its interests from the second posture than from the first.

To buttress this point, McNamara referred to the recent NATO experience during the Berlin crisis, in which an increase in manpower, ready divisions, ships, and air squadrons showed Western determination and forced the Kremlin to back down in its demand over the city. He cautioned that he was not arguing that a forward defense "must be able to defeat in non-nuclear action every conceivable element of Soviet strength that might be thrown against it. Our nuclear forces would rapidly come into play if an all-out attack developed. We believe the Soviets can hardly doubt that; hence, we think it quite improbable that a major attack would develop out of a crisis."

McNamara then outlined what had so far been achieved in the conventional force buildups called for by the revised version of SACEUR's requirement plan, MC 26/4, and what still needed to be done. He noted that NATO had shown some real progress, especially in the combat division equivalent measure, which reflected substantial improvement in the readiness of individual units. But the totals were still far from what MC 26/4 called for: NATO would have to add 5⅔ division units to the front line and would have to improve its combat readiness by almost 50 percent.

Next he pinpointed the main areas of NATO conventional weaknesses that would require improvement to meet the MC 26/4 ceiling.

Manning levels still promise to be inadequate, and many needed combat support units are missing or weak. . . . There are also alarming weaknesses in our service support systems. Defects which degrade our ability to support sustained non-nuclear combat include exposed positioning of stocks, lack of depth in depot systems, low levels of war reserves of ammunition and repair parts, and much obsolescent or absent material.

He noted that these problems suggested important inefficiencies in the way NATO was using its resources; with more men under arms than the Warsaw Pact, NATO still considered itself conventionally inferior in spite of the obvious importance of manpower in conventional warfare. "To a considerable extent," McNamara said, "this inferiority stems from specific, remediable deficiencies. As long as they continue to exist, they will serve to undermine our over-all efforts."

He then listed what the Kennedy administration had done, and was planning to do, to improve U.S. nonnuclear forces: an added $10 billion to previously programmed expenditures on nonnuclear forces for fiscal 1962 and 1963; an increase in U.S. combat-ready divisions from 11 to 16; the pre-positioning of two full division sets of equipment to help in rapid reinforcement on the front. And he offered American help, in the way of credit and matériel, to European efforts to improve logistical support and equipment shortages. In summary, he stated: "With improvements in ground force strength and staying power, improved non-nuclear air capabilities, and better equipped and trained reserve forces, the Soviet Union can be assured that no gap exists in the NATO defense of this vital region, and that no aggression small or large can succeed."

With the bulk of his argument behind him, McNamara now turned to specific issues on the NATO agenda. Regarding the exchange of information on nuclear weapons, he said, "Our own view is that the flow of information should be greater than it has been in the past. We welcome the new procedures for handling sensitive information and we plan to provide information about our nuclear forces and consult about basic plans and arrangements for their use on a continuing basis." Indeed, this speech represented a large step in this direction. "In the coming months," he promised, "U.S. military personnel will be prepared to discuss other aspects of our common problems."

McNamara noted with approval the adoption of general guidelines on the use of nuclear weapons by the alliance, the so-called Athens guidelines. These guidelines presumably outlined, in broad political terms, the consultative obligations under which the United States would proceed on a decision whether to use its nuclear weapons in defense of the alliance. He turned briefly to a reiteration of one of his earlier themes, the coverage of targets threatening Europe:

[The strategic retaliatory] force works in conjunction with NATO committed forces and is devoted to a very considerable degree to countering Soviet forces that are able to attack Western Europe. This mission is assigned not only in fulfillment of our treaty commitments but also because the indivisible character of nuclear war compels it. More specifically, the U.S. targets key elements of Soviet nuclear striking power, including MRBM's, with as high priority to that portion that can reach Western Europe as to that portion that also can reach the United States.

Next he reaffirmed Kennedy's May 1961 commitment at Ottawa to assign five, and subsequently more, U.S. Polaris vessels to NATO under SACLANT command. But, he carefully noted, "operations, targeting, and firing timing of the Polaris submarines must be responsive to the over-all requirements of the Alliance as a whole. Their use, therefore, will not be limited to the support of any single theater or major commander." In effect, he reserved the right to withhold these vessels for other theaters as deemed appropriate.

Finally, McNamara noted that the United States was willing to discuss with other NATO members the need for an MRBM force for NATO. It is unclear whether he was referring to the MLF—in which case he was envisioning a surface fleet configuration not dependent on the already developed Polaris A-3 MRBM—or to the Norstad configuration of mobile land-based MRBMs. Both configurations are cited in the technical appendix to the speech. He did, however, say: "We expect our allies will wish to consider very carefully the full implications of undertaking this venture. There are many complicated questions to be dealt with. In the meantime, the U.S., although it is not committed to the procurement or development of an MRBM weapon system, is proceeding with the design of such a weapon."

In summary, McNamara reiterated his call for across-the-board conventional force improvements, ending on a direct note:

The question is not one of the ability of the Alliance but of its will. The obstacles are real. We all have our special problems of conscription, or budget level, or the balance of payments. However, the brute facts of technology and the realities of military power cannot be denied. They call for us to take common action.

In a little under an hour, Robert McNamara had given the NATO ministers an unprecedented, detailed look at the new U.S. strategy of flexible response. The Europeans had heard him discuss at length the rationale for what was to become known as the no-cities strategy; the nature of the limits on the strategic deterrent; the dangers of a posture that relied heavily on the tactical use of nuclear weapons to compensate for conventional force inadequacies; the dangers of small, weak, independent national nuclear forces within the alliance; and the crucial need for conventional force improvements. McNamara had also announced U.S. willingness to be more open with the allies regarding technical data on nuclear weapons and plans for their use, a willingness lent credibility by his candor on these matters.

The European Reaction

The immediate European reaction was muted, perhaps reflecting a legitimate need to digest the material and to explore its implications before responding. In any case, the quiet did not last. McNamara chose to go public with his ideas in a commencement speech at Ann Arbor on June 16; in this address he made the same major points as in the Athens speech, at times using verbatim excerpts from it.[39] This time the reaction was swift.

THE FRENCH POSITION. The French took the greatest exception to the new strategy enunciated at Athens and at Ann Arbor. Between 1962 and 1965 French military and political leaders repeatedly attacked flexible response in private and in public.[40] Their reaction was conditioned by the increasingly open differences between Kennedy and de Gaulle regarding the proper political orientation of Western Europe; by the perception of blatant U.S. discrimination against France, heightened by the repeated rejection of French requests for aid in their nuclear program and the apparent willingness of Washington to ignore its own arguments against independent nuclear arsenals after Nassau; and by the general

39. Robert S. McNamara, "The United States and Western Europe: Concrete Problems of Maintaining a Free Community," speech delivered at the commencement exercises at the University of Michigan, Ann Arbor, June 16, 1962, pp. 626–29.
40. Wilfrid L. Kohl, *French Nuclear Diplomacy*, pp. 227–29.

deterioration of Franco-American relations after de Gaulle's January 14, 1963, press conference (described in chapter 5). Even under better circumstances, McNamara's logic would not have met with a warm reception from a government that had already staked so much international prestige on the attainment of an independent strategic nuclear capability; under the actual circumstances, the debate turned rancorous.

The rationale the French had already begun to develop for pursuing an independent strategic capability formed the basis for the repudiation of flexible response. In essence, it denied the credibility of the American pledge to use strategic nuclear weapons in defense of Europe. To quote General Pierre Gallois, whose many articles detail the rationale explicitly: "If resort to force no longer implies risking merely the loss of an expeditionary army but hazards the very substance of national life, it is clear that such a risk can be taken only for oneself—and not for others, including even close allies."[41]

In response to the claim that a counterforce strategy could provide a way to limit damage while holding enemy cities hostage, Gallois argued that the development of invulnerable sea-based strategic forces rendered a counterforce option obsolete: "Neither of these two countries will be able any longer to use a counterforce strategy against the other and each will have to be content with 'peaceful coexistence' with its main opponent, or risk national suicide."[42] Deterrence based on the threat of countervalue retaliation—upon which the superpowers will now have to rely—is ultimately stable:

The Soviets will be able to destroy American urban centers, but their aggression would set off a counterattack, led by submarines armed with Polaris missiles, which, in turn, would reduce the principal Soviet cities to ashes. Conversely, this reasoning applies to a U.S. initiated attack. For the two Great Powers, equipped with nearly invulnerable retaliatory weapons, peaceful coexistence is the only solution, since resort to force would lead to the near-extinction of both belligerents.[43]

For the United States to extend this stability of deterrence over the West Europeans was impossible; however, by implication, nations like France would be able, with some effort, to buy stable anti-city deterrents of their own. "Once a few dozen nuclear weapons are enough to destroy the few dozen urban areas on which the life of a nation depends, it is

41. Pierre M. Gallois, "U.S. Strategy and the Defense of Europe," p. 233.
42. Ibid., p. 232.
43. Ibid.

hard to see the purpose of the huge stocks of weapons which the two Great Powers have accumulated in the attempt to provide themselves with the instruments of a counterforce strategy."[44]

In McNamara's efforts to endow NATO with a serious conventional capability, the French saw an implicit recognition of the weakness of the American strategic guarantee. Against an enemy armed with nuclear weapons, it was argued, concentrations of troops, logistic networks capable of handling large volumes of matériel, and lines of communication—all requirements for conventional defense—become attractive targets for nuclear attack. "The more the European nations on the Continent equip themselves conventionally, the more vulnerable they will be to nuclear attack and therefore the stronger will be the temptation for the opponent to use nuclear weapons."[45] Furthermore, by abdicating the nuclear initiative to the enemy, NATO would be demonstrating a lack of resolve that in itself could damage the alliance's deterrent. Faced with evidence of American strategic illogic, Gallois sought another explanation for U.S. preoccupation with conventional defense and uncovered what he—and many French political leaders—believed to be the ulterior motive. Afraid that, as a price of U.S. strategic commitment to the alliance, a European nuclear war would escalate to a level that would involve strikes against U.S. cities, the United States was determined to prevent any conflict in Europe from becoming nuclear. Aware of the suicidal consequences of having to make good on its strategic guarantee, the United States was now transparently trying to back out of the guarantee unnoticed, to decouple U.S. and Western European strategic interests: "By substituting for the nuclear system an enlarged conventional system, backed up by a dubious threat of strategic nuclear action, the lower rungs of the nuclear ladder on which many Europeans think that their safety hinges would be removed—and 'escalation' would, hopefully, be halted at the bottom."[46]

THE WEST GERMAN POSITION. As Catherine Kelleher relates, West Germany went through two phases in its reaction to flexible response. The first phase, which lasted roughly until October 1962, saw the formation of a vigorous critique of flexible response under the vocal leadership of Defense Minister Strauss. The second phase, associated

44. Pierre M. Gallois, "The Raison d'Etre of French Defence Policy," p. 353.
45. Gallois, "U.S. Strategy and the Defense of Europe," p. 247.
46. Ibid.

with Adenauer's successor, Ludwig Erhard, and his minister of defense, Kai-Uwe von Hassel, witnessed a cooling of rhetoric but no fundamental shift in position.[47]

As developed in the first phase, the critique maintained that nuclear weapons were essentially countervalue, not counterforce, weapons. A shift to a counterforce strategy, or to any strategy that made the response of the West more predictable or calculable, would reduce the potential risks perceived by the Warsaw Pact in contemplating aggression against NATO and thereby weaken deterrence. Furthermore, an emphasis on conventional defense was incompatible with West Germany's closely held objective of "forward defense," namely, a defense that attempts to halt Warsaw Pact aggression at the inner-German border. Tactical nuclear weapons would have to be used early on in countering any serious conventional offensive. Finally, it was held that once tactical nuclear weapons were used, the conflict would quickly, almost automatically, escalate into a strategic nuclear exchange; but, in contrast to Alain Enthoven and others who feared this tendency, Germans saw it as reinforcing deterrence by automatically raising the stakes for the Warsaw Pact in any aggression against NATO.[48]

To be sure, not all elements of the West German defense community shared this opinion. For example, Helmut Schmidt, the defense expert for the opposition Social Democratic party, publicly supported a shift toward serious consideration of a conventional option, as did ranking officers within the Bundeswehr. But influential members of the ruling Christian Democrats held the dominant views, which were furthered by the growing influence of pro-French elements of the party who found that the French criticism of flexible response addressed many of their own concerns. This fact goes a long way toward explaining the interest Bonn had in the MLF. If McNamara's speeches indicated a growing reluctance by the United States to extend its nuclear umbrella over Europe, then it would be important for Germany to gain direct influence over the disposition of the strategic nuclear forces of the alliance. It also explains Bonn's insistence, during the early MLF negotiations, that the United States not foreclose devolution of control over the MLF to the European participants in the force.

The transition from Adenauer to Erhard, from Strauss to von Hassel,

47. Kelleher, *Germany and the Politics of Nuclear Weapons*, pp. 179–227.
48. Ibid., pp. 156–78. See also Helmut Schmidt, *Defense or Retaliation?*

also saw a transition in Bonn's reaction to flexible response. This was probably the result of many factors. For one, Erhard and von Hassel belonged to the group within the Christian Democrats that opposed the Gaullist tendencies of Adenauer and Strauss. Their political positions within the party and within the country rested on their commitment to maintain closer relations with Washington; they therefore rejected de Gaulle's vision of a Europe outside American influence. A second factor may have been the development of more regular, frequent meetings between President Lyndon Johnson and Erhard, and between Mc-Namara and von Hassel, to coordinate U.S.-German positions on NATO strategy.

By November 1964 this transition had resulted in a public acceptance of flexible response, although the version of flexible response proclaimed by von Hassel, distinctly German in approach, bore many similarities to the position taken by Strauss a year earlier. "I do not suppose," von Hassel wrote in a direct repudiation of Gaullism's central tenet, "that European members of NATO would question the fact that in view of the world situation, Western Europe can be effectively protected only by NATO, that is, only in the closest partnership with the United States."[49] He went on to endorse one of McNamara's main points:

Since any war would be a catastrophe not only for Europe but for all the nations of the alliance, it is of the highest importance to see that the risk for the potential aggressor remains incalculable and that deterrence remains credible. The maintenance of that credibility in the atomic age calls logically for a system of graduated deterrence, since resort to a system of total nuclear defense, which would be tantamount to self-destruction, is not credible. Hence, all levels of possible aggression must be matched with the appropriate means of defense.[50]

So far von Hassel had not taken issue with American policy. But he now departed in substance from the Athens version of flexible response and brought up specifically German concerns.

This means, so far as concerns the defense of Europe, in contrast to other parts of the world, that the atomic threshold must be very low, because Western Europe—considered as part of the whole NATO territory—is only a strategic bridgehead without depth which can accept neither loss of terrain nor diminution of its potential.

That is why the strategy of forward defense along the Iron Curtain, which

49. Kai-Uwe von Hassel, "The Search for Consensus," pp. 209–16. For a contrasting, somewhat Gaullist view from a German, see General Paul Stehlin, "Atlantic Policy: The Evolution of Western Defense," pp. 70–83.
50. Von Hassel, "Search for Consensus," p. 210.

SACEUR made official on September 1, 1963, is the essential prerequisite, not only for the Federal Republic of Germany but for its European partners as well. This is a matter of life and death for my country. To regard the Federal Republic, or even a larger part of Western Europe, solely as a battlefield, which NATO forces would have to liberate afterward, would forecast the total destruction of Western Europe. This appears to me hardly a valid objective of defense policy.[51]

Declaring that the objective of flexible response is "to force the enemy to give up his idea of aggression by demonstrating that his only alternative will be willfully and deliberately to initiate escalation, which would be equivalent to his own self-destruction," von Hassel explained that raising the atomic threshold too high would carry grave dangers:

Apart from the fact that this would lead the potential aggressor to think that he could calculate his risk, it would create a situation in which he could seize pawns for future negotiations.

In order to prevent this, atomic demolition mines, nuclear air defense weapons and, if need be, nuclear battlefield weapons must be made ready for employment in an early phase of a recognizable attack on Europe. Only in this way, as I see it, can a last determined warning be given the enemy without involving escalation as a consequence. Further supporting this view is the fact that a prolonged conventional war would lead rapidly to attrition of forces, jeopardize the operational readiness of the nuclear capability and thus rapidly shift the balance of power in favor of the enemy.[52]

Absent from this position was any direct challenge to the credibility of the American strategic guarantee; in fact, the position implied a continuing reliance on the guarantee, since the deterrent effect of the threat to escalate rested on the ultimate threat of U.S. strategic nuclear response. But von Hassel was clear on another point: if McNamara and his colleagues believed they could get Europeans—particularly Germans—to accept as a basis for alliance defense planning the possibility of an extended phase of conventional warfare confined to the Continent, they were mistaken.

THE BRITISH POSITION. The position of Britain in response to the proposal of a flexible response strategy was closely linked to the Conservative party's determination to maintain its independent strategic deterrent.[53] McNamara's "clarification" that he was not referring to the British arsenal in his Athens and Ann Arbor presentations, since the British force was integrated into the defense plans of the alliance, was

51. Ibid., pp. 210–11.
52. Ibid., p. 211.
53. Andrew J. Pierre, *Nuclear Politics,* pp. 259–62, contains an excellent summary of the British reaction to flexible response under Douglas-Home.

hardly satisfactory to a government whose rationale for the force had been predicated on the contention that the deterrent could be used independently if Britain so desired. If McNamara's logic held for France, it should apply as well to Britain. Thus government leaders felt compelled to challenge that logic on the same grounds as the French did: that the ultimate strategic nuclear guarantee might not be credible. Minister of Defense Peter Thorneycroft stated the issue in Parliament:

As an increasing number of more and more powerful missiles will be aimed at Washington and New York, can we be certain that a threat directed against our country would always be answered by an American counterthreat? And should we admit this certitude, would the Russians be equally persuaded? Is a deterrent under the exclusive control of America absolutely reliable?[54]

At the same time, British government officials, though not as wedded to the forward-defense concept as their colleagues in Bonn, were skeptical of the renewed emphasis on conventional defense for many of the same reasons. They were reluctant to accept the Pentagon's claim that a conventional option would work; they also worried that overreliance on a conventional posture would weaken the deterrent effect of NATO's nuclear posture.

As in other European countries, not everyone in Britain agreed with the official position. The Labour party in particular took issue with the whole direction of the government's defense policy. Like the opposition in the Federal Republic, Labour leaders were sympathetic to McNamara's proposed new strategy; unlike the German Social Democrats, however, they were in a position to unseat the party in power in the October 1964 general election. British defense policy thus became a leading campaign issue. The party's defense and foreign policy specialists, Denis Healey and Patrick Gordon Walker, put together a formidable assault on the policies of Douglas-Home and Thorneycroft, based largely on positions consonant with McNamara's.[55]

The first, and most important, plank of their platform was a pledge to renounce Britain's independent strategic nuclear capability, which they claimed was neither independent nor credible. The results of the Nassau conference, they maintained, had made Britain permanently dependent on the United States for strategic weapon technology, and in fact Britain

54. Cited in Gallois, "U.S. Strategy and the Defense of Europe," pp. 248–49.

55. See Pierre, *Nuclear Politics,* pp. 262–72, for an excellent summary of Labour's position in the 1964 elections. For a definitive statement of the Labour position, see P. C. Gordon Walker, "Labor Party's Defense and Foreign Policy."

had for years been dependent on the United States for strategic planning as well. Furthermore, the Cuban missile crisis had proved that "nuclear weapons could never, of purpose and intent, be deliberately used."[56] While accepting the need for the West to maintain a nuclear capability for deterrent purposes, Gordon Walker wrote, "We do not, however, believe that Britain herself should seek to make or possess nuclear weapons of her own. . . . It seems to us pointless and wasteful to have a weapon that could not be used by itself and which adds nothing to the power of the American nuclear armory."[57]

A second plank in the Labour platform endorsed McNamara's efforts to shift NATO's attention and resources to conventional improvements.

From the point of view of Britain's own military power we have come to the conclusion that, since the Cuba crisis, it has become clear that the only usable form of force is conventional. This applies equally to the superpowers. Provided that the nuclear balance is maintained, America's actual power in the world depends upon the conventional forces that she maintains in Germany and elsewhere and upon such conventional capacity as "Big Lift." This applies *a fortiori* to a power like Britain.[58]

Recognizing that to renounce the nuclear option would require changes in the Nassau Agreement, Gordon Walker advanced an idea obviously derived from the writings of Alastair Buchan (see chapter 5):

But we do not wish simply to cancel it [Nassau]. We want to negotiate a far-reaching new arrangement with Washington. . . . We would want to have a real share with the United States in shaping nuclear policy and strategy and we accept, both as a fact and as something desirable, that the last decision must be in the hands of the President. But we want to participate fully, intimately and without limit in the formulation of the ideas, policy and strategy that together make up the doctrine upon which any particular decision of the President must depend. We would want to share in the decisions about the deployment and targeting of nuclear weapons and in future production plans. We would also seek to conclude agreements under which we could execute enough specialist work to benefit from the industrial fall-out that comes from the production of nuclear weapons.

This would be a lot to ask from America. But in exchange we would recognize and support the ultimate nuclear monopoly of the United States in the West.[59]

After its victory in October 1964, the Labour party found many reasons to reverse its pledge to renounce the independent strategic

56. Gordon Walker, "Labor Party's Defense and Foreign Policy," p. 391.
57. Ibid., p. 392.
58. Ibid., pp. 392–93.
59. Ibid., pp. 393–94.

deterrent. But, as Andrew Pierre wrote, this reversal was not the result of sudden doubts about the credibility of the U.S. guarantee, or of second thoughts about the viability of a conventional option for NATO, but rather the result of cost considerations, domestic political liabilities, and a stubborn bureaucracy.[60] Throughout the years of Harold Wilson's government, Britain fully supported McNamara's efforts to gain adoption of flexible response by NATO, and at the same time, through the Nuclear Planning Group, made important contributions to the debate over NATO's nuclear posture.

The American Debate

Not surprisingly, the American debate over flexible response was loud enough to be heard across the Atlantic. Those who objected to the new policies found various grounds for displeasure.[61] Some argued that counterforce options, by threatening the enemy's retaliatory forces, were destabilizing, since they gave the enemy an important incentive to attack first in times of crisis. Others argued that counterforce options were illusory; that any strategic nuclear exchange, however limited, would entail ghastly consequences for both sides; and that, whatever its intentions, the United States would quickly find it impossible to limit strategic nuclear war to avoid counter-city exchanges. They also feared that by fostering the illusion that a general nuclear war could be controlled and limited, flexible response would make political leaders more reckless and hence weaken deterrence.

Some argued that McNamara's attack on independent nuclear forces was ill-conceived and ultimately futile. If France and Britain felt they needed their own arsenals as a hedge against the unreliability of the American guarantee—a belief shared by some Americans—why should the United States spend fruitless effort trying to dissuade them from this view? Why not offer to help them in whatever way they wanted? Would not that kind of policy bring France back into the fold? These same doubts about the wisdom of trying to maintain the American strategic nuclear monopoly were shared by the multilateralists.

60. Pierre, *Nuclear Politics,* pp. 283–92.
61. There are many useful sources for this debate. One of the best is Moulton, *From Superiority to Parity,* pp. 72–107. See also Henry A. Kissinger, *The Troubled Partnership,* pp. 91–125.

Finally, some took issue with the renewed emphasis on a conventional option. At various times they disagreed with the analyses suggesting that the conventional option was feasible; claimed that a posture relying on tactical nuclear response was a more credible, more threatening deterrent than one relying on conventional response; and argued that for many political and financial reasons the Europeans could never be induced to spend what was needed to provide a serious conventional option.[62]

McNamara generally rejected all these arguments and pressed on with flexible response. Recognizing the dangers and uncertainties inherent in any attempt to limit damage or to control a strategic nuclear conflict, he nevertheless continued to worry about the implications of the various choices open to the president in the event deterrence failed; consequently he maintained the options introduced into the single integrated operational plan in 1962. He did, however, begin to back off from emphasis on counterforce damage limitation in his public statements to Congress, emphasizing instead the deterrence derived from a force capable of withstanding a surprise attack from Soviet missiles and of responding with a retaliatory blow against Soviet urban-industrial targets so devastating that any Soviet first strike would be suicidally irrational. This was the so-called assured destruction capability, somewhat arbitrarily defined as the ability to wipe out in a second strike 25 percent of the Soviet population and 70 percent of its industrial capacity.

Much confusion surrounds the significance of McNamara's public shift from emphasis on damage-limitation counterforce options to assured destruction capability. Some apparently assumed that McNamara had seen the potential dangers of counterforce and thus shifted U.S. strategic nuclear policy toward reliance on an assured destruction posture.[63] Hence their arguments that Secretary of Defense James A. Schlesinger had somehow *revived* counterforce in 1974–75 after an interment of a decade.

Here it is probably best to make the distinction, first articulated by Paul Nitze, between *declaratory policy* and *action policy*.[64] U.S. declar-

---

62. Brodie was the most influential of these critics. See Bernard Brodie, "What Price Conventional Capabilities in Europe?" pp. 25–33, and Brodie, *Escalation and the Nuclear Option.*

63. Moulton, *From Superiority to Parity,* pp. 283–89, seems to come close to this conclusion.

64. Paul H. Nitze, "Atoms, Strategy and Policy," pp. 187–98.

atory policy did gradually move away from counterforce options toward a posture of assured destruction. But on the level of war plans, the action policy of the United States, the SIOP was never revised to reflect this shift in declaratory policy. McNamara never had counterforce options removed from U.S. strategic war plans, and as new counterforce targets appeared, new U.S. weapons were allocated to these targets. Operationally, McNamara and his successors never incorporated assured destruction as an action policy.[65]

This fact raises an interesting question, one that lies at the heart of much misunderstanding of U.S. strategic nuclear policy, as will be seen in the next chapter. Why the shift in declaratory policy if McNamara was unwilling to codify assured destruction into the war plans? Several answers have been proposed, all speculative. One focuses on McNamara's desire to calm domestic and European fears that a counterforce strategy was provocative and that it weakened deterrence. Another focuses on the bureaucratic battles McNamara was engaged in with the air force over the size and composition of the strategic force. At first reluctant to accept the new planning guidelines set forth in 1961, the air force had become more enthusiastic when it realized that these guidelines left the calculation of strategic requirements somewhat open-ended. Any target of military importance could be pressed for inclusion in the SIOP on the ground that its destruction would reduce Soviet capability to wage war against the United States. Furthermore, as the Soviet strategic arsenal grew, the required level of U.S. strategic forces grew. This allowed the air force to press for higher rates of missile procurement, which McNamara, faced with competing claims on a constrained defense budget, could not easily authorize. Counterforce targeting principles did not define a level of *sufficiency,* as those who analyzed the results of Hickey's study on strategic force requirements quickly realized.[66]

Assured destruction, however, did provide a rough measure of

65. On this point Rowen, Ball, and Enthoven agree. See Rowen, "Formulating Strategic Doctrine," Ball, *Politics and Force Levels,* and Enthoven's testimony before the Senate Armed Services Committee in April 1968, in which he said: "Our targetting policy, as reflected in the guidance for the preparation of the targetting plan, has not changed. From 1961–62 on, the targetting plan has been based on the principle that we should have different options that target the strategic forces and cities." *Status of U.S. Strategic Power,* Senate Hearings, p. 138. For more on this issue, see the Senate hearings *Nuclear Weapons and Foreign Policy* and *U.S.-U.S.S.R. Strategic Policies.*

66. These points are taken up in Enthoven and Smith, *How Much Is Enough?* pp. 165–96.

sufficiency—the capability to destroy 25 percent of the Soviet population and about 70 percent of its industrial capacity—and conveniently permitted force sizing to affordable levels. Thus, it is argued, McNamara latched onto assured destruction to put a ceiling on the procurement requests of the air force. In fact, he directed top air force officers to cease requesting additional funds on the basis of counterforce requirements.[67] By the time McNamara left office, each leg of the strategic triad—ICBMs, SLBMs, and bombers—was sized to fit the assured destruction criteria, but not much more.

Another answer, not offered by many observers of the McNamara era but worth considering in light of events described in chapter 5, would point to the MLF experience and the Skybolt crisis as a partial explanation for the shift in declaratory policy. For Europeans, the multilateral nuclear force was primarily a countervalue weapons system; as a counterforce system its use would be sharply limited by its relatively small size, and thus it would be heavily dependent on coordination with the supposedly unreliable U.S. strategic arsenal to execute meaningful counterforce missions. Gallois, for one, was quick to point out the apparent contradiction between the new U.S. counterforce policy and Washington's pursuit of the MLF.[68]

McNamara was probably well aware of the contradiction, which may in turn help to explain his initial reluctance to give his full support to the MLF. But as already seen, the Skybolt crisis gave him little choice but to acquiesce to the State Department's ill-fated efforts to promote the MLF. His public shift of emphasis toward assured destruction had the effect of resolving the contradictions noted by Gallois and others, and possibly this effect was intended.

Two Versions of Flexible Response

As can be seen by comparing the West German position in support of flexible response with McNamara's Athens speech, two versions of this strategy existed. These were discussed and debated over the next few years. Both versions maintained that NATO must threaten to respond appropriately to aggression on any level for the threat to constitute a credible deterrent. Where the two versions differed was on the role accorded to escalation.

---

67. Ball, *Politics and Force Levels,* pp. 201–02.
68. Gallois, "U.S. Strategy and the Defense of Europe," pp. 240–45.

The version presented in Athens by McNamara foresaw grave dangers in escalation, particularly in escalation over the nuclear threshold. This is the direct implication of his warnings about the feasibility and desirability of a tactical nuclear response to conventional aggression. In this version, the goal of flexible response was to be able to challenge conventional Warsaw Pact aggression with conventional response so effectively that the *enemy* would have to make the decision to escalate to the nuclear level, and face all the awesome risks and uncertainties associated with that decision. Such a posture, it was held, would be an effective deterrent without forcing NATO to have to make a divisive and potentially catastrophic decision to initiate use of nuclear weapons.

The other version, explicitly supported by von Hassel and others, held that a stronger deterrent lay in the credibility of NATO's threat to escalate. If this threat was not credible, it was argued, the Warsaw Pact might come to believe that it could calculate the consequences of limited aggression and that these consequences were acceptable enough to justify the risk of initiating aggression. Thus NATO must be visibly prepared to bring the conflict across the nuclear threshold relatively early in the engagement.

Implicit here was the assumption that NATO's conventional defense could never hope to impose costs out of proportion with the benefits to be derived by the Warsaw Pact from conventional aggression. This, in turn, rested on one of two assumptions: that the Warsaw Pact would inevitably have superiority on the conventional level, or that the allies would never be able to afford a conventional posture capable of forcing the Soviets to escalate a conflict from the conventional to the nuclear level.

Whatever the relative merits of the two versions, the main constraints on NATO's choice of one or the other were political, having to do with the reluctance of the Europeans to spend more on conventional forces or to move away from their reliance on the threat of early nuclear response as a deterrent. As U.S. officials discovered, these constraints were formidable and finally led NATO to adopt the latter rather than the former version of flexible response.

Flexible Response in Limbo

The response of NATO to McNamara's Athens speech was complex. At SHAPE, SACEUR General Norstad was known to be skeptical of the feasibility of a conventional option; by July 1962 he had tendered his resignation as SACEUR, in a move widely but erroneously interpreted as a protest to McNamara's new strategy.[69] His replacement, General Lyman Lemnitzer, was mistrusted by Europeans because of his involvement in the Bay of Pigs fiasco. Lemnitzer's appointment caused a mini-crisis in U.S.-German relations, with Adenauer and Strauss expressing grave fears that the United States was maneuvering to revoke its nuclear pledge to NATO. Kennedy and McNamara repeatedly denied that the appointment of Lemnitzer as SACEUR, and Maxwell Taylor as chairman of the Joint Chiefs of Staff, reflected any such renunciation; they insisted that U.S. policy remained committed to using whatever weapons were necessary to counter a Warsaw Pact invasion.

At the same time, however, the staff at SHAPE recognized the similarities between the Athens speech and the 1957 study conducted by Stilwell.[70] The Stilwell report was dusted off in June 1962 and under the new name of Draft MC 14/3 was submitted to NATO's Standing Group for possible adoption to supersede MC 14/2, which outlined a strategic concept for NATO calling for immediate nuclear response to Warsaw Pact aggression. Governments were asked to return MC 14/3 with comments by September 15. Given the doubts entertained by the Europeans, it is not surprising that only the United States met the September 15 deadline. No comment was forthcoming from any of the other allies. France, of course, totally rejected the concepts outlined in MC 14/3; Britain and West Germany also had doubts. The other European allies were loath to respond, largely because doing so would embroil them in disputes either with France, if they accepted MC 14/3, or with the United States, if they rejected it. By the end of the year it was clear that NATO would have to postpone formal action on adopting the new strategic concept of flexible response.

Between late 1962 and mid-1965, discussions of flexible response were almost entirely superseded by alliance consideration of the multi-lateral force. By that point, however, it was becoming clear that the MLF discussions were leading nowhere. Also becoming clear was de Gaulle's intention to radically redefine France's role in NATO. France's announcement in March 1966 that it was withdrawing from the military

69. See, for example, *New York Times,* July 21, 1962; and Charles J. V. Murphy, "NATO at a Nuclear Crossroads," pp. 85ff.

70. The rest of this section is based on Rowny, "Decision-Making Process in NATO," pp. 193–204.

organization of the alliance paved the way for the new strategy to be adopted by the North Atlantic Council, especially since government changes in West Germany and Britain brought support for flexible response.

Moreover, another event took place in 1965 that eased the process of formal adoption of flexible response: the creation of the Special Committee of NATO defense ministers, the forerunner of the Nuclear Planning Group.

Nuclear Consultation and the Nuclear Planning Group

Until 1962 the United States had maintained an extraordinary shroud of secrecy over its strategic nuclear planning process, as impervious to the allies as it was to the Soviet Union. Only Britain—after more than a decade of effort—had succeeded in gaining limited access to the data and the rationale behind American strategic nuclear planning.

This secrecy created problems on two levels. For McNamara, it prevented the allies from fully appreciating the reasons behind the new strategic nuclear policy contained in flexible response. Without access to the data, analysis, and war games upon which the counterforce doctrine was based, the Europeans could not have confidence in Mc-Namara's claims about the advantages of the doctrine. If McNamara was to succeed in convincing the allies of the soundness of the new strategy, he would have to modify the tradition of secrecy that kept them from having access to the basis of U.S. strategic planning.

On another level, the secrecy was having broader political repercussions. For Europeans, it reinforced, in a particularly arrogant way, the unequal relationship between Washington and its NATO partners. This inequality naturally added to the suspicion and resentment with which the allies viewed unilateral American pronouncements of strategic policy. If the allies had no voice in determining the strategic nuclear policy of the alliance, how could they be expected to have confidence in it? Furthermore, that one of their members, Britain, was treated as an exception only heightened the general resentment and placed Britain in an awkward political position with respect to the Continent, particularly to France. Finally, the resentment was only intensified when the Athens speech made clear that the United States had embarked on a dramatic new policy without prior consultation with other members of the alliance.

This result of the Athens speech was ironic, for McNamara had intended his unprecedented candor to be the first step away from the secrecy surrounding previous U.S. policymaking. The allies might not have been so resentful if McNamara had been able to follow through on his pledge to continue frequent consultation with the allies on strategic nuclear matters. Personally he did follow through. Each of his subsequent briefings to NATO ministerial meetings demonstrated the same candor and openness displayed at Athens. But when he tried to create an ongoing strategic seminar in which the United States would lead the allies in an open discussion of the problems of strategic nuclear planning, his efforts failed.[71] The Joint Chiefs of Staff demanded to be put in charge of organizing the seminar and turned it into a military briefing on U.S. policy. The allies were clearly not interested in that sort of "seminar," correctly perceiving that it would give them no voice in the American planning process. By the end of 1962, therefore, this preliminary effort came to an end.

McNamara was still intent on improving the consultative mechanisms for setting alliance nuclear policy. By May 1963 he had gained support for a new effort, this time to establish regular staff liaisons between SHAPE and the U.S. Joint Strategic Target Planning Staff in Omaha, where U.S. SIOP planning takes place.[72] Officers representing Britain, France, West Germany, and Italy at SHAPE were assigned on a rotating basis to the planning staff starting in May 1963, to observe in a limited way the process by which U.S. military staffs carried out the complex tasks of nuclear planning. Still, these officers retained the status of observers, not participants in the process. Furthermore, close consultation between military staffs in Omaha did not directly translate into a greater sense of political participation back home.

By mid-1965 the time seemed appropriate to McNamara to renew efforts to regularize closer political consultation on nuclear planning within the alliance.[73] Several factors made this period particularly opportune. First, the MLF was recently moribund, leaving unsatisfied

71. See John D. Steinbruner, *The Cybernetic Theory of Decision*, pp. 209–13.
72. Thomas C. Wiegele, "Nuclear Consultation Processes in NATO," pp. 484–86.
73. The following description of the evolution of the Nuclear Planning Group is based on several excellent accounts: ibid., pp. 472–83; Harlan Cleveland, *NATO*, pp. 53–65; Arthur Hockaday, "Nuclear Management in NATO," pp. 3–7; Harvey B. Seim, "Nuclear Policy-Making in NATO," pp. 11–13; Paul Edward Buteux, "The Politics of Nuclear Consultation in NATO, 1965–1974" (Ph.D. dissertation); and Robert Max Krone, "NATO Nuclear Policymaking" (Ph.D. dissertation).

West Germany's desire for a greater share of control over alliance nuclear weapons. Though McNamara never explicitly linked his initiative to compensation for the failure of the MLF—it was still somewhat impolite to discuss its death openly—a new initiative to create regular consultative arrangements would work to reconcile German leaders to the political impossibility of obtaining control over strategic nuclear weapons within the alliance. Second, Denis Healey was now Britain's minister of defense, and while he could not deliver on his pledge to renounce Britain's independent strategic deterrent, he would clearly press for a "renegotiation" of Nassau to "participate fully, intimately, and without limit in the formulation of the ideas, policy and strategy that together make up the doctrine upon which any particular decision of the President must depend."[74] His efforts in this direction took on added weight from the support of the influential Alastair Buchan, who had been arguing for years that America's misplaced zeal for creating the MLF would have been more wisely directed toward meeting the allies' real desire: to have regular input into the determination of U.S. nuclear policy and to have the right of criticism and comment.

The Initial Proposal

With all these factors in mind, McNamara proposed, at the June 1965 meeting of the NATO defense ministers in Paris, the creation of a special committee of NATO members to examine ways in which to implement consultation on nuclear planning. The exact size and composition was left open to further clarification in subsequent discussions among the permanent representatives to NATO. But the United States made it clear from the beginning that it envisioned a committee large enough to be broadly representative but small enough to encourage freewheeling discussions and to facilitate action. What McNamara probably had in mind was a committee composed of the defense ministers of the United States, Great Britain, France (if it so desired), West Germany, and perhaps Italy and one or two smaller allies on a rotating basis.

From the outset it was apparent that France would not participate. By then, France's independent course had been charted; within a year it would announce its withdrawal from the military organization of NATO. The French ridiculed the proposal as being too trivial for high-

74. Gordon Walker, "Labor Party's Defense and Foreign Policy," pp. 393–94.

level political participation and too irrelevant to France's own security interest to merit its participation.

The reception of the proposal in other countries ranged from positive to ambivalent. The Wilson government was predictably enthusiastic; after all, the idea for such a committee had been raised frequently by Healey.[75] In Bonn the reaction was mixed. On the one hand, Bonn wanted to play a more active role in the making of alliance nuclear policy; on the other hand, it was reluctant to give up efforts to create the MLF, and if the select committee was merely a way to divert attention from nuclear control-sharing arrangements, some members of Erhard's government were not eager to participate. These factions gained greater influence as Erhard began to prepare for the elections in September. The German Gaullists were particularly worried that the select committee would permit the United States to isolate de Gaulle further from the rest of NATO.

Italy and other countries like Canada and the Netherlands were also reluctant to show eagerness for a committee that, depending on how select the participation was, might lock them out of influence on matters important to the alliance.

By the end of November, Erhard, with elections behind him, was in a stronger position to renounce interest in the MLF and to accept de facto compensation by way of membership in the select committee. The smaller allies, led by Italy, prevailed over U.S. reservations and were able to gain broad representation on the committee. Thus, on November 27, 1965, the Special Committee of Defense Ministers was formally constituted, with ministers from Belgium, Great Britain, Canada, Denmark, Greece, Italy, the Netherlands, Turkey, West Germany, and the United States taking part.

The Formation of the Special Committee

The committee, with American encouragement, immediately decided that its agenda was best addressed by splitting the committee into smaller working groups on specific areas. One working group, consisting of defense ministers from the United States, Great Britain, West Germany,

---

75. Some even claim that Healey was the driving force behind the creation and operation of the Nuclear Planning Group. See Bruce Reed and Geoffrey Williams, *Denis Healey and the Policies of Power.*

Italy, and Turkey, was to examine problems related to planning for the use of nuclear weapons. This working group on nuclear planning was widely recognized as the most important one. Two other working groups dealt with exchanges of data and with communications during crises. Allocation of seats on each group became a serious political problem, especially on the nuclear planning working group. But McNamara persisted in his demand for a relatively small membership in each working group, and the participation problems were eventually resolved. As McNamara later said:

Whenever I want to be really efficient, I get a building about half the size that anybody wants and say that's what we're going to build Ford cars in or that's what we're going to have for the Navy or whatever it may be. Well, we followed the same procedure here and we designed small tables and said that nobody can talk that doesn't sit at the table and there are only X number of spaces at the table. Now, this sounds childish maybe, but it isn't childish. There's a very direct inverse relationship between the number of participants and the degree or extent of accomplishment.[76]

The Working Group on Nuclear Planning

The working group on nuclear planning met four times between February 1966 and September 1966, when it forwarded its report to the special committee. In February it met in Washington under the chairmanship of McNamara, who proceeded to stimulate the most wide-ranging discussion of strategic nuclear policy to have taken place within the alliance up to that time. The secretary of defense told John McNaughton, who was Nitze's successor at ISA and who helped McNamara prepare for this first meeting: "We are going to insist that the Germans stop talking about a finger on the trigger without a plan to use it. . . . We are going to make them resolve the question of whose finger, and when it is to push."[77]

In subsequent discussions during the Washington meeting McNamara emphasized the complexities and frustrations of the nuclear planning process, from the problems of target selection and warhead allocation, to the development of attack packages, to the coordination of command and control, and so on.

In London at the end of April, the working group met again to consider

76. Cited in Cleveland, *NATO,* pp. 56–57.
77. Cited in Krone, "NATO Nuclear Policymaking," p. 24.

the role of nuclear weapons deployed in Europe for tactical missions. Briefings were given by SACEUR General Lemnitzer and SACLANT Admiral Thomas Moorer, followed by a briefing by Denis Healey on the analysis of extensive simulations of the effects of a prolonged tactical nuclear campaign in Europe. These simulations suggested the none-too-surprising conclusion that large areas would be destroyed and millions of people killed in a tactical nuclear war, even one confined to relatively small kiloton-range weapons.

One would assume that because Healey and his British colleagues appreciated the dangers of a tactical nuclear posture, they would have accepted the need for the improvements in conventional capabilities called for by McNamara ever since May 1962. But Healey did not share his American counterpart's enthusiasm for the conventional option, especially since he was trying to deal with the budgetary problem posed by maintaining the British Army of the Rhine at its current levels. As a result, Healey argued throughout this period—and he brought the issue up at the London planning session—that SACEUR was too much concerned with fighting a prolonged conventional war in Europe.[78] Any such war, he said, would quickly become nuclear, and furthermore it was politically unrealistic to expect Europe to allocate the necessary resources to counter such an unlikely threat. Instead, SACEUR should plan to use the already formidable conventional forces at his disposal to deal with accidents or minor incursions during crisis and, if the Warsaw Pact did launch a major conventional attack, to gain time for consultation among the allies about the use of nuclear weapons, in the tradition of Norstad's pause concept.

McNamara took issue with Healey at this meeting and subsequently. U.S. officials were convinced that a serious conventional option to counter a major Soviet nonnuclear attack was within the grasp of the alliance and, considering the dangers associated with nuclear alternatives, well worth striving for.

After the London meeting, McNamara apparently believed that the alliance had progressed further on nuclear matters in the previous few months than in all the time since he had taken office.[79] His belief was reinforced by the evident enthusiasm of the Europeans for the new arrangement. At subsequent meetings of the working group, in June in

78. Buteux, "Politics of Nuclear Consultation in NATO," p. 78.
79. Cleveland, *NATO*, p. 55.

Paris and in September in Rome, it became clear that the main recommendation of the group would be to institutionalize a forum for discussing nuclear planning within the alliance.

The Creation of the Nuclear Planning Group

In December 1966 the Defense Planning Committee, which consisted of the NATO defense ministers (France excepted), took up these recommendations and created a two-tiered forum for institutionalizing the nuclear planning working group. One tier, the Nuclear Defense Affairs Committee (NDAC), would be open to all interested members of the alliance, to meet the political requirement for an equal chance to participate in matters critical to the security of the alliance. The other tier would be the Nuclear Planning Group (NPG), comprising the United States, West Germany, Great Britain, Italy, and three other members of the NDAC in rotation, which would carry on the main work of detailed consultation and discussions. This arrangement met McNamara's stated preference for a smaller group more capable of efficient deliberation. All NATO members except France, Luxembourg, and Iceland joined the NDAC; initially neither Portugal, Denmark, nor Norway wished to be considered for rotating membership in the NPG, which left Canada, Greece, the Netherlands, and Turkey as the rotating members of the smaller body. Manlio Brosio, secretary general of NATO, was selected chairman of both committees, an honor particularly fitting because of his central role in mediating the discussions on participation.

Ever since April 1967 the Nuclear Planning Group has met on a ministerial level twice a year and has taken up a wide range of subjects, such as ABM systems for Europe (which it rejected), guidelines for the use of tactical nuclear weapons, SALT, and mutual and balanced force reductions (MBFR).

Though the creation of the NPG and the formal adoption of flexible response by the North Atlantic Council in December 1967 may not be directly related, the candid give-and-take in NPG sessions probably convinced Europeans doubtful of the American nuclear guarantee that they could significantly affect U.S. strategic nuclear policy without having physical access to the weapons themselves. A report by the Western European Union—never a proponent of the MLF—concluded that the deliberations of the special committee working group in nuclear planning "seemed to indicate that the non-nuclear members of the

Alliance recognise that, through improved consultation, they will secure a more real share in the planning of nuclear defense of the Alliance as a whole than they could hope to obtain by participating in a small joint nuclear force, the use of which would inevitably be subject to a veto by the United States."[80]

McNamara's behavior during the crucial 1966 meetings showed his determination not to let the working group degenerate into another of the "kindergarten" briefings that the Europeans resented in previous attempts to improve consultation. He reportedly went far in opening for scrutiny and criticism the analysis and assumptions behind American plans, convinced that doing so would serve two purposes: the allies would feel that the United States cared about their perspectives on matters of nuclear security, and they would learn about the technical complexities of nuclear planning, complexities that might make them better understand the frustrations of the United States in trying to maintain a credible strategic nuclear deterrent for the alliance.

The Adoption of Flexible Response

During this period the United States and NATO returned to the task of revising NATO's 1957 military guidance on general strategy, MC 14/2, to reflect the growing acceptance of flexible response, a task that the alliance had put aside because of French intransigence in late 1962. The details of how this directive was supplanted by MC 14/3, which raised flexible response to the level of alliance strategy, have never been fully revealed. But it is known that in mid-to-late 1966, U.S. Vice Admiral John Lee, assigned to the American delegation staff at NATO, learned that SHAPE was considering a revision of MC 14/2 based on a draft that, according to Lee, did not embody the concept of flexible response.[81] Whether this draft was a revision of the Stilwell report is not known, though that would seem unlikely, since the Stilwell report apparently promoted many ideas and concepts in line with flexible response. Determined to prevent this draft from being adopted, Lee went to Washington and enlisted the help of William W. Kaufmann, a Pentagon colleague, to

---

80. Cited in Buteux, "Politics of Nuclear Consultation in NATO," p. 88.
81. The following information was provided to the author by Admiral Lee, August 5, 1980.

generate an alternative revision of MC 14/2, one more in keeping with flexible response. Together they came up with a new draft, which Lee then proceeded to have cleared within the U.S. government.

By the end of the year, the United States had informed the NATO Military Committee that it had its own proposal for a revision of MC 14/2, a proposal that reportedly differed only in minor ways from that drawn up by Lee and Kaufmann. What the Military Committee finally adopted as MC 14/3, though not identical to the U.S. proposal, integrated large parts of it into the text. The North Atlantic Council also took the somewhat unusual step of formally adopting a Military Committee directive, so that MC 14/3 is both a Military Committee document and a council document. According to Harlan Cleveland, the U.S. ambassador to NATO at the time, the guidance the council passed along to NATO commanders directed them "to provide for the employment as appropriate of one or more of direct defense, deliberate escalation, and general nuclear response, thus confronting the enemy with a credible threat of escalation in response to any type of aggression below the level of a major nuclear attack."[82] Thus May 1967 saw the culmination of a process that had begun on May 5, 1962, in Athens.

Conclusions

The creation of the Nuclear Planning Group was important in defusing pressure for nuclear control sharing, in reconciling the allies to American strategic concepts, and in convincing them that the United States cared what its partners thought about nuclear matters and was willing to make nuclear planning an *alliance* function. But by itself the NPG does not explain the apparent ease with which MC 14/3 was adopted in 1967. Another crucial factor was de Gaulle's decision to withdraw France from the military functions of the alliance, announced in March 1966. Up till then, France had raised strong objections to flexible response on many grounds. De Gaulle and his aides had, in the process, created doubt about the American nuclear guarantee in the minds of other European political leaders, particularly within the pro-Gaullist wing of Germany's Christian Democratic party. Even had these pro-Gaullist

82. Cited in Cleveland, *NATO,* p. 81. See also *New York Times,* April 20, 1967, and May 10, 1967.

forces not existed, West Germany and other European partners would have been reluctant to make a choice between France and the United States over the proper direction of alliance policy. For these countries, full endorsement of the flexible response strategy expounded at Athens and elsewhere would have amounted to a choice of Washington over Paris. Eager to preserve whatever unity Europe had achieved in the two decades since World War II ended, and reluctant to break with the superpower on which they had relied for their security so long, the allies successfully tried to postpone such an agonizing choice. Thus inaction was the direct consequence of a Franco-American controversy that extended beyond the realm of military strategy to a disagreement over the fundamental political relationship between Europe and America.

Of course, France was in a formal position to block adoption of the new strategy as long as it was a full member of the alliance. France maintained a seat on the North Atlantic Council, where it could exercise an effective veto over any decision that came before the council. Even so, once it withdrew from the military organization, it effectively removed the main obstacle to the adoption of flexible response.

Analysts continue to disagree about whether de Gaulle's action of 1966 was prompted largely by U.S. pressure on the alliance to adopt flexible response, by the creation of the Nuclear Planning Group, or by more fundamental political objectives. Some argue that had it not been for American pressure on the alliance to adopt a strategy so clearly opposed to France's perceived strategic and political interests, France would not have found itself in such an isolated position by early 1966 and thus might not have felt compelled to withdraw from NATO.[83] The timing of the withdrawal announcement—soon after the creation of the special committee—lends some plausibility to this argument.

Others argue, however, that France had been isolated for some time; it did not take part, for example, in the MLF deliberations that occupied much of the alliance's attention from early 1963 until late 1965.[84] They maintain that France had isolated itself, by its strict adherence to a strategic doctrine that seemed to make the concept of a military alliance irrelevant and by its refusal to concede a leadership position to the West's most powerful nation; that the United States had made many

83. Kissinger, in *The Troubled Partnership*, is critical of U.S. rigidity, although his book came out before France's withdrawal from NATO.
84. Robert R. Bowie foreshadowed this argument explicitly in "Strategy and the Atlantic Alliance," pp. 729–30.

efforts to facilitate a rapprochement with France if de Gaulle had wanted it; and that the final split was the inevitable result of the irreconcilability not of opposing views of nuclear deterrence but of de Gaulle's vision of Europe and Kennedy's Grand Design.

Whatever the relative merits of the two positions, one thing can be said confidently: if France had chosen to remain a full member of the alliance, the adoption of MC 14/3, with or without the deliberations of the NPG, would have been problematic, if not impossible.

Events in Germany also facilitated the adoption of flexible response. When Erhard resigned as chancellor in late 1966, he was followed by Kurt-George Kiesinger, who named Willy Brandt, a Social Democrat, as foreign minister and replaced von Hassel with Gerhard Schroeder as defense minister in what came to be known as the grand coalition between the Social Democrats and the Christian Democrats. This shift to the left, with Brandt beginning his first tentative moves toward a policy of *Ostpolitik,* reduced whatever lingering interest Bonn had had in gaining direct access to nuclear weapons through nuclear control sharing.

The shift also had a positive effect on Bonn's interest in the continuing negotiations at the United Nations over a treaty on nuclear nonproliferation.[85] Throughout 1965 and 1966 Bonn had viewed the treaty with suspicion. First, the treaty had been partly responsible for the demise of the MLF, because the Soviet Union had repeatedly claimed that progress on the treaty would be incompatible with the realization of the MLF. Second, the treaty seemed to be directed at West Germany out of fear that Bonn's 1954 nonproliferation pledge was somehow suspect; but Bonn's nuclear aspirations had proved illusory, and the German government had been adamantly opposed to any nonproliferation policy that seemed to single Germany out as the main proliferation problem. U.S.-German tensions over the treaty had probably contributed to Bonn's reluctance to meet the American demands for formal adoption of flexible response. With Brandt as foreign minister, eager to smooth the way for a diplomatic opening to the East, these tensions virtually disappeared, thus facilitating the adoption of MC 14/3.

Finally, and perhaps most important, the adoption of MC 14/3 was made easier by the willingness of the United States to accept a somewhat limited and ambiguous endorsement of flexible response. As has been

85. Kelleher, *Germany and the Politics of Nuclear Weapons,* pp. 298–301.

seen, the version of flexible response finally adopted made the threat of deliberate escalation explicit. Despite the potential dangers it saw in a posture relying on escalation, especially escalation across the nuclear threshold, the United States agreed to this version, in part because of the political problems associated with building up a serious conventional option. As a result, by the middle of 1968—well after flexible response had been adopted—NATO had some 28⅔ M-day divisions on the central front, still short of the MC 70 requirements. NATO outnumbered the Warsaw Pact on the central front in terms of manpower in divisions and in leading categories of equipment, such as antitank weapons and mortars; it had come a long way since 1960. But readiness, reserve structure, and mobilization all needed improvement, for which the alliance was either unwilling or unable to pay. Operationally, NATO still seemed to rely heavily on tactical nuclear capabilities, with over 7,000 nuclear warheads deployed in Europe by 1968.

To explain this reliance, one must again fall back on the distinction between declaratory policy and action policy. In declaratory policy, NATO had fully accepted flexible response as its strategic concept by the end of 1967. In action policy, however, formidable ambiguities remained. How many resources should the allies devote to a conventional capability able to defeat a major, prolonged Warsaw Pact invasion? Would a war in Europe be likely to remain conventional for long? How early should NATO consider introducing nuclear weapons into conventional operations? These operational issues, shrouded in uncertainties if for no other reason than that they raised politically divisive problems for the alliance, must remain outside the scope of this chapter. But until some clarification of these operational questions is forthcoming, the efforts of McNamara and others to have NATO adopt a strategy of flexible response as the basis for operational planning must be judged only partly successful.

Nevertheless, flexible response and the creation of the NPG did resolve some of NATO's problems. For more than a decade, the strategic nuclear guarantee of the United States was rarely, if ever, questioned openly. Gone were the many mini-crises over strategic nuclear matters, tactical nuclear weapons, and forward defense that marked the period between 1958 and 1967. The attention of the alliance now turned to some equally troublesome but less divisive matters—Vietnam, SALT, and *Ostpolitik*.

Several plausible explanations for this apparent success can be offered. One centers on the persuasive efforts made by McNamara and others during this period. Three characteristics made these efforts particularly successful. First, they were sustained and repetitive. McNamara renewed his Athens pleas at each subsequent meeting of the NATO defense ministers, and his aides continually made the same arguments in private and public. These actions had two effects: they convinced the Europeans of the seriousness of the American leadership in sponsoring the new strategy, and they kept the Europeans exposed to a relatively new, unfamiliar way of thinking.

Second, McNamara's ideas were logically consistent. Some critics tried to find inconsistencies in the logic, and at times thought they had succeeded in doing so. But their judgments were almost always based on a selective interpretation of the American position. When presented in full detail, such as in the Athens speech, the policy of flexible response was remarkably coherent. It was so coherent, in fact, that it forced opponents to attack it on its underlying assumptions: that counterforce targeting strategy was feasible, that the conventional balance was rectifiable, and that the American nuclear guarantee was credible.

Third, McNamara's efforts directly challenged prevailing doubts and assumptions about the American nuclear guarantee, about the feasibility of the conventional option, about the alleged benefits derived from small independent nuclear forces, and about the relative deterrent effects of conventional and nuclear forces. These challenges were in sharp contrast to the other initiatives pursued by the United States, which took those doubts for granted and tried to devise policies to accommodate them. The challenges, in turn, put the burden of the argument back onto those who had the doubts, and in so doing forced a healthy rethinking about the general nuclear dilemmas facing the alliance. In creating the Nuclear Planning Group, the United States went one step further: it gave the allies the information and the forum for exploring the validity of these doubts.

A second explanation for the U.S. success rests on the fortuitous political trends that made acceptance of flexible response easier. These include the progressive isolation and final withdrawal of the main opponent of flexible response, France, from the alliance; the shift from Adenauer to Erhard to Kiesinger, and from Strauss to von Hassel to Schroeder, in West Germany, a trend that undermined the influence of forces in West German politics sympathetic to the Gaullist position; and the assumption of power in Britain by Labour party leaders who shared many of the concerns and perspectives of McNamara and his colleagues.

A third explanation focuses on the general intellectual and political fatigue that had resulted from years of inconclusive, divisive debate over the nuclear dilemmas of the alliance. Especially after the time-consuming negotiations on the multilateral force, everyone concerned may have wished to put the issue aside as soon as politically possible.

CHAPTER SEVEN

Long-Range Theater Nuclear Modernization and Arms Control

FROM 1977 through 1979 NATO debated the deployment of a new generation of long-range theater nuclear forces (LRTNF).[1] As a result of this extended debate NATO foreign and defense ministers met on December 12, 1979, and agreed to pursue a two-track decision: LRTNF modernization and arms control.[2] On one track, Britain, Italy, and West Germany each agreed to accept deployments of American ground-launched cruise missiles (GLCMs) on their territories, and West Germany agreed in addition to the deployment of 108 American extended-

1. In the second half of 1981 the Reagan administration adopted new terminology, subsequently adopted throughout NATO, that did away with the name *theater nuclear forces*. Instead, these forces are now described according to their range capability; longer-range intermediate-range nuclear forces (LRINF), shorter-range intermediate-range nuclear forces (SRINF), and short-range nuclear forces (SNF). The LRINF category is roughly equivalent to the old LRTNF category. The change was made at the insistence of Europeans, who wanted to emphasize that the European continent is more than a "theater" and felt that the old terminology carried connotations that were decoupling. My decision to retain the old terminology does not reflect a belief that Europe can or should be strategically decoupled from the United States. Rather, the old terminology seems more descriptive of the location and mission of these forces.

2. The December 1979 decision was procedurally unique. It could not be taken by the North Atlantic Council, since France was a member of that body and at the same time stood aside from endorsing the decision. Nor could it be taken by the Defense Planning Committee, which, though it did not include France, could not give the decision the high political significance that was sought. In the end, the decision was taken by NATO foreign and defense ministers (minus France) meeting jointly in extraordinary session.

193

range Pershing II missiles on its territory. Belgium and the Netherlands were also scheduled for deployments of American GLCMs; however, though they endorsed the NATO plan, they both postponed final decision on whether to join the other three countries in participating in deployments of GLCMs. At the same time, the United States agreed to proceed along a second track of arms-control negotiations with the Soviets concerning these weapons.

Many observers have remarked on the similarities between this initiative and earlier American efforts to deal with NATO's nuclear dilemmas.[3] This chapter examines the nature and extent of these similarities. In the process, it seeks to go beyond the simple observation that the December 1979 decision is yet another attempt to address NATO's nuclear dilemmas through the introduction of new weapons into Europe. It tries to use NATO's nuclear history to provide a richer context for understanding why NATO made this decision and what are its prospects for success.

But first it is essential to understand some of the changes in the international environment that occurred after 1967. The debate that culminated in NATO's December 1979 decision on LRTNF is incomprehensible without this background.

Changes in the International Environment, 1967–77

Among the many changes in the international environment relevant to this chapter, three are particularly important: shifts in the Warsaw Pact–NATO balance of forces; changes in political relationships within the alliance, particularly among the United States, Great Britain, France, and West Germany; and the emergence of détente as a prime political objective.

The NATO–Warsaw Pact Balance

Starting in 1967 there was a gradual but sustained growth in the military forces of the Soviet Union and the Warsaw Pact. The buildup of intercontinental strategic nuclear forces is perhaps the most dramatic.

3. For example, see Gregory F. Treverton, "Nuclear Weapons and the 'Gray Area,' " p. 1075.

Table 7-1. *U.S. and Soviet Strategic Launchers, 1967–77*

	United States			Soviet Union		
Year	ICBMs	SLBMs	Bombers	ICBMs	SLBMs	Bombers
1967	1054	656	600	570	107	160
1968	1054	656	545	858	121	155
1969	1054	656	560	1028	196	145
1970	1054	656	550	1299	304	145
1971	1054	656	505	1513	448	145
1972	1054	656	455	1527	500	140
1973	1054	656	442	1527	628	140
1974	1054	656	437	1575	720	140
1975	1054	656	432	1618	784	135
1976	1054	656	387	1527	845	135
1977	1054	656	373	1477	909	135

Source: International Institute for Strategic Studies, *The Military Balance, 1977–1978*, p. 80.

Table 7-1 illustrates the gross characteristics of the trend in the balance between the United States and the Soviet Union. Any such simple comparison inevitably obscures critical factors that must be taken into account in drawing conclusions from the trend—for example, numbers of deliverable warheads, accuracy of delivery, reliability, readiness and alert status, and passive and active defenses. More useful are dynamic analyses that use these static inputs to suggest how the forces would operate under certain plausible circumstances. But even that kind of dynamic assessment does not deal with the ability of each country to achieve its desired political goals through the use of these weapons.

But from the trend shown in the table, one can conclude that the United States no longer has the clear-cut strategic nuclear superiority over the Soviet Union that it allegedly had as late as 1967. In the early 1970s various labels began to be applied to this nuclear relationship, such as *rough equivalence, parity,* and *essential equivalence.* These terms are virtually synonymous and indicate that during 1966–77 the Soviet strategic forces became roughly comparable to those of the United States in the damage they could do to a wide range of civilian or military targets.

The Soviets' nuclear deployments against Europe were dominated by two new theater-oriented delivery systems, the SS-20 mobile IRBM, with a 3-MIRV (multiple independently targeted reentry vehicle) warhead, and the Backfire bomber. The deployment of these weapons became a *cause célèbre* within NATO. NATO also improved its in-theater nuclear capability over the years. Deployments of American F-111 nuclear capable bombers in Britain began in 1969. In the mid-1970s various improvements were made in NATO's tactical nuclear delivery systems, most notably by the introduction of a new missile, the Lance, with a range of about seventy miles, as a substitute for the Sergeant missile. Besides these theater nuclear forces, French nuclear forces grew substantially during the 1970s, first with the deployment of eighteen new IRBMs, which began in 1971, then with the addition of the short-range Pluton missile in 1974, and finally with the launching of the first four ballistic missile submarines, carrying sixteen submarine-launched ballistic missiles (SLBMs) apiece. NATO's nuclear forces were being improved, but by 1977 the alliance had no formal plans for deploying land-based missiles on the Continent comparable to the Soviet SS-20.

A serious assessment of trends in the nonnuclear military balance between NATO and the Warsaw Pact is too complex to be done here. People not only disagree on what units should be counted and compared: divisions, division equivalents, manpower in divisions, manpower in division slices, tanks, antitank weapons, or firepower in division or in division slices. They also disagree on whose forces should be counted: some exclude French divisions stationed in West Germany, because France is no longer a member of the military organization of NATO; some exclude Moscow's satellite divisions, assuming that Germans will be reluctant to fight Germans, that Poles will be more likely to fight Russians than Germans, and that Czechs will simply not fight at all; and some include only those Soviet divisions stationed in Eastern Europe and in the western military districts of the Soviet Union. The most useful assessments of the nonnuclear balance, like the strategic nuclear balance, attempt to understand how the nonnuclear forces would operate over time in a war. These assessments focus on the effect of different rates of mobilization on the outcome of the war. They also focus on the effect of attrition of manpower and firepower on the course of the battle.[4]

Such assessments are by nature too long to incorporate here. Nevertheless, some general observations are in order. Since August 1968, when the Soviet Union invaded Czechoslovakia, Warsaw Pact manpower has grown substantially, though divisional counts have remained fairly constant. In equipment, Warsaw Pact trends are also worth noting.

4. An informative treatment of this methodology can be found in General Accounting Office, *Models, Data, and War.*

The Warsaw Pact added some 6,000 to 8,000 tanks to its forces in Eastern Europe between 1968 and 1977; however, it retained in its forces old and increasingly obsolescent tanks of 1950s vintage, which could be of only marginal use in combat.[5]

NATO has responded to these developments, although the most important conventional improvements took place after deliberation over LRTNF began in 1977. In large part they were fostered by a debate in the mid-1970s within the alliance over the problem of surprise attack. Reports by retired Lieutenant General J. F. Hollingsworth and Senators Dewey Bartlett and Sam Nunn questioned NATO's ability to respond effectively to a surprise, "bolt out of the blue," Warsaw Pact attack. As a result of the ensuing debate, a U.S. brigade was shifted to the North German plain, new equipment sets for a reinforcement corps were prepositioned, and renewed attention was given to improving deficiencies in rapid reinforcement airlift.[6]

In the course of this debate, political attention focused primarily on the strengths of the Warsaw Pact and the weaknesses of NATO. Whether merited or not—and analyses by Alain C. Enthoven, Robert Lucas Fisher, John Mearsheimer, and Congressman Les Aspin provide some reasons for doubting the gloom-and-doom school—this focus had political implications. It shook NATO's confidence that the alliance had either the basic resources or the political will to compete effectively with the Warsaw Pact on the conventional level. At the same time it eroded the confidence of the allies in America's effectiveness as a leader. Not surprisingly, it also called attention to the trends in the theater nuclear balance, with complex implications for the 1979 LRTNF decision.

Political Trends

Military trends take on a richer meaning in the context of the changing patterns of political power and influence within the alliance. The often

5. This assessment is derived from an examination of the data contained in International Institute for Strategic Studies, *The Military Balance*. See also *Department of Defense Annual Report, Fiscal Year 1980*, pp. 204–05.

6. A good source for the debate, which contains the Hollingsworth report and speeches by Senator Sam Nunn, is *First Concurrent Resolutions on the Budget—Fiscal Year 1978*, Senate Hearings, vol. 1, pp. 197–246. See also Alain C. Enthoven, "U.S. Forces in Europe," pp. 513–32; Robert Lucas Fisher, *Defending the Central Front*; and John J. Mearsheimer, "Why the Soviets Can't Win Quickly in Central Europe," pp. 3–39.

observed weakening of America's political position in NATO—resulting
from the interaction of Vietnam, Watergate, the decline of the dollar,
and the chronic energy crises of the 1970s—is only one part of these
changing patterns. The decline of Britain's influence in alliance politics—
a result primarily of chronic economic problems that eroded the strength
of the British economy within the European Community and within
international trading patterns—also changed the environment in which
the alliance countries operated.

As Britain declined in political influence, West Germany rose.
Throughout the 1970s West Germany was clearly the strongest economy
of Western Europe by almost any indicator—industrial output, gross
national product per capita, employment rate, inflation, balance of trade,
and stability of currency in foreign markets. During this time West
Germany's economic efforts were blessed with relative political stability.
The Social Democrats were in power for the whole decade, with only
one change of leadership, when Helmut Schmidt replaced Willy Brandt
as chancellor in 1974.

Amid this economic strength and political stability West Germany
forged ahead with development of its Bundeswehr, which by the mid-
1970s had reached the legal limit prescribed in the 1954 Paris accords of
12 standing divisions. By general assessment, the West German army
was the premier European army in quality and quantity of men and
matériel. West Germany thus gained perhaps the strongest position of
influence on alliance matters of all the European allies. It did so,
moreover, by explicitly recognizing the need for American leadership of
the alliance.

France had changed a good deal since the heyday of Gaullism in the
mid-1960s. Even though France withdrew from the military organization
of the alliance, its military staffs maintained liaison with NATO staffs.
This sub-rosa cooperation gradually flourished, through the various ups
and downs of Franco-American and Franco-NATO political relations.
Most alliance observers no longer doubted that if general war broke out
between the Warsaw Pact and NATO, French divisions would actively
participate in NATO's defense.

After de Gaulle's death, French political leadership gradually moved
away from the national chauvinism preached and practiced by the
general. Under Georges Pompidou and Valéry Giscard d'Estaing, the
French made special efforts to renew intimacy with their neighbors,
particularly West Germany, and even to a limited extent with the United

States. They no longer used the European unity movement to drive a wedge between Great Britain and the Continent, accepting Britain's second application for European Community membership in 1973. Even though the French remained aloof from the discussions and decisions in NATO relating to concrete security problems, they no longer tried to block important initiatives before the alliance.

As for the smaller members of NATO, their political power and influence within the alliance remained roughly constant during the 1967–77 period; however, they shifted their political attention from initiatives to integrate Europe toward efforts by West Germany and the United States to pursue détente with the Soviet bloc.

These dynamic political trends had complex and significant implications for the United States. No longer could it rely on British influence among the allies to help translate American objectives and concerns into a language comprehensible to the Continent. At the same time West Germany had in some ways replaced Britain in this capacity; the growth of West German power, influence, and self-confidence took place within the context of close U.S.-German relations. But Bonn's new-found position also created a potential for self-assertion, for an increasing impatience with strategic and political dependence on the United States.

The personalities of the situation also influenced these broad political trends. Specifically, beginning in 1974 West Germany was under the vigorous leadership of Helmut Schmidt, a man who has never hesitated to speak his mind on controversial political and strategic issues. He brought to the chancellorship an impressive record of involvement in the security affairs of his country and the alliance: one of the vocal leaders of the opposition in the 1958 nuclear debates, who gradually moved up in the Social Democratic party to become its chief defense spokesman; author of a well-received book that intelligently challenged conventional wisdom about the security problems of the alliance; an occasional participant in the activities of London's International Institute for Strategic Studies, which exposed him to the thinking of men like Alastair Buchan, the founder of the institute, and Denis Healey; and finally defense minister under Chancellor Willy Brandt.

Because of this record, Schmidt believed that his views on national security and alliance defense were not those of a mere politician dabbling in an unfamiliar area. And he was justified in that belief. Given the new role West Germany assumed within the alliance as the 1970s progressed, Washington could hardly afford not to take his views seriously. But

Schmidt's attitude created tensions between the United States and its strongest NATO partner, especially when Schmidt felt that Americans were not taking his opinions into account or were lecturing to him as if to a schoolboy.

Détente

The concept of détente—basically the easing of tensions between East and West—was as much a European concern as an American one. Tensions between the superpowers peaked in October 1962, and a period of relaxation ensued between 1963 and 1968 that produced two important arms-control treaties, the limited test ban and the nonproliferation treaty. Without this relaxation, *Ostpolitik* would have been unlikely. But when Willy Brandt, first as foreign minister and later as chancellor, initiated diplomatic activity with East Germany and the Soviet Union designed to bring to an end more than twenty years of recurring crises over the status of Berlin and the division of Germany, many Germans—and many other Europeans—found their own stakes in détente to be compelling. Détente had a humanitarian side, reuniting German families split for years by the Iron Curtain. It had direct financial benefits in the form of greater East-West trade. It had psychological benefits, gradually reducing the fear that war on the central front was likely. It had strategic benefits, removing some—though not all—of the conflicts of interest that might lead, intentionally or not, to war. Finally, détente offered the possibility—small but too important to ignore—that more contacts between East and West would increase the pressure for liberalization in Eastern Europe. This, in turn, might lay the foundation for a gradual dismantling of East-West divisions, perhaps eventually leading to the reunification of Germany.

While Europe moved beyond initial agreements defining the status of Berlin and the relation between East and West Germany to a broad program of increased economic, political, and cultural ties, the United States pursued détente for somewhat different reasons, and chose other methods to pursue it. One important goal was to stabilize the superpower strategic nuclear relationship. There were many reasons for wanting to do this. The arms competition was costly and added little to each country's security. Yet for the United States merely to take itself out of the competition might make the Soviet leadership miscalculate U.S. resolve in the face of political and military challenges around the globe. For some U.S. officials, the possibility of managing the arms race to enhance technical strategic stability was particularly attractive. A relaxation of tension, which would accompany successful strategic arms limitation talks, would create an atmosphere that would reduce the likelihood of war. Others hoped that SALT could put pressure on the Soviet Union to stop challenging American interests in various parts of the world. Détente in this light became the prerequisite for the politics of linkage.[7]

Since the American pursuit of détente depended heavily on SALT, these negotiations took on a special importance to Europeans. For them, SALT was the essential thing, in the absence of which all the potential perceived benefits from closer political, economic, and cultural ties would be almost impossible to achieve.

In the early 1970s the arms-control approach to détente became more complex when NATO and the Warsaw Pact decided to pursue an agreement to limit the deployment of military forces in the central region of Europe, the mutual and balanced force reduction negotiations. NATO was able to overcome the formidable problem of arriving at a common, coordinated negotiating position, only to find that the talks stalled on the basic issue of data on military deployments in the central region. This disappointment was somewhat mitigated by the surprising political effect of another broad détente negotiation, the Conference on Security and Cooperation in Europe, which arrived at a final agreement endorsing the pursuit of broad humanitarian goals on both sides of the Iron Curtain and, to the dismay of the Kremlin, gave impetus to dissident movements in Eastern Europe and the Soviet Union.

As the difficult process of relaxing political tensions between East and West came to hinge on specific arms-control negotiations, most notably SALT, arms control became a high-priority political issue on the agenda for the West. However much the United States valued arms-control negotiations, European political elites valued them even more, for all the reasons associated with their enthusiasm for détente.

The Prelude to the Schmidt Speech

The first pages of this study examined a speech delivered by West German Chancellor Helmut Schmidt in London in October 1977, which

7. This last view, an interesting if somewhat partisan one, on the potential usefulness of détente can be found in Henry A. Kissinger, *White House Years,* especially pp. 132–33.

by asserting that the superpower strategic arsenals had been neutralized by SALT, and by pointing out the growing imbalance between East and West in long-range theater nuclear weapons, set off the active diplomacy that resulted in NATO's December 1979 decision. Though the Schmidt speech was a catalyst of sorts, it was not the main cause of the initiative. Events had been taking place during the previous three years that had paved the way for the Schmidt speech and provided a receptive environment for the activity it engendered: the development of the cruise missile and its relationship to SALT II during the Ford administration, the Soviet theater nuclear modernization program, the neutron bomb debate, the Carter administration's handling of SALT II, and the leak of Presidential Review Memorandum (PRM) 10.

Cruise Missiles, Kissinger, and SALT II

Most important was the growing interest within defense establishments on both sides of the Atlantic in a new strategic technology, the cruise missile.[8] Actually, the cruise missile—essentially a pilotless aircraft armed with a warhead—was an old idea. The German V-1 missile of World War II was a primitive cruise missile, and the United States and the Soviet Union had each developed many cruise missiles since the war. But owing to technical limitations and the high priority given to the development of ballistic missiles, U.S. interest in cruise missiles waned throughout the 1960s. Interest revived in the early 1970s because of technical developments that promised to make cruise missiles highly effective. Warhead miniaturization had progressed to the point where a sophisticated nuclear warhead could be made small enough to fit into the nose of a small, pilotless aircraft. And jet engine technology had experienced dramatic breakthroughs, pointing to the possibility of building lightweight engines with high thrust and long range that were small enough to fit into a small cruise missile. Perhaps most important, new computer technologies were wedded to guidance systems to form guidance packages capable of periodically updating vehicle location and

8. A good technical introduction to the cruise missile is Kosta Tsipis, "Cruise Missiles," pp. 20–29. For a useful introductory essay on the political and strategic consequences of cruise missiles, see Richard Burt, "The Cruise Missile and Arms Control," pp. 10–17. A particularly good set of essays is found in Richard K. Betts, ed., Cruise Missiles.

of making associated course corrections from preprogrammed flight profiles, all small enough to fit into the nose of the missile. The new cruise missiles would thus be able to fly at low altitudes, avoiding radar detection, and correlate their positions with specific features of the terrain, delivering payloads to targets with virtual pinpoint accuracy. Their small size—some 18 to 20 feet long, and 1.5 to 2.0 feet in diameter— would further complicate enemy efforts to locate them and destroy them in flight. Their relatively low cost would, it was argued, permit procurement in large enough numbers to saturate enemy air defenses, which would also have trouble coping with the small size and low flight path of these new missiles.

In 1973, however, the new cruise missiles were only in early development. Secretary of State Henry Kissinger was reportedly skeptical of the claims being made for this allegedly revolutionary technology.[9] But he saw them as ideal bargaining chips in the ongoing strategic arms limitation talks between the United States and the Soviet Union; that is, the United States could promise to cancel development or deployment of the missiles in exchange for tangible reductions in Soviet strategic force deployments. Accordingly, he pressed successfully for increased funds for cruise missile development.

In doing so, however, Kissinger undercut his own strategy. For the claims being made for the new technology turned out to be substantially correct. As a result, influential groups within the Pentagon, and within the broader U.S. defense community, became committed to the eventual production and deployment of cruise missiles on a large scale. They viewed the cruise missile not as a *bargaining chip* but as a *defense bargain,*[10] and resisted the notion of trading the cruise missile option for any Soviet concessions.

Undoubtedly SALT heightened the visibility of cruise missiles as a defense issue on both sides of the Atlantic. After the Vladivostok summit of November 1974, the Soviets contended that the 2,400 ceiling on strategic nuclear launch vehicles agreed to tentatively at Vladivostok included the American cruise missile. This contention may have been a response to the U.S. position that the Soviet Backfire bomber should be

9. Strobe Talbott, *Endgame,* p. 35.

10. These terms are taken from Robert L. Pfaltzgraff, Jr., and Jacquelyn K. Davis, *The Cruise Missile: Bargaining Chip or Defense Bargain?*

included under the same ceiling. The United States was initially unwilling to accept this Soviet demand but in mid-1977—for reasons discussed below—decided that cruise missiles could be included under certain restrictive arrangements in SALT II. The publicity surrounding these discussions naturally heightened European interest in cruise missiles, particularly because the SALT II negotiations between early 1975 and May 1978 focused on the so-called noncircumvention-nontransfer clauses under consideration. A brief word on the history of this issue will show how directly European interests were being affected by SALT II.[11]

Throughout the early part of SALT I, the Soviets had insisted—not without logic—that any system capable of delivering a nuclear warhead onto Soviet territory, irrespective of its location, was by definition strategic. This definition would have included so-called American forward based systems (FBS) in Europe—nuclear delivery vehicles, primarily aircraft based in Britain and on aircraft carriers in the Mediterranean, capable of striking Soviet territory—as well as U.S. central strategic systems. The Soviets had no comparable FBS. The United States was able to persuade the Soviets to focus solely on ABMs, ICBMs, and SLBMs for the purposes of SALT I. But when SALT II began, the Russians renewed their claim, arguing that the Soviet Union should be allowed an aggregate ceiling as large as the U.S. central systems, FBS, and systems of U.S. allies *combined*. Such a great asymmetry was unacceptable to the United States, which offered a compromise: the United States would insist on equal aggregate ceilings on ICBMs and SLBMs but would not "circumvent" those ceilings by augmenting FBS. At Vladivostok the Russians dropped their insistence on including FBS under aggregate ceilings, but soon thereafter proposed an even more extensive version of the noncircumvention clause, containing a nontransfer provision, apparently designed to tie American hands with respect to the European cruise missile option by requiring the parties "not to transfer strategic offensive arms to other states, and not to assist in their development, in particular, by transferring components, technical descriptions or blueprints for these arms."[12] The United States categorically rejected this provision, and no further progress was made on the issue until the first year of the Carter presidency.

11. The discussion of the nontransfer issue is based on the excellent summary in *SALT and the NATO Allies,* Committee Print, pp. 29–32.
12. Ibid., p. 30.

Nevertheless, many Europeans viewed the nontransfer clause with alarm; they feared generally that the United States would come to an agreement directly affecting European security without enough consideration of its allies' positions, and specifically that the provision would proscribe European access to this new technology that had applications in the theater, specifically interdiction missions currently assigned to tactical air forces based in Europe. The allies continually warned the United States against agreeing to the nontransfer provision; they also had their doubts, frequently expressed to American officials, about the noncircumvention clause as well.

The high visibility of the issue in the context of SALT II drew increasing European attention to the alleged merits of cruise missiles deployed in Europe and to the potential dangers of a SALT II agreement made over the heads of the Europeans that restricted such deployments. Interest was also stimulated by the work of a nongovernmental body of academic experts in Europe and the United States that began to study seriously the various missions for cruise missiles in Europe. This group, known as the European-American Workshop Organizing Committee, included such well-known American experts as Albert Wohlstetter, Henry S. Rowen, James F. Digby, and Thomas Brown; Uwe Nerlich of West Germany's Foundation of Science and Politics at Munich; Johan Jørgen Holst, who was director of research at the Norwegian Institute for International Affairs; and strategic analyst Laurence Martin. The group sponsored a series of workshops and seminars throughout 1975 in Europe and the United States, and in 1977 the papers developed during these conferences were published in a book, *Beyond Nuclear Deterrence*. This widely read volume traced the evolving requirements for improving NATO's flexible response capability and highlighted the importance of the new generation of American cruise missiles for this capability.[13]

To determine the precise degree of influence this group had on subsequent events is difficult. Some have chosen to view it as a "cabal" that stimulated a hitherto nonexistent European interest in cruise missiles. Others have seen the group as a reflection of a growing interest occasioned by other factors, mainly SALT. Certainly other factors were at work, and it would be oversimplistic to view the European-American

13. Johan J. Holst and Uwe Nerlich, eds., *Beyond Nuclear Deterrence*.

Workshop, as some have, as the main force behind the European interest in improving NATO's long-range theater nuclear capability.[14]

Soviet Theater Nuclear Modernization

One factor has already been noted: SALT II seemed to be focusing attention on ways to bring cruise missiles into arms-control arrangements. Another factor was the growth of a new generation of Soviet nuclear weapons aimed at the European theater. In the early 1970s the Soviet Union began to deploy a new medium bomber, known by its NATO code name, Backfire.[15] Debates raged in the U.S. intelligence community over whether the Backfire was capable of performing intercontinental missions. By the late 1970s the consensus had been reached that the new bomber had the capability of performing missions against the continental United States, given certain assumptions about its flight profile. At the same time, however, there was some justification for the Soviet claim that Backfire had been intended only as a theater weapon for deployment against European and Asian targets. The basing, training missions, and technical characteristics of the aircraft all pointed to this conclusion. Eventually, the American insistence on including Backfire under SALT II ceilings was dropped in exchange for the Kremlin's extra-treaty pledge not to change basing or training to make intercontinental missions more feasible. In the process, the debate naturally highlighted Backfire's considerable potential against Europe, a potential that created general European political concern.

In the mid-1970s the Soviet Union also began to improve its theater missile capabilities. In 1976–77 it introduced a new MRBM into its arsenal, the SS-20. This mobile missile, with a range of some 3,000 nautical miles, is MIRVed with three independently targetable nuclear warheads. The missile was evidently intended to replace the aging SS-4 and SS-5 IRBMs that had been targeted against NATO Europe, though, as many observers noted, it did not change Europe's long-standing vulnerability to theater nuclear forces in the Soviet Union. But NATO had no directly comparable capability; for those who worried about the

14. Fred Kaplan tends to view it in this way in an otherwise informative account, "Warring over New Missiles for NATO," pp. 46 ff.

15. For the technical characteristics of the Backfire, see John W. R. Taylor, ed., *Jane's All the World's Aircraft: 1979–1980*, pp. 212–13.

political implications of an absence of theater parity in the arsenals of the two blocs, the SS-20 required some sort of response.

The Neutron Bomb Debate

The issue of the enhanced radiation warhead, or neutron bomb, dates back to a review of the U.S. tactical nuclear weapons posture during James Schlesinger's tenure as secretary of defense from 1973 to 1975. One result of the review was a comprehensive report to Congress, detailing the disposition, rationale, strengths, and weaknesses of the U.S. tactical nuclear stockpile.[16] Another result was a decision, foreshadowed by more than a decade of discussion, to proceed with "cleaning up" some of the warheads in this arsenal. In 1973 the Pentagon found that the nuclear weapons stationed in Europe as part of the tactical nuclear stockpile were "dirty"—that is, rather high-yield devices that had a high fission-fusion ratio and that upon detonation would probably produce high levels of long-term radioactivity, blast, and fallout. As such, they were likely to cause substantial collateral damage to civilian populations and were too powerful to use in a "discriminate" way against enemy military forces. Since 1958 a group of weapon designers, led by S. T. Cohen, had been arguing that low-yield, clean weapons could be developed that could minimize blast and long-term radiation, releasing more of their energy in the form of fast, lethal neutrons almost immediately on detonation. Secretary of Defense McNamara and his colleagues had resisted the idea largely because of cost and skepticism about being able to maintain a limited tactical nuclear engagement without quick escalation to general strategic war. Schlesinger was more receptive: the idea fit into his attempt to develop a posture that could enhance control of nuclear escalation; he disagreed with those who claimed that such weapons, by making a nuclear war more fightable, would make policymakers more willing to take the risks associated with initiating nuclear war.

Accordingly, Schlesinger approved the cleaning up of the tactical nuclear stockpile, and work on the new warheads for deployment on Lance missiles and artillery shells proceeded. By 1977, when the Carter administration took office, this development work was essentially complete. President Carter and Secretary of Defense Harold Brown contin-

16. Department of Defense, *The Theater Nuclear Force Posture in Europe.*

ued funding for the warheads; as far as can be determined, this was not considered at the time an important decision.

In June 1977, however, Walter Pincus of the *Washington Post* took notice of the budget item for these warheads and, after investigating the matter, published an article in which he described the ongoing program.[17] This press coverage touched off an emotional debate at home and abroad over the merits of the new warheads, which were quickly dubbed neutron bombs because of their enhanced neutron flux.[18] In the United States, opponents claimed variously that the weapons were immoral, in that they were specifically antipersonnel; that they fostered the illusion that a tactical nuclear battle was fightable in the traditional sense of the term; that they would be prone to escalatory pressure like other tactical nuclear weapons; that they would make political leaders less reluctant to cross the threshold between conventional and nuclear operations in time of war; and that, even if the technical claims for the weapons were correct, they would have to be applied in such quantity to affect the course of battle that their use would have the same effect as the older weapons.[19] Proponents countered that the weapons were no more immoral than any other horrible weapon, either conventional or nuclear, in the NATO arsenal; that they would permit a degree of discrimination and control that could help limit escalation, hence making the threat to use them more credible; and that their technical characteristics would make them ideal for use against ground units, both armored and infantry.[20]

In Europe the debate was even more heated, especially in the Netherlands and in West Germany, where the bulk of the new warheads would be deployed. Opponents highlighted the "immoral" nature of the warheads, which would "kill people but spare buildings." They also claimed that these weapons would make nuclear war in Europe more thinkable and increase the likelihood of the destruction of West German

17. *Washington Post,* June 6, 1977.

18. Two excellent descriptions of the technical basis for the enhanced radiation weapon exist: Fred M. Kaplan, "Enhanced-Radiation Weapons," pp. 44–51; and Walter Sullivan, "Neutron Bomb Is a Modification of H-Bomb with a Smaller Blast," *New York Times,* June 27, 1980. A recent comprehensive treatment can be found in Milton Leitenberg, "The Neutron Bomb—Enhanced Radiation Warheads," pp. 341–69.

19. Kaplan, "Enhanced-Radiation Weapons."

20. Sam Cohen is perhaps the most vocal of the proponents. See S. T. Cohen, "Enhanced Radiation Warheads," pp. 9–17; and Brigadier General Edwin F. Black and S. T. Cohen, "The Neutron Bomb and the Defense of NATO," pp. 53–61.

society. Here the lingering memories of the Carte Blanche exercise in 1955 influenced the debates, even though, as its proponents observed, neutron bombs were intended to make outcomes like Carte Blanche less likely. The Soviets weighed in heavily on the side of the opponents, derisively terming these weapons "the capitalist bombs." The Soviets' massive propaganda campaign was particularly influential with the left wing of the ruling West German Social Democratic party, headed by Herbert Wehner and Egon Bahr, who led a spirited fight against the weapons in the Bundestag.[21]

Faced with this opposition and subject to an increasingly volatile and emotional public debate over the issue, Schmidt had little room to maneuver. Reportedly he had no strong feelings one way or the other about the new weapons. It was also the first year of the Carter presidency; even though the chancellor had begun to doubt the new president's ability to lead the alliance, he was still reluctant to force a confrontation with Carter. If Carter insisted on deploying neutron bombs in West Germany, Schmidt would ultimately agree, providing that other European partners would join him, but for obvious political reasons he was in no position to petition for these weapons. Yet Carter, faced with the increasingly volatile domestic and foreign debate, now made this petition a *condition* for a positive U.S. production decision. And at the same time Schmidt began to get pressure from the United States—especially from the Defense Department—to put forward this request. Schmidt could not help feeling that American plans for developing, producing, and deploying these weapons had been made without detailed consultation—though the matter had been taken up in a general way in the NATO Nuclear Planning Group.[22]

The Carter Administration and SALT II

By October 1977, then, Schmidt faced mounting pressure from American officials to take the politically unpalatable position of asking for these new weapons. This alone would have placed strains on the U.S.-German relationship. But other factors were at work to exacerbate the growing tensions. One was the continuing effort of the Carter

21. For a sampling of this debate, see Theo Sommer, "The Neutron Bomb," pp. 263–66.

22. *New York Times,* April 8 and 9, 1978.

administration to hammer out an agreement on SALT II. In March 1977 the administration's dramatic comprehensive proposal, a substantial departure from what had tentatively been agreed to at Vladivostok, was summarily rejected by the Soviet Union. In the subsequent American effort to get the talks back on track, Leslie Gelb, then director of the State Department's Bureau of Politico-Military Affairs, and William Hyland, a specialist on Soviet affairs in the National Security Council, worked out a formula for rescuing the negotiations. They came up with a three-tiered approach. The first tier, the formal SALT II treaty, would expire at the end of 1985 and would place Vladivostok-type limits on the central strategic systems of the superpowers. The second tier was a shorter-duration protocol to the treaty, which would place constraints on cruise missile development and deployment through 1981. The third tier was an agreed statement of principles to guide the agenda for subsequent SALT discussions.

The timing of the press leaks of this development raised suspicions that the United States was intent on foreclosing the European cruise missile option in exchange for a speedy SALT agreement. A central concern was the issue of the extension of the protocol. True, the protocol would be in effect only through the end of 1981, during which time cruise missiles would not be technically ready for deployment. But fears were raised on both sides of the Atlantic, particularly in the increasingly feverish U.S. debate over SALT II, that the protocol would be extended past the date when cruise missiles were fully ready for deployment, hence depriving NATO of its cruise missile option. As in many past cases already examined, it is hard to know where these fears first arose— from Americans eager to multiply potential objections to the treaty, or from Europeans who feared the foreclosing of this option without consultation. In the end, though, both groups shared the concern, in spite of repeated U.S. government statements that extension of the protocol would not be automatic and would take into account both the full range of opinion within the United States and the alliance and the trends in Soviet activities.

In the early summer of 1977 European interest in cruise missiles peaked—no doubt stimulated by rumors of the protocol—and the United States received several requests from European governments for a detailed briefing on these new systems. Up till then, the United States had limited discussions of cruise missiles with the allies to SALT briefings and even then had touched only casually on the capabilities and missions

MODERNIZATION AND ARMS CONTROL

of these weapons. In Washington cruise missiles were seen strictly as central strategic systems and solely in the context of SALT II. According to some participants, the United States may have even been reluctant to brief the Europeans fully on this missile for fear of stimulating their interest and further complicating SALT II.[23]

In any case, by the summer of 1977 Washington felt it had little choice but to respond to these direct European requests. Officials in the State Department, under Gelb's direction, drafted a briefing paper on the political, military, and arms-control aspects of the cruise missile. When this draft circulated to other agencies for comment, it created a big interagency fight. The Defense Department argued strongly that the substance should be narrowly technical and that the briefing should be delivered to the Nuclear Planning Group by Defense officials. State's position was that the issues had broad and critical political implications and that State should be the agency to brief not the NPG but the North Atlantic Council. In the end, State won the task of giving the briefing, and Gelb led an interagency delegation to the North Atlantic Council for this purpose. The content of the briefing, however, was a hodgepodge of State and Defense positions and had little direction and focus. The result was that the Europeans felt they were being stalled while the United States gained time to trade away cruise missiles in SALT II. According to at least one official, this briefing raised suspicions about American intentions that were to plague the entire subsequent process of arriving at a decision on the LRTNF.[24]

In another attempt to breathe life into the stalled strategic arms limitation talks, the administration took up the noncircumvention problem once again, this time bringing before the North Atlantic Council a proposal to have the Soviets drop their insistence on nontransfer in exchange for a general statement on noncircumvention. Two versions of this proposal were discussed, the second to be put forth as a fallback if the first was rejected:

23. The following description of U.S. government and alliance deliberations leading to the December 1979 decision is derived from in-depth interviews with government officials, who talked to the author on condition that their statements not be attributed to them. These data have been used cautiously and include only those pieces of information that can be corroborated through other sources, either published works or interviews.

24. Interview material. See also Library of Congress, Congressional Research Service, "The Modernization of NATO's Long-Range Theater Nuclear Forces."

In order to ensure the viability and effectiveness of this Treaty, each Party undertakes not to circumvent the provisions of this treaty.

[Fallback] In order to ensure the viability and effectiveness of this Treaty, each Party undertakes not to circumvent the provisions of this Treaty, through any other state or states, or in any other manner.[25]

The allies approved the U.S. pursuit of the first provision; if the Soviets rejected it and refused to alter their demands for a nontransfer clause, the United States should return to the North Atlantic Council for consultation over the second version. The clause "through any other state or states" in the second version, while more likely to gain Soviet withdrawal of its stringent nontransfer clause, might prove to have the same effect as the nontransfer clause—although the United States insisted that even the second version merely reaffirmed the obligations incumbent upon each party to any international agreement. In August 1977 the United States tabled the first version; throughout the fall and winter there was considerable anxiety in Europe over the possibility of Soviet rejection.

The tensions within the alliance over noncircumvention-nontransfer, already evident by the time of the Schmidt speech, continued to play a role in intra-alliance politics well after October 1977. In January 1978 the Soviets rejected the August 1977 U.S. proposal. In February the United States returned to the North Atlantic Council to discuss tabling of the second, more restrictive version. European members expressed considerable concern that the version would amount to nothing more than a nontransfer clause in disguise. The United States insisted that the clause would leave open all the more relevant options for long-range theater nuclear force modernization then being considered by the alliance; to obtain council approval, the United States gave assurances that it would make a statement offering a unilateral interpretation of the clause after its adoption, stressing that such modernization would be permitted under the terms of the treaty. In April the United States and the Soviet Union agreed to use the fallback version of the noncircumvention clause in exchange for Soviet withdrawal of its nontransfer demands. During these April discussions, the United States developed this interpretative statement in consultation with the European allies, in particular West Germany, which took a special interest in the terms of the statement. When SALT II was initialed in June 1979, the allies were finally convinced that the United States had traded away neither its

25. *SALT and the NATO Allies*, p. 30.

option to deploy cruise missiles in Europe after the expiration of the protocol nor the options for future trans-Atlantic defense cooperation in a wide range of areas. But for almost two years the noncircumvention-nontransfer issue, like the protocol, increased the tension of intra-alliance discussions and put pressure on the alliance to come to an agreement on long-range theater modernization.

Presidential Review Memorandum 10

In early August 1977 another press leak from Washington confirmed the growing impression in Bonn that Carter and his aides were insensitive to the political-strategic problems facing West Germany. This time the leak purported to describe the conclusions of a recently completed interagency review of U.S. defense policy, Presidential Review Memorandum 10. This document allegedly advocated that NATO should accept the Weser-Lech line as its main line of defense. Doing so would, in effect, concede about one-third of West German territory in the event of a Warsaw Pact attack.[26]

The administration immediately denied that PRM 10 contained any such recommendation. According to several of those who drafted the memorandum, it used the Weser-Lech line purely as a notional line of defense to generate planning requirements for conventional defense and in no way advocated a fallback to the Weser-Lech as an operational strategy—although top officials may have informally observed that defense along this line was possible.

Immediately after the leak, Secretary of Defense Harold Brown testified that he would oppose any shift in NATO strategy and posture from the forward-defense concept, thus repudiating the notion of a fallback to the Weser-Lech. But these assurances rang somewhat hollow in Europe, since the press leak also reported that high-level sources recommended that U.S. officials should not publicly withdraw support from the forward-defense concept, even though plans might change, because of the political consequences to the allies of such a shift. Publicly, Schmidt and his European colleagues were silent over this particular leak, apparently accepting Brown's assurances; privately, they were furious, and none more than Schmidt. Forward defense, that is, defense at the interbloc border, was the cornerstone of West German

26. *Washington Post,* August 3, 4, 5, and 8, 1977.

defense policy; as seen earlier, controversy over forward defense brought U.S.-German relations to a mini-crisis during the 1961 Berlin crisis. For Schmidt, the fact that top American officials called forward defense into question privately, without consultation with their West German counterparts, must have seemed incredibly insensitive; to have these discussions leaked to the press compounded insensitivity with indiscretion.

The Schmidt Speech, October 1977

In this way, then, a breach in U.S.-German relations was rapidly approaching, with dire implications for the rest of NATO as well. Schmidt had held his silence through the first nine months of the Carter administration, though privately he was known to question the seriousness and even the competence of the new American leadership. Indeed, he later claimed to have made some of his concerns known in a speech to the NATO summit meeting in May 1977.[27] He took the occasion of a speech to London's International Institute for Strategic Studies, in memory of Alastair Buchan, a friend of Schmidt's from the time Schmidt was defense expert for the Social Democratic party, to publicly air the fears aroused by recent events.[28] That he chose to voice his general concerns in the form of the particular issue of the theater nuclear balance in Europe probably reflects not only his worries about the political effect of the continuing deployment of the SS-20 but also the ideas of his closest defense adviser, Walther Stutzle. Stutzle had been following the debate on the European cruise missile option in some detail and had been impressed with the strategic rationale for LRTNF improvements in Europe. In any case, Schmidt's message was direct:

SALT neutralizes [the superpowers'] strategic nuclear capabilities. In Europe, this magnifies the significance of the disparities between East and West in nuclear tactical and conventional weapons. . . . It is of vital interest to us all that the negotiations between the two superpowers on the limitation and reduction of nuclear strategic weapons should continue and lead to a lasting agreement. The nuclear powers have a special, an overwhelming responsibility in this field. On

27. "Remarks by Chancellor Helmut Schmidt," pp. 177–78. I am indebted to Catherine Kelleher and Jorg Baldauf for calling my attention to this speech.
28. Helmut Schmidt, "The 1977 Alastair Buchan Memorial Lecture," pp. 2–10.

the other hand, we in Europe must be particularly careful to ensure that these negotiations do not neglect the components of NATO's deterrence strategy.

We are all faced with the dilemma of having to meet the moral and political demand for arms limitation while at the same time maintaining a fully effective deterrent to war. We are not unaware that both the United States and the Soviet Union must be anxious to remove the threatening strategic developments from their relationship. But strategic arms limitations confined to the United States and the Soviet Union will inevitably impair the security of the West European members of the Alliance *vis-à-vis* Soviet military superiority in Europe if we do not succeed in removing the disparities of military power in Europe parallel to the SALT negotiations. So long as this is not the case we must maintain the balance of the full range of deterrence strategy. The Alliance must, therefore, be ready to make available the means to support its present strategy, which is still the right one, and to prevent any developments that could undermine the basis of this strategy.[29]

To Americans, the most important statement here was that "strategic arms limitations confined to the United States and the Soviet Union will inevitably impair the security of the West European members of the Alliance *vis-à-vis* Soviet military superiority in Europe if we do not succeed in removing the disparities of military power in Europe parallel to the SALT negotiations." What this statement implied, in contrast to NATO policy over the previous twenty years, was that somehow the balance of military forces in the European theater could be considered separately from the overall military balance between the two blocs. By implication, therefore, the statement seemed to be questioning the ability of U.S. forces outside the theater—especially the strategic nuclear forces—to deter conflict in Europe and expressing the fear that parity achieved in strategic nuclear arsenals through SALT might make the theater nuclear balance, the so-called Eurostrategic balance, more important. Finally, it seemed to be a call for the rectification of existing theater imbalances; one of the most obvious of these was the growing imbalance of forces in the LRTNF category, highlighted by deployment of the SS-20 with no response from the West.

But did Schmidt really intend to call the U.S. strategic nuclear guarantee into question? Did he intend to direct attention to the rectification of the Eurostrategic balance? Were his words meant to elicit a strong American response?

These are difficult questions to answer. Some have claimed that Schmidt subsequently regretted having voiced his displeasure over U.S.

29. Ibid., pp. 3–4.

European policy in this way, that he had not intended to call the strategic guarantee into question. This seems plausible. Schmidt had often challenged the Gaullist position on the lack of America's strategic credibility; he had opposed heavy reliance on tactical nuclear response to conventional Warsaw Pact aggression and had continued to support McNamara's flexible response proposal with its emphasis on supplying NATO with a serious conventional option. These positions do not suggest that he was overconcerned about an LRTNF imbalance in Europe.[30]

More likely Schmidt did not intend his message as a challenge to U.S. strategic policy. Rather, he was increasingly worried about the lack of political sensitivity and coherent political direction with which the United States was pursuing its policy toward the alliance. And what was often forgotten, Schmidt had also mentioned in his speech the need to pursue arms control of theater nuclear forces as well as to modernize them. Moreover, close observers of Schmidt have often noted his tendency to go on a verbal rampage when frustrated or angered; he did so during the 1958 Bundestag debate on the arming of the Bundeswehr with nuclear weapons and subsequently regretted his incautious rhetoric. This side of Schmidt's personality may partly explain the October 1977 speech. And finally, as noted, some of his close defense advisers, particularly Stutzle, were increasingly convinced of the political and military need to modernize NATO's LRTNF. With rumors circulating that Carter's SALT II negotiating position might constrain NATO's freedom to do so, these advisers might have seen the Buchan memorial address as a well-timed opportunity to raise this issue within the context of Schmidt's growing concern about the general course of U.S. policy toward Europe.

The Reaction to the Schmidt Speech

All this must remain speculative, however, as must the reasons behind the response to the speech in Washington. Within the U.S. government the speech served to catalyze activity toward exploring ways to rectify the imbalance highlighted by Schmidt. According to one participant in the U.S. decisionmaking at the time, before the October speech many U.S. officials had hoped that the general fears in Europe raised by the deployment of the SS-20 could be handled quietly, without resort to

30. See, for example, Helmut Schmidt, *Defense or Retaliation*.

hardware, through discussions in the Nuclear Planning Group; but they felt that the Schmidt speech, with all the publicity surrounding it, effectively foreclosed that option. Exactly why is unclear. In any event, the U.S. government made no high-level attempt to challenge Schmidt's premises or conclusions. Just as the State Department had reacted to the statements by Strauss on the MLF, much of the U.S. bureaucracy decided that the German concerns had some merit and that the best course of action would be to deal with them on their own terms.

The High Level Group

This attitude was reflected in the activity of the Defense Department over the next few months. In early October 1977 the Nuclear Planning Group, at American instigation, created a so-called High Level Group (HLG) of allied foreign and defense ministry representatives to carry out the assignment of "Task Force 10" in the long-term defense plan. The latter was an American sponsored plan, presented in May 1977, that called for across-the-board buildups in NATO defense capabilities. One of the designated areas of improvement was nuclear weapons. Task Force 10 was supposed to study problems in this area and recommend improvements. Its mission was quickly taken out of the NPG's hands; some in the Pentagon suggested this move deliberately, having been disappointed by the NPG's failure to foresee the crisis the neutron bomb would create in European governments. While not necessarily agreeing that the NPG staff group had failed to foresee the controversy over the neutron bomb, others, in both the United States and Europe, concurred with the Pentagon's desire to create a group of individuals who had access to key political figures in their own countries *and* who had operational responsibility for defense planning within their governments. The High Level Group fitted the bill.[31]

The HLG first met soon after the Schmidt speech, in December 1977, with David E. McGiffert, assistant secretary of defense for ISA, as chairman. This meeting consisted of briefings and discussions on NATO doctrine, NATO nuclear capabilities, and Warsaw Pact nuclear capabilities. The SS-20 was discussed, but only as part of the panoply of Soviet

31. Interview material. See also Stephen R. Hanmer, Jr., "NATO's Long-Range Theatre Nuclear Forces," pp. 3–6. The HLG was, however, formally a creation of the NPG and reported to the NPG ministers.

nuclear assets directed at NATO. American officials returned from the meeting feeling that a consensus could be reached on what needed to be done about theater nuclear force modernization. At the Pentagon, ISA officials and others developed an option paper for presentation to the next meeting of the HLG. It described four alternative ways to deal with LRTNF modernization:

—do nothing;

—build a serious battlefield nuclear capability for the theater, without the capability to strike targets in the Soviet Union;

—make a modest improvement in long-range theater nuclear weapons;

—develop a theater capability to wage a counterforce and counter-value strategic nuclear war against the Soviet Union.

At another meeting in February 1978 the HLG examined these options in a freewheeling general discussion, made more candid by the agreement that the opinions of its members were not formally binding on the participating countries. The first option was dismissed because of the perceived political need to respond to SS-20 deployments and to make sure that SALT II would not constrain the European cruise missile option. The second was dropped because of European reluctance to adopt a serious nuclear battlefield capability, with its terrible conse-quences for European societies, and because of general agreement that new weapons should be able to strike the Soviet Union. One American participant recalls the comment from a European: "The Poles are not enemies, they are victims."[32] The fourth option was dismissed out of hand, because its creation could imply the decoupling of American central strategic forces from the defense of Europe. This left the third option, which was attractive for several reasons:

—It would not raise the specter of decoupling.

—At the same time it would be a visible response to Soviet SS-20 deployments.

—It was the least provocative of the three action options and hence most acceptable to the elites in domestic settings that favored the pursuit of détente.

However, the HLG agreed that this modest, evolutionary upward adjustment in NATO's long-range theater nuclear capabilities should include the ability to strike targets in the Soviet Union, thus combining elements of the third and fourth options.

So by March 1978 McGiffert had led the group to an important

32. Interview material.

consensus: LRTNF modernization was necessary; it should be an evolutionary upward adjustment; and it should endow NATO with an enhanced capability to strike targets in the Soviet Union.

During this period West German officials began to argue that, though they agreed in principle on the need for modernized LRTNF for deployment in West Germany, they were not willing to have the weapons deployed under dual-key arrangements in their own armed forces. They held this position throughout the talks, much to the surprise of those who feared that demands for control sharing would inevitably follow from LRTNF modernization and would create another MLF kind of dilemma for the alliance. Bonn apparently felt, and still feels, that to deploy these new systems under dual-key arrangements within the national armed forces would make West Germany's quasi-independent pursuit of détente with the East insupportable.

The Debate in Washington

During this same period long-range theater nuclear forces were also on the minds of officials on the National Security Council staff and in the State Department. Informal discussions and study gradually led to the development of a strategic rationale for new LRTNF deployments that, while slightly different from the one suggested by Schmidt, caused these officials to support further investigation into options for modernizing LRTNF. The rationale accepted as premises both the credibility of the American nuclear guarantee and the fundamental soundness of NATO's flexible response strategy.

One political argument for modernization was the serious potential problem of political perceptions arising from the growing disparity between the Warsaw Pact and NATO in LRTNF. The Soviet Union was busily upgrading its own LRTNF in Europe, yet NATO was involved in no comparable modernization program. This situation, if not rectified, could signal to Moscow that the alliance lacked the resolve to compete effectively with the Pact in peacetime and to commit the necessary resources for its own defense. Moreover, such a signal would weaken U.S. leadership in the alliance, by leaving open to question Washington's political will to lead the alliance effectively in countering the new Soviet deployments. As seen, this particular problem had already been worsened by various inconsistencies in President Carter's policy to date. The time had come to send a strong message both to the Kremlin and to European capitals that the United States had the resolve, strength, and sense of purpose to lead the alliance to maintain parity with the Warsaw Pact across the spectrum of the military balance.

A second political argument had to do with SALT II. Within the State Department, SALT II had top priority during this period, and one of the most important tasks the department faced was to convince the allies of the merit of these negotiations. If LRTNF modernization was needed to persuade the allies that the United States was sensitive to European security issues and that it was not ready to bargain away their interests in SALT II, then LRTNF modernization was worth pursuing.

A third argument for LRTNF was more military, centering on the implications of force disparity for NATO's ability to pursue its flexible response strategy. As noted in chapter 6, NATO had finally chosen a flexible response strategy based on the explicit threat of escalation should NATO's attempts to counter aggression on a given level fail. If Soviet SS-20 and Backfire deployments continued unabated, with no Western response in kind, the alliance would face a serious gap in the "continuum of deterrence." As a Senate Foreign Relations Committee staff report in 1978 explained:

This concept, which assumes that nuclear weapons could be introduced into a European conflict in such a way as to control the escalation of their use, arises from the precept that NATO should have a progressive series of responses, or "rungs," constituting a "ladder" of nuclear escalation options, with each level adapted to specific situations and uses. According to NATO planners, the Alliance deterrent is missing a "rung" because it lacks an adequate component of weapons capable of striking Soviet targets without engaging Western systems normally considered strategic.

They argue that if, for example, a NATO commander should want to use only one or two warheads against Soviet territory—as a signal of intent as well as a military response—he could be inhibited by the present structure of NATO nuclear forces. Attacking Soviet targets with bombers or fighter bombers, they point out, would be slow and possibly ineffective because of improving Soviet air defenses. Alternatively, a decision to use only a single SLBM would not only involve fourteen relatively inaccurate warheads: it could also be impeded by a U.S. president hesitant to risk the Soviet counterstrike against U.S. territory which might result from the use of a "strategic" weapon.

To NATO analysts, the question is one of credibility; and to answer it they seek an increment in theater nuclear forces which, by demonstrating Western resolve to respond to Soviet theater improvements and by filling the long-noted "gap" with new nuclear options, will reinforce Soviet perceptions of the Alliance deterrent.[33]

33. *SALT and the NATO Allies*, p. 19.

At first, some at the NSC staff and elsewhere were reluctant to accept this argument. Did it not imply, they wondered, that such a capability might make it more conceivable to confine a nuclear war to the European continent? Would not this be tantamount to decoupling? Whatever doubts these questions might have raised were set aside in subsequent discussions with the allies and particularly with the West Germans, who saw the addition of a modernized LRTNF rung to NATO's escalation ladder as making the threat of strategic retaliation even more credible; otherwise, they argued, escalation may stop at the battlefield nuclear level, since the next step—central strategic war—would seem too awesome a step to take, with apocalyptic consequences.

Within the bureaucracy, arguments against new LRTNF deployments were being voiced as well.[34] First, it was at best uncertain that the Soviet Union would choose a level of nuclear response based on the location from which an enemy weapon was launched rather than on the target that the enemy weapon hit. Strikes against Soviet territory would probably lead directly to central strategic war, irrespective of the location from which those strikes may have been launched. Second, even if the Soviets were sensitive to the political and strategic signals of the modernized LRTNF, they might not be technically capable of determining the launch point of a weapon quickly enough to respond in an appropriately limited way. Third, U.S. central strategic systems had evolved with the flexibility of command and control and targeting to launch limited (or selective) strikes against Soviet territory, largely because the president (and NATO) required options other than conventional war, tactical nuclear engagements, or massive countervalue strategic exchanges. To many observers, this flexibility of targeting and command already provided the West with the capability to plug the gap in the continuum of deterrence. Moreover, the evolution of the U.S. central strategic systems had made possible a highly coordinated U.S. war plan that was integrated with SACEUR's target list and nuclear strike requirements. But additional forces in the theater might not be subject to the same centralization of command and reliability of control, especially since a strong conventional attack might overrun these weapons, forcing the West to "use them or lose them." Thus modernized LRTNF might be not only redundant but also destabilizing.

The military rationale for modernized LRTNF was also not convincing

34. Interview material.

to some who emphasized the conventional elements of flexible response. If NATO had a strong enough conventional option, these people argued, the *Soviets* would have to decide whether or not to escalate to the nuclear level; and they would always be uncertain about the West's response. The prudent Soviet planner could never be sure that the West would hesitate to use its strategic nuclear capability, especially since that capability was flexible and discriminate enough to carry out a no-cities option if so desired. This line of argument naturally led to a discounting of the alleged weakness of NATO's overall deterrent despite Soviet SS-20 and Backfire deployments.

A further anticipated problem led some to doubt the wisdom of LRTNF modernization. If the Europeans—primarily the West Germans—desired new LRTNF because of fear that the United States would lack the political will to engage the Soviet Union in strategic war in defense of Europe, they would probably insist at some point on a share of operational control over the new weapons deployed in Europe. This had certainly been West Germany's position on such deployment in the mid-1960s, during the Norstad MRBM and the MLF initiatives. If such a phenomenon recurred, many anticipated a replay of the fruitless control-sharing debates examined in previous chapters. No one—particularly those in the United States who had lived through that period—was eager to go through the debate again. Furthermore, control sharing would create significant arms-control problems; principally it would undermine U.S. efforts to keep U.S.-Soviet negotiations bilateral.

There were also questions about whether SS-20 and Backfire deployments fundamentally changed the threat facing Western Europe. True, it was conceded, the SS-20 was mobile, MIRVed, and accurate, an impressive qualitative improvement over the SS-4 MRBM and SS-5 IRBM, which had confronted Europe for almost two decades. Equally true, the Backfire represented a qualitative improvement over the aged Badger and Blinder aircraft deployed against Europe during the same period. But Europe had been vulnerable to more than 600 MRBMs and IRBMs and more than 400 medium-range nuclear bombers, not to mention intercontinental-range forces that might be used against Europe, for quite some time. Was there a pressing need for responding dramatically to what some perceived as an evolutionary development?

Finally, it was argued that if the intent of the initiative was to reduce the threat to Europe posed by the SS-20 and Backfire, then the weapons deployed should be able to target and destroy these systems. But the

SS-20, once moved out of its storage facility, would be difficult to target with any missile system, and Backfires at air fields could be knocked out with the existing inventory of strategic nuclear forces. In fact, SALT II ceilings were likely to be high enough to permit extensive target coverage of military sites in Eastern Europe and the Soviet Union without recourse to new systems based on the Continent. Such systems as submarine-launched ballistic missiles would have the added advantage of being less vulnerable to attack from enemy forces than LRTNF. In sum, the military justification for deployments of new long-range theater nuclear weapons on the Continent seemed open to question.

The Prelude to Decision

From October 1977 to April 1978 these various arguments were considered by officials in the State Department and the National Security Council.[35] Although the Defense Department was pursuing modernization through its leadership in the High Level Group, there was not an interagency consensus on this policy, partly because of the unsettled debate and partly because of a reluctance to undertake another inter-agency review of a big defense issue so soon after the fiasco of PRM 10. In fact, when the NSC staff learned of the deliberations of the HLG, it determined to put its own representative on the U.S. delegation to slow up HLG discussions until the interagency bureaucracy had time to develop a consensus on LRTNF modernization.

The Neutron Bomb Debacle

But in April 1978 President Carter decided, for reasons that may never be fully understood, to postpone production of the neutron bomb, just when the Defense Department had succeeded in getting West Germany to agree to ask for the weapon if other European countries followed suit. Schmidt had finally prevailed over the left wing of his party, though at considerable political cost. Now the president had effectively pulled the rug out from under Schmidt and the Pentagon.

It would be difficult to overstate the effect that Carter's decision had in Europe. Despite considerable public opposition, West European

35. Most of this section is based on interviews.

governments seemed willing to follow the American lead on the neutron bomb issue, and had agreed to put themselves in the politically dangerous position of *demandeur,* because the United States, as leader of the alliance, had apparently decided that this was necessary. But in April Carter had suddenly, without consultation, reversed his position. In Europe the embarrassing question was raised: why should the alliance follow the leadership of a government so obviously unable to define a direction for alliance policy?

In Washington officials resolved to reaffirm American leadership in the strongest way possible. The Defense Department had been convinced of the need to proceed with LRTNF modernization ever since the February 1978 HLG consensus. Now others, particularly at State, shared this belief. As one participant noted, the neutron bomb episode might have left the Soviet Union—and the allies—with the impression that the Kremlin had a veto over NATO deployments. This impression had to be reversed. LRTNF modernization would now become the issue on which the United States would demonstrate firm leadership; within the government, doubts began to take on secondary importance.

PRM 38

The first manifestation of this new determination was the sudden willingness of the bureaucracy to examine the LRTNF issue in a formal interagency setting. By June 1978 President Carter had issued, at the recommendation of the NSC staff, a broad interagency directive, Presidential Review Memorandum 38 (PRM 38), entitled "Long Range Theater Nuclear Capabilities and Arms Control," to generate an interagency study on the implications of new LRTNF for the NATO–Warsaw Pact military balance and on the arms-control implications of new LRTNF deployments. The State Department was charged with the section giving an overview and history of the issues to date; this work was carried on by Gelb and his staff at the Bureau of Politico-Military Affairs. The Defense Department, under the guidance of David McGiffert and his staff, was charged with presenting the military rationale for deployment and deployment packages. The Arms Control and Disarmament Agency was to study the implications for arms control and to identify options for inclusion of LRTNF in arms-control discussions. The CIA was to assess the evolving Soviet LRTNF threat and its implications for possible NATO responses. The NSC staff was responsible for coordinating these efforts and for generating an executive summary for consideration by the Special Coordinating Committee of the National Security Council, consisting of the president, the secretaries of defense and state, the director of central intelligence, and the president's national security adviser.

Throughout June and July this work was carried out in the individual agencies; in late August a series of meetings between National Security Adviser Zbigniew Brzezinski's deputy, David Aaron, Gelb, and McGiffert (along with various aides) coordinated the work. By October the meetings had resulted in a general consensus:

—The role of U.S. central strategic forces in alliance defense required no revision.

—There were both political and military needs for the new LRTNF deployments in NATO, for the reasons outlined in the previous section.

—Any arms-control efforts to limit Soviet SS-20 and Backfire deployments would probably not succeed unless NATO demonstrated its willingness to modernize its LRTNF.

—The United States should support the High Level Group, which was moving toward recommending an LRTNF deployment option for NATO.

In interagency discussions, and in subsequent papers generated from HLG deliberations, the notion of trying to establish a theater balance or a Eurostrategic balance was rejected, since it would raise European doubts about the credibility of the American strategic nuclear guarantee—an issue that U.S. officials were intent to avoid as far as possible.

To summarize, the rationale that began to take shape in early 1978 in the United States, and that found further development during these summer months, was threefold:

—It was necessary to modernize aging NATO long-range theater nuclear forces; failure to do so would have negative practical political consequences for the alliance.

—LRTNF would serve to bolster the alliance's capability for limited nuclear options.

—Without a decision to modernize LRTNF, the West would be unable to bring theater deployments under arms-control arrangements.

HLG Deliberations

Once this consensus had been reached and a response to PRM 38 generated, the Special Coordinating Committee directed Defense officials to prepare a military options paper for presentation to the High

Level Group as a basis for discussion. The paper the group received in October 1978 examined five weapons systems and many deployment packages involving these systems.

GLCM: The ground-launched cruise missile, to be produced by General Dynamics, would be transported around NATO Europe on board transporter erector launchers, which would carry four missiles. Each launcher would be accompanied by launch-control vehicles, security personnel, and various other support elements.

Pershing II XR: The Pershing II XR (extended-range) was a new version of the Pershing IA missile already deployed in West Germany. Originally developed by the army to enhance the accuracy of the Pershing IA to 25 meters, in 1978 the Pershing II XR was given an extended range of about 1,000 miles, from its old range of 450 miles, largely in response to the growing realization that some form of LRTNF modernization would eventually take place.[36]

MRBM: The air force had developed plans, in response to the search for military options for LRTNF deployment, for a new medium-range ballistic missile called Longbow. With a range of about 1,500 miles, Longbow would use technology already developed for other purposes— a Mark 12A warhead developed for Minuteman III and standard, off-the-shelf missile guidance and engines—and even use the same launcher, with the same support systems, as the General Dynamics GLCM.

FB-111H: The FB-111H was a variant of the FB-111A bombers assigned to the Strategic Air Command and based in the United States. The FB-111H presumably was to be based in Europe and to have somewhat longer ranges and higher payloads.

SLCM: The sea-launched cruise missile was considered for deployment on submarines assigned to the NATO area.

McGiffert presented this paper to the High Level Group. In subsequent discussions by the group in November 1978 and February 1979 various deployments were considered; some were rejected, but none were adopted. For example, GLCMs and Pershing IIs were quickly supported over SLCMs, largely because they had greater visibility and would thus enhance deterrence. SLCMs had the problem of being sea-based and too similar to U.S. SLBMs to provide limited nuclear options in theater, as distinct from strategic options. Interestingly enough, the

36. For an excellent technical piece on the new Pershing II XR, see F. Clifton Berry, Jr., "Pershing II," pp. 1303–08.

option of an SLCM-based multilateral force was once raised, in which a fleet of SLCM-carrying submarines or surface ships would be multinationally manned, owned, and operated; however, those who had lived through the MLF controversy were not sympathetic, and little interest developed among Europeans.

In April 1979 the High Level Group submitted its final report to the Nuclear Planning Group. It concluded the following:

—NATO should modernize its LRTNF through an "evolutionary upward adjustment," for both the political and military reasons discussed earlier.

—The deployment package should consist of land-based cruise missiles and ballistic missiles. Because of the longer time it would take to make Longbow operational and the hope that the political provocation to the Soviet Union could be minimized by claiming that Pershing II XR was merely an upgrading of an existing system, it was felt that Pershing II XR should be chosen over Longbow for the ballistic leg of the new LRTNF.

—The total number of missles deployed should be greater than 200, in order to have a substantial effect, but less than 600, so that the possibility of decoupling would not be too great. (This seems to have been a political rather than a technical calculation.)

—Deployment should be shared among as many NATO allies as possible. This would ensure that West Germany would not be the only continental ally to host the new LRTNF, a situation that West German political leaders, wary of damaging détente with the East, insisted on avoiding.

—A final decision on LRTNF deployments should be made by December 1979. This would be necessary to avoid complications that might arise during the election campaigns in West Germany and the United States in 1980 and to provide enough time to prepare for deployments when the systems would be ready in 1983.

After considering the report, the NPG directed the HLG to come up with a specific deployment package.

White House Involvement

While the HLG had been deliberating the various American papers, a parallel set of negotiations and consultations was taking place at a higher level. The origin of these higher-level contacts dates from late

1978, when members of the NSC staff came to several important conclusions.

First, to avoid a replay of the neutron bomb debacle, and to eliminate any lingering European suspicion that the newest American initiative would suddenly fall apart like the neutron bomb initiative, it would be necessary to involve the White House directly in the initiative. Furthermore, the White House and the NSC should play a stronger role in coordinating and directing the American initiative.

Second, to avoid a replay of the MLF episode, it would be necessary to line up support from top-level Western European officials, since the HLG decisions were formally nonbinding on governments. The tactical lesson learned from the MLF experience was that an LRTNF initiative could fall apart at the last minute unless a strong consensus among European political leaders could be developed before the decision deadline. In fact, several members of the NSC staff who were familiar with the MLF experience were concerned in late 1978 and early 1979 that the LRTNF initiative had all the makings of a new MLF debacle. Specifically, they believed that domestic political pressures within European countries could work to undermine the initiative when a decision had to be made. After some discussion, it was decided that efforts should begin immediately to assure this would not happen.

Guadeloupe and the Aaron Mission

President Carter took the occasion of the January 1979 summit at Guadeloupe, attended by British Prime Minister James Callaghan, Chancellor Schmidt, and French President Giscard, to raise the issue and explore the attitudes of the European leaders on LRTNF modernization. To what extent they gave their support to the LRTNF initiative at Guadeloupe is not clear, though it is probable that some discussion of the need for LRTNF arms control took place. Enough interest was generated to warrant further briefings.

In late January, David Aaron and his staff went to London, Bonn, and Paris to present the U.S. position on LRTNF requirements, based on the work of the High Level Group. In London political leaders gave their strong support for the initiative; in Paris the French were positive, but for political reasons maintained a public silence on the matter. In discussions with Schmidt and his colleagues, however, Aaron now found some political ambivalence about the program. The same factions in

Schmidt's party that had opposed the neutron bomb as a wrecker of détente were likely to oppose new LRTNF deployments in West Germany. Schmidt felt he could handle these factions, but he would need assurances from the United States that West Germany would not be the only continental ally required to deploy the new weapons and that efforts would be made to include LRTNF in an arms-control package along with a deployment package.

As mentioned earlier, LRTNF arms control had been studied during the PRM 38 period; and low-level officials in the State Department and the Arms Control and Disarmament Agency (ACDA) continued this work afterward, mindful of European concern about postponing the issue of forward-based systems until the next round of SALT, in exchange for the cruise missile protocol. But it was clear that FBS would be considered in upcoming SALT negotiations. For Americans as well as Europeans, East-West negotiations to limit LRTNF offered an attractive opportunity to put a ceiling on the deployment at least of Soviet SS-20s and probably of Backfires as well. But the West would need some bargaining leverage of its own. Hence the need for a NATO decision to deploy before arms-control negotiations could begin.

Arms control was attractive to Europeans for other reasons too. Many believed that tangible benefits had resulted from the period of relaxed East-West tensions ushered in by the June 1972 SALT I agreements. They were loath to see a reversion to pre–SALT I tensions and feared that LRTNF deployments could stimulate such a reversion. A focus on arms control could mitigate whatever East-West tensions would be stimulated by LRTNF deployments alone. Ideally, the Europeans hoped, arms control could reach the point where the regional NATO deployments could be held to a minimum.

When Aaron returned to European capitals in March 1979 to broaden the basis of consensus to meet Schmidt's requirements, he found these arguments very much on the minds of political leaders in Belgium, the Netherlands, and West Germany. Once again, there was broad agreement that for political reasons NATO required a visible response to Soviet SS-20 deployments. But in Brussels and Amsterdam, political leaders were so concerned about how to manage the domestic political repercussions of LRTNF modernization they were reluctant to give their outright support, preferring to await the approach of a formal decision by NATO before dealing with the issue.

In Bonn, Aaron found the same concerns among West German

leaders, magnified by a recent debate over the issue led by Herbert
Wehner, a Social Democratic parliamentarian, who had launched an
attack on LRTNF modernization on the ground that a militarily superfluous decision now seemed likely to wreck détente. Schmidt had deftly
overcome this opposition within his own party but now felt even more
pressure to require some serious arms-control initiatives from the High
Level Group.

In Rome, Aaron met with somewhat surprising enthusiasm for LRTNF
modernization. The new prime minister, Francesco Cossiga, was aware
of the domestic political problems he faced in assuring Italian participation but seemed eager to accept the challenge. He had decided to retain
Attilio Ruffini, who was personally keen on LRTNF modernization, as
minister of defense. Perhaps because of Italy's myriad domestic problems, Cossiga felt more confident in focusing on the foreign policy
matters on his agenda.

To this extent Cossiga was helped by the Italian Socialist party, which
made LRTNF deployments a test of the Italian Communist party's
avowed loyalty to NATO. The Communist party was faced with a choice
between a position guaranteed to enrage Moscow and many of its
domestic followers, and one that would not only cast doubt on its own
pledge to support NATO but also make its chief competition on the
Italian left, the Socialist party, look more respectable to the rest of Italy.
Because of the exclusion of Italy from the Guadeloupe summit, bolstering
Italy's role in the alliance became a leading concern. In fact, Cossiga
had reportedly told associates that if Italy cooperated on LRTNF, he
expected no more Guadeloupes. Whether by coincidence or design, the
June 1980 economic summit of industrial leaders took place in Venice.
Under the circumstances, the Italian Communist party chose not to
choose. In any event, Cossiga was able to assure Aaron of Italy's
interest, support, and participation in new LRTNF deployments.

During this period, then, the United States began to recognize the
political need for NATO to take up the arms-control issue as soon as
possible. Also evident was the need for renewed work to develop a
specific deployment plan for presentation to the HLG when it began to
consider how to implement a deployment decision. McGiffert and his
staff at ISA spent the summer of 1979 hammering out the details of a
deployment package, which were then discussed in several interagency
meetings. In essence, they chose one of the packages already identified
in earlier Pentagon studies, which called for replacement of the 108

Pershing IAs already deployed by the United States in West Germany with 108 Pershing II XRs and for the deployment of 464 ground-launched cruise missiles spread out among participating countries, with 160 in Britain, 112 in Italy, 96 in West Germany, and 48 each in Belgium and Holland. During the summer Aaron brought this deployment plan to the five relevant European capitals to obtain reactions from political leaders. The results were the same as in his March mission: Britain, Italy, and West Germany showed serious interest in the plan; Belgium and the Netherlands deferred to the judgment of the High Level Group so as to delay their own decisions.

The Special Group

In April, at German and Dutch insistence, NATO had created a Special Group (SG), composed of national government officials at the same level as in the HLG, to study arms-control initiatives parallel to the LRTNF deployment schedule. The SG held a series of meetings chaired by Gelb, and later by his successor Reginald Bartholomew, to consider these matters. Gelb and his deputy, David Gompert, drew up a set of objectives and principles, buttressed by analysis, to guide future LRTNF discussions. They presented these objectives in draft form to the SG for comment and criticism, then returned to Washington to incorporate the comments and changes into a subsequent draft to be resubmitted at the next SG meeting. During this process, which was repeated several times, they also cleared the draft with the relevant Washington agencies—Defense, NSC, ACDA—to achieve a coordinated U.S. position on an evolving basis. The paper eventually developed into a final report for the SG. It discussed three problems in particular: the appropriate forum for future LRTNF arms-control talks; the appropriate channels of participation and consultation in their talks; and the utility and validity of various arms-control principles, such as equal aggregates, equal ceilings by specific category, and reductions.

The general conclusions were that future LRTNF arms control should formally take place within the framework of the projected SALT III negotiations between the United States and the Soviet Union. That framework would involve fairly simple procedures and would avoid giving the Soviet Union a reason for claiming that British or French forces should be included. Nevertheless, some sort of continuing liaison between the United States and NATO on positions to be taken regarding

LRTNF should be created, perhaps by extending the life of the Special Group. Provisions for limitations and reductions should be based on general principles of mutuality and equality and should be adequately verifiable. Bartholomew (who by then had replaced Gelb) and Gompert were also able to get the SG to accept the idea that LRTNF arms control was a complement to, not a substitute for, LRTNF modernization.

Thus by the end of September, both the High Level Group and the Special Group had issued their final reports to their parent bodies, the Nuclear Planning Group and the North Atlantic Council. The HLG report contained the 108 Pershing II XR/464 GLCM deployment package; the SG report contained an analysis of the arms-control issues for future consideration once the deployment decision was made.

The Integrated Decision Document

At this point U.S. negotiations had overcome many of the bureaucratic and political obstacles that had existed in January 1979. NATO had the LRTNF decision on its formal agenda for the December ministerial meeting. Italy had expressed its willingness to participate, which met the principal West German condition that Germany not be the only continental power to deploy the new systems. And throughout the whole process European political leaders had been kept informed of American efforts in the HLG and SG; indeed, they had made important contributions to those efforts. Still, Belgium and Holland had not agreed to LRTNF deployments, and West Germany, though formally satisfied with the participation of Italy, was eager to broaden participation as much as possible.

Most important, however, the reports of the HLG and the SG had yet to be converted into a document that NATO could agree to in December. During late September and early October, another series of interagency meetings involving the National Security Council, the State Department, ACDA, and the Defense Department combined the two reports into what became known as the Integrated Decision Document. The document was to be placed before the NATO ministers at their meeting in December. In anticipation, and following the general consultative procedures developed over the previous year, Aaron, Bartholomew, and McGiffert went to the capitals of potential host countries in October to present the document for comment and criticism to political leaders in advance of the NATO meeting. Once again, in Italy, West Germany, and Britain no problems were raised. In Holland and Belgium, however, the same problems recurred. In Holland, in particular, the government felt constrained about committing itself to LRTNF deployments because of vocal left-wing opposition. In Belgium, as mentioned earlier, the government was now facing some grave domestic political problems that threatened to topple the current cabinet; the resulting political crisis was clearly not conducive to important Belgian initiatives.

Kissinger's Challenge

In September 1979 a widely noted, controversial speech by former Secretary of State Henry Kissinger added a note of confusion and doubt to NATO's LRTNF deliberations. It will be recalled that the European allies had made a point of refusing any operational control over the new systems. Aaron had made control sharing under a dual-key arrangement part of the offer as early as January 1979 and renewed the offer on several occasions. The West Germans refused largely on political grounds. They did not want to appear too provocative. The British and the Italians were probably influenced by this consideration, but more strongly by cost. Under a dual-key arrangement, the host country would buy the missiles and man the bases, while the United States would retain control over the warheads. For Britain and Italy this added expense was not attractive.

In any case, the allies' refusal of control sharing had led American officials to believe that the LRTNF question would not become an explicit test of European faith in the U.S. strategic guarantee. Indeed, until this point the Schmidt speech was the only public hint of European concern about the U.S. guarantee. Of course, Americans involved in the HLG deliberations knew this issue was always present, lurking beneath the surface of the group's discussions, ready for the proper moment to reemerge. No one expected it to be raised publicly by an American, much less one of Kissinger's formidable political stature.

Nevertheless, Kissinger did so in a presentation to a conference of academic and government experts meeting in Brussels to commemorate the thirtieth anniversary of the founding of the alliance.[37] He bluntly challenged the credibility of the American strategic guarantee and the credibility of new LRTNF deployments:

37. The text of Kissinger's speech, apparently edited, appears in "NATO: The Next Thirty Years," pp. 264–68. See also Bridget Gail, "NATO, Kissinger, and the Future of Strategic Deterrence," pp. 58–64.

No one disputes any longer that in the 1980s . . . the United States will no longer be in a strategic position to reduce a Soviet counter-blow against the United States to tolerable levels. Indeed, one can argue that the United States will not be in a position in which attacking the Soviet strategic forces makes any military sense, because it may represent a marginal expenditure of our own strategic striking force without helping greatly in ensuring the safety of our forces. . . .

Now we have reached that situation so devoutly worked for by the arms control community: we are indeed vulnerable. Moreover our weapons had been deliberately designed, starting in the 60s, so as to not threaten the weapons of the other side. . . .

While we were building assured destruction capabilities, the Soviet Union was building forces for traditional military missions capable of destroying the military forces of the United States. So that in the 1980s we will be in a position where (1) many of our own strategic forces including all of our land-based ICBMs, will be vulnerable and (2) such an insignificant percentage of Soviet strategic forces will be vulnerable as not to represent a meaningful strategic attack option for the United States. Whether that means that the Soviet Union intends to attack the United States or not is certainly not my point. I am making two points. First, that the change in the strategic situation that is produced by our limited vulnerability is more fundamental for the United States than even the total vulnerability would be for the Soviet Union because our strategic doctrine has relied extraordinarily, perhaps exclusively on our superior strategic power. The Soviet Union has never relied on its superior strategic power. It has always depended more on its local and regional superiority. Therefore, even an equivalence in destructive power, even assured destruction for both sides is a revolution in NATO doctrine as we have known it. It is a fact that must be faced.[38]

In light of the development of U.S. strategic policy examined in previous chapters, and in light of subsequent efforts by Secretary of Defense James Schlesinger in 1974–76 to introduce even greater counterforce flexibility into the U.S. strategic posture, Kissinger's characterization of U.S. strategic policy as primarily one of "assured destruction" must be viewed as idiosyncratic. But from this Kissinger went on to draw ominous conclusions:

One cannot ask a nation to design forces that have no military significance, whose primary purpose is the extermination of civilians and to expect that these factors will not affect a nation's resoluteness in crisis. . . . therefore I would say, which I might not say in office, the European allies should not keep asking us to multiply strategic assurances that we cannot possibly mean, or if we do mean, we should not want to execute because if we execute, we risk the destruction of civilization. Our strategic dilemma isn't solved with reassurances.

38. Kissinger, "NATO," pp. 265–66.

There is no point in complaining about declining American will or criticizing this or that American administration, for we are facing an objective crisis and it must be remedied.[39]

In Kissinger's assertion that his assurances, while in office, and the assurances of U.S. administrations since the founding of NATO, had never been meant, his European audience found little comfort, and much to worry about. His assessment of NATO's tactical and theater nuclear deployments was even more distressing:

In the fifties and sixties we put several thousand nuclear weapons into Europe. . . . one reason we did not have a rational analysis for the use of these forces was for the very reason that led to the strategic theory of assured destruction. Let us face it: the intellectually predominant position in the United States was that we had to retain full control of the conduct of nuclear war and we therefore had a vested interest in avoiding any firebreak between tactical nuclear weapons and strategic nuclear weapons. The very reasoning that operated against giving a rational purpose to strategic forces also operated against giving a military role to tactical nuclear forces and this was compounded by the fact that—to be tactless—the secret dream of every European was, of course, to avoid a nuclear war but, secondly, if there had to be a nuclear war, to have it conducted over their heads by the strategic forces of the United States and the Soviet Union. But be that as it may, the fact is that the strategic imbalance that I have predicted for the 80s will also be accompanied by a theater imbalance in the 80s. How is it possible to survive with these imbalances in the face of the already demonstrated inferiority in conventional forces?[40]

These arguments are difficult to reconcile with the efforts of American and SHAPE military planners to develop specific plans for targeting NATO tactical nuclear weapons and the fact that by and large the targeting principles guiding SACEUR's strike plan had coincided with the counterforce targeting pursued by U.S. strategic planners for almost two decades. In contrast, it may be true that political leaders within the alliance had never developed a clear idea of how to achieve political objectives through nuclear operations on a battlefield or within the European theater. But this failure reflects the natural reluctance of European political leaders to think about precisely how they would prefer to see the nuclear destruction of their homelands unfold; the myriad political and strategic dilemmas the United States faced as leader of an alliance with disparate political and strategic interests; and the fact that military and civilian targets in Europe are too close together to let planners be confident that a nuclear battle, even one restricted to military

39. Ibid., p. 266.
40. Ibid.

targets, would not destroy European society. The failure is the consequence not of an alleged assured destruction doctrine for tactical nuclear
weapons in Europe, but rather of the technical characteristics of nuclear
weapons, the compact, crowded nature of Western Europe, and the
resulting difficulty of controlling the tendencies of a nuclear war in
Europe to escalate.

Reaction to Kissinger's speech in Europe was a mixture of bafflement,
outrage, and embarrassment. Some European leaders, especially the
French, reacted as if Kissinger were telling them only what they had
suspected all along. Others who were more familiar with the long history
of American attempts to improve the strategic posture so as to make the
nuclear guarantee more credible simply rejected Kissinger's arguments
as clear misstatements of fact. Still others reacted with deep uneasiness,
as can be seen in the remarks of one European defense analyst:

You must remember that Europe has never really debated the strategic
balance. It has simply observed the American debate over the balance, and it
has never really closely followed that. We have had no real access to your war
planning, to your analyses and games as they touch upon war fighting capability,
or to the details of your intelligence. The few officers who have been let into
your strategic planning club are there on sufferance, not to question or to raise
embarrassing issues.

It may have been a bit foolish, but we simply trusted in your confidence, in
your strategic forces and virtually all of NATO never went any further than the
political level. Now the most senior policy man you have has said at the policy
level that you cannot provide an extended deterrent. We have never paid
attention to your hawks, and all military officers are expected to issue dire
warning. But this . . . this is word after word of abdication without defining a
reason for hope.

Why is it really credible that you will risk attacking Soviet strategic forces
any more than you will risk attacking cities? Why will different U.S. strategic
forces be any more credible? Will you risk triggering strategic war with all the
attention being given on both sides to counterforce conflicts? How do you make
such distinctions credible?[41]

Despite the profoundly negative effect of Kissinger's speech on
European confidence in the United States, the Carter administration
failed to challenge the former secretary of state in a public forum.
McGeorge Bundy, a former national security adviser who was now a
private citizen unconnected with the administration, gave a speech one
week later at the International Institute for Strategic Studies that directly

41. Quoted in Gail, "NATO, Kissinger, and the Future of Strategic Deterrence,"
p. 62.

challenged Kissinger's assessments and conclusions.[42] But Europeans certainly expected a high-ranking administration official to go to Europe to offer personal, high-level reassurances to political leaders. No such trip was forthcoming, although lower-level private assurances were offered at High Level Group and Special Group meetings soon afterward. Yet it is difficult to imagine that these assurances carried the same weight as did the words of a former secretary of state, particularly one with Kissinger's prestige. Even so, in the last few months before the December ministerial meeting, the credibility of the U.S. guarantee was not a problem in alliance discussions. Whether out of apathy, embarrassment, or shock, Europeans simply did not make an issue out of Kissinger's remarks. What they believed privately, however, is a matter that will greatly concern those whose task it will be to implement the December 1979 decision.

Brezhnev's October 1979 Offer

Dutch and Belgian reservations were further deepened in October by a Soviet diplomatic initiative designed to destroy the momentum behind the imminent December deadline. Up till then, the Soviet leadership had remained fairly silent about the ongoing NATO deliberations. To those familiar with past Soviet behavior, especially during the debates over allocating nuclear weapons to the Bundeswehr and over the MLF, this silence was surprising. Perhaps the Soviet leaders believed a president who had backed down on the neutron bomb issue would be incapable of following the new initiative through to the end, or perhaps they were confident they could repeat the success of their neutron bomb propaganda campaign within the short span of two months. Another factor may have been their reluctance to force an East-West confrontation while there was still hope that SALT II, agreed to in June 1979, would be swiftly negotiated and then ratified by the U.S. Senate.

In any event, the Soviets did break their silence in early October, when, in a speech in East Germany, Brezhnev sharply criticized the alliance for its apparent determination to go through with the LRTNF initiative, announced a unilateral cutback of up to 20,000 Soviet troops in East Germany and a withdrawal of 1,000 tanks, and offered to negotiate

---

42. McGeorge Bundy, "The Future of Strategic Deterrence," speech delivered to the IISS, pp. 268–72.

on Soviet LRTNF deployments.[43] The speech was followed by a series of public statements, notes, and the like warning the Western European nations of the dire consequences for détente if NATO decided to deploy LRTNF on the Continent. So well coordinated was the alliance position by this point that each of the relevant European nations rejected the Soviet warning out of hand, with little prompting from American leaders. But the offer worsened the domestic political problems of Belgium and the Netherlands, where strong pressure was now placed on the governments to seek postponement of the decision until the avenues for arms control for LRTNF had been fully explored. As a sweetener for the Belgians and the Dutch the United States added to the Integrated Decision Document the provision that the United States would remove some 1,000 existing nuclear systems from the stockpile in Europe, a gesture that had been under consideration for some time in the context of NATO–Warsaw Pact negotiations on mutual and balanced force reductions. This additional provision made it easier for Schmidt to gain acceptance from the left wing of his party, but it apparently did little to bring domestic opposition in Belgium and Holland into line. Despite repeated assurances from American officials, including President Carter, that the alliance would proceed with vigorous arms-control efforts in conjunction with LRTNF deployment, the Dutch Parliament voted in early December to reject the NATO initiative. The Belgians remained hesitant till the end, and when the NATO ministers met in Brussels on December 12, 1979, to consider adopting the Integrated Decision Document, both Belgium and Holland endorsed it but deferred agreement to participate in GLCM deployments, the former for six months, the latter for two years, to await demonstrated progress on arms control.

The December 1979 Decision

In the end, then, although NATO agreed that five countries should deploy American GLCMs and Pershing II XRs on their territory, two of the countries reserved, pending progress in arms control. The Integrated Decision Document adopted at the December 1979 meeting remains classified; however, NATO's communiqué on the decision reveals the rationale for deployment and the importance accorded future arms-

43. *New York Times,* October 7, 1979.

control efforts in this area. Noting the trends in Soviet LRTNF deployments and the simultaneous improvement of Warsaw Pact conventional and battlefield nuclear capabilities, the communiqué stated:

These trends have prompted serious concern within the Alliance, because, if they were to continue, Soviet superiority in theatre nuclear systems could undermine the stability achieved in intercontinental systems and cast doubt on the credibility of the Alliance's deterrent strategy by highlighting the gap in the spectrum of NATO's available nuclear response to aggression.[44]

The communiqué went on to outline plans for "pursuing two parallel and complementary approaches of TNF modernization and arms control." The deployment would consist of 108 Pershing II XRs, to replace the 108 Pershing IAs deployed by the United States, and 464 GLCMs. In addition, 1,000 U.S. nuclear warheads would be withdrawn from Europe "as soon as feasible." The High Level Group would then proceed to examine "the precise nature, scope, and basis of the adjustments resulting from the LRTNF deployment and their possible implications for the balance of roles and systems in NATO's nuclear armory as a whole," and would present a report to the Nuclear Planning Group ministers in the fall of 1980.

Turning to arms control, the communiqué noted:

Ministers attach great importance to the role of arms control in contributing to a more stable military relationship between East and West and in advancing the process of détente. This is reflected in a broad set of initiatives being examined within the alliance to further the course of arms control and détente in the 1980's. Ministers regard arms control as an integral part of the Alliance's efforts to assure the undiminished security of its member States and to make the strategic situation between East and West more stable, more predictable, and more manageable at lower levels of armaments on both sides. In this regard they welcome the contributions which the SALT II Treaty makes towards achieving these objectives. . . .

Ministers consider that, building on this accomplishment and taking account of the expansion of Soviet LRTNF capabilities of concern to NATO, arms control efforts to achieve a more stable overall nuclear balance at lower levels of nuclear weapons on both sides should therefore now include certain US and Soviet long-range theatre nuclear systems.

Having endorsed future efforts by the United States to bring LRTNF to the negotiating table, the communiqué set forth principles that should guide the U.S. negotiating position:

A. Any future limitations on US systems principally designed for theatre

44. "Special Meeting of Foreign and Defense Ministers—Communiqué," pp. 25–26.

missions should be accompanied by appropriate limitations on Soviet theatre systems.

B. Limitations on US and Soviet long-range theatre nuclear systems should be negotiated bilaterally in the SALT III framework in a step-by-step approach.

C. The immediate objective of these negotiations should be the establishment of agreed limitations on US and Soviet land-based long-range theatre nuclear missile systems.

D. Any agreed limitations on these systems must be consistent with the principle of equality between the sides. Therefore, the limitations should take the form of de jure equality both in ceilings and in rights.

E. Any agreed limitations must be adequately verifiable.

The communiqué went on to note the establishment of a Special Consultative Group (SCG), composed of alliance members, to follow arms-control negotiations on a continuing basis and to report periodically to the NATO ministers. In effect, this extended the life of the Special Group and gave it a new name.

In summary, the communiqué concluded:

A modernization decision, including a commitment to deployments, is necessary to meet NATO's deterrence and defense needs, to provide a credible response to unilateral Soviet TNF deployments, and to provide the foundation for the pursuit of serious negotiations on TNF.

Success of arms control in constraining the Soviet build-up can enhance Alliance security, modify the scale of NATO's TNF requirements, and promote stability and detente in Europe in consonance with NATO's basic policy of deterrence, defence, and detente as enunciated in the Harmel Report. NATO's TNF requirements will be examined in light of concrete results reached through negotiations.

Summary

Learning from history is difficult. Clear analogies between episodes in history—even episodes that are as closely related as those in this study—are hard to draw. Tempting as it may be to see the December 1979 decision on long-range theater nuclear forces as merely a replay of the multilateral force debacle of the previous decade, to do so is to miss some striking differences between the two initiatives. The prospects for the success of the 1979 initiative can be appreciated only by looking at the differences, as well as the similarities, between previous episodes.

Hardware Initiatives

The most obvious similarity between the LRTNF and the MLF cases—that each involved a hardware solution to European anxieties over the nuclear guarantee—has significant implications. As the experiences with the MLF and earlier with the Thor and Jupiter offers made clear, hardware solutions tend to preclude the creative ambiguity in national positions that can facilitate dealing with political problems. In the end, the five NATO nations scheduled for LRTNF deployments will either accept them or reject them. The Dutch and Belgian decision to await an evaluation of progress in the Geneva negotiations on these weapons will probably just delay this painful, direct choice. As a result, the success or failure of the initiative will be clear-cut, a fact that no amount of diplomatic persiflage can obscure. With the political stakes so high, and the criteria for success so obvious, there will be tremendous pressure within NATO to implement the decision, and potentially catastrophic consequences for failure.

The hardware solution also focuses attention on whether the specific weapons will perform the missions for which they are intended. Invested with such political significance, highly complex and fragile technologies hold hostage the political objectives to which they are directed. For example, under normal circumstances, the failure of the first flight test of the Pershing II missile in July 1982 would not have engendered much public discussion. Flight test failures for missile systems under development are commonplace and an important part of the debugging process. But because Pershing II is such an integral part of the December 1979 decision, the first flight test was covered by national and international news media; its rather spectacular explosion only fourteen seconds after launch was viewed in millions of American homes and received widespread coverage in Europe. The result was to make the public question the seriousness and competence of those responsible for the development of such a high-priority weapon.

Even the most mundane technical or operational considerations are likely to assume a political significance far greater than what they would otherwise merit. For example, NATO's public pledge to begin deployments at the end of 1983 unless there is an agreement with the Soviets imposes a critical political deadline on the cumbersome technical process of arranging for basing in each of the host countries. After the host government has given its approval, potential sites for basing have to be surveyed and analyzed. After the complex task of comparison and selection has been completed, the United States and the host country must agree on elaborate technical schedules to define what work needs to be done, when it needs to be done by, who will do it, and who will pay for it; the work must begin and proceed on schedule, with a minimum of interruptions or delays. And all this must be done with a sensitivity to the public controversy surrounding the decision. Under even the best circumstances, schedules are likely to slip. Yet the consequences of missing the initial December 1983 deadline could be significant. Substantial delays in the Italian GLCM program could, for example, place West Germany in the position of accepting Pershing II deployments well before any other Continental ally would actively participate in LRTNF deployments, creating the situation Germany was trying to avoid when it insisted that at least one other Continental ally join it in LRTNF deployments as a prerequisite for German participation. Delays could also undermine the strength of the U.S. position at the negotiating table in Geneva, where NATO's demonstrated resolve to deploy these systems is one of the few incentives the Soviets have to negotiate seriously.

Control Sharing

But even from this standpoint the analogy to hardware solutions of the past has its limitations. With the MLF a hardware proposal prompted extensive—and ultimately fatal—discussions over operations related to the control of the hardware. Contrary to predictions, control sharing never became an important issue in the deliberations leading up to December 1979. From a purely strategic standpoint, this was surprising; doubts about America's willingness to use nuclear weapons against the Soviet homeland in response to aggression against Western Europe would seem to have demanded some form of control sharing. At a minimum, one would have expected host nations to require that the systems be integrated into the command structure of host nation armed forces, with the United States retaining custody of the warheads. David Aaron in fact suggested such an arrangement but found no takers.

From a broader political perspective, however, the lack of interest in control sharing is easy to understand. The West Germans in particular wanted nothing to do with it; for Schmidt, a German finger on the trigger would be too provocative to the Soviet Union and could undermine the *Ostpolitik* to which he and his party were strongly committed. To some extent other host nations shared the German concern about the viability of détente if Western European nations had control over nuclear assets that would directly threaten Soviet territory. Where political considerations were not decisive, economic considerations—particularly the U.S. requirement that if the host wanted a share of control, it would have to buy the systems from the United States—tipped the balance against control sharing.

Consultative Procedures

Another important difference between the MLF initiative and the December 1979 decision is the relative success of consultative procedures in the later case. The MLF initiative moved forward in fits and starts; careful coordination among U.S. government agencies, and among NATO allies, was often lacking; and political commitment to the project at the highest level changed from one moment to the next.

U.S. decisionmakers learned their lessons from the MLF episode well. During the summer of 1978 the U.S. position was carefully developed by a fully staffed interagency committee and presented in the PRM 38 study; the president was directly engaged at the end of the process and supported the conclusions of the study, which had the backing of all relevant agencies; operationally responsible officials from host governments were regularly and frequently engaged in the collegial forums of the High Level and Special groups; top-level political support was obtained almost a year before the December 1979 NATO ministerial meeting; and bilateral meetings between the United States and key allies were regular and frequent, serving as backups to the more formal multilateral discussions. The result was a decision based on a consensus among the officials of allied governments who would be responsible for implementing the decision, who were able to keep their respective ministers informed on the status of deliberations, and who were sensitive and responsive to the concerns of those ministers. If there ever has been an important NATO decision that was a product of true intergovernmental consensus, it was the December 1979 decision.

In the context of this study, the consultative process, established through the creation of the High Level Group–Special Consultative Group system, raises interesting questions. Are U.S. and alliance interests better served through the new process than through the old Nuclear Planning Group process? Can the HLG and SCG supplant the NPG as a consultative forum? Has the NPG outlived its usefulness?

To answer these questions, one must contrast the strengths and weaknesses of the two consultative systems. The NPG system ensures that the defense ministers of almost all NATO countries will meet regularly to discuss broad nuclear issues—a system that allows for substantive interchange at the highest political levels. The HLG and SCG by themselves do not guarantee such direct high-level political involvement in nuclear issues. As such, it can be argued, the NPG system serves a useful and unique function that should be preserved.

The NPG system does not, however, include officials at the working level of defense and foreign ministries, those responsible for taking actions to implement decisions made by ministers. The HLG-SCG system does exactly that; one would expect—and the December 1979 decision confirms this—that when specific action is required, the HLG-SCG system will facilitate implementation of this action in a more timely way than the NPG. The NPG does have a staff in Brussels, but this staff has no direct responsibility for implementing decisions taken by member governments. Furthermore, the staff in Brussels, physically separate from the ministries and governments it is supposed to represent, tends to become distant from the concerns, interests, and constraints of these ministries and governments. In this respect, staff members of ministries in capitals have an advantage over the NPG staff, even in issues directly related to nuclear planning.

It is critical to recognize that the December 1979 decision did not entirely circumvent the NPG system. The HLG was, and remains, a creation of the NPG, and reports directly not to the North Atlantic Council but to the NPG ministers. Furthermore, the NPG staff undoubtedly gave support in Brussels to HLG meetings, although its mandate for involvement in Special Group matters was probably more circumscribed, since the SG was a creation of the North Atlantic Council. Complete circumvention of the NPG system was probably thought politically unwise, given the symbolic importance of consultations within this forum. These considerations are likely to dominate future discussion of how to get things done on nuclear policy within NATO. Thus the issue will never be an either/or decision, either the NPG or the HLG-SCG system. Rather, the issue will be: should mid-level officials from capitals be brought together for discussions in Brussels to review the alliance's nuclear agenda to supplement the work of the Nuclear Planning Group and its staff? Because of the success of the process leading up to December 1979, the answer is likely to be yes.

Though the new NATO consultative procedures have some strong advantages over the previous system, their continuation may eventually entail costs that could reduce their usefulness. The creators of the HLG-SG process in 1977–79 realized that the LRTNF issue was extraordinary and required extraordinary action. With such an important item on the agenda, it was easy to get mid-level officials to come to Brussels frequently, easy to justify their increased attention to the issue, and easy to justify the devotion of scarce manpower resources in capitals to this joint venture. In many capitals the number of officials directly involved in nuclear planning is surprisingly small; furthermore, these poorly manned staffs often have other important briefs as well and can devote only a small amount of time to nuclear matters over a long period. The NPG staff is valuable because it relieves what would otherwise become an intolerable burden on national staffs, which sometimes number no more than five people.

If the HLG-SCG mechanism continues indefinitely and deals with issues more routine than LRTNF, one can expect pressure for fewer meetings, lower-level attendance, or even the creation of an HLG-SCG staff in Brussels to manage routine matters of alliance nuclear policy. At that point the mechanism will have lost much of its advantage over the less responsive NPG system. The obvious solution is to use the HLG-SCG mechanism only in extraordinary cases. Bureaucratically, however, these forums will be difficult to hold in abeyance.

A distinction should be made between the work of the High Level Group and that of the Special Consultative Group. The HLG has a broad mandate. Growing out of Task Force 10 of the long-term defense plan, it can legitimately seek to examine all elements of NATO's nuclear posture. Indeed, much of the work it has done since December 1979 has been focused on issues other than LRTNF. In contrast, the SCG's mandate is well defined—to serve as a consultative forum for the theater nuclear force arms-control negotiations. If these negotiations produce an agreement, presumably the purpose of the SCG will have been fulfilled, and it will cease to function.

Arms Control

Another sharp contrast between the December 1979 decision and the previous initiatives is in the role played by arms-control efforts. The earlier initiatives were all pre–SALT I, though serious U.S.-Soviet arms-control efforts became entangled with the MLF debate, when the United States, Britain, and the Soviet Union were beginning to negotiate a nuclear nonproliferation treaty. Because of the MLF initiative the Soviet Union could charge that the United States was trying to undermine the intent of the treaty. To some extent, one may assume that those who were actively seeking the treaty within the U.S. government viewed the MLF as a danger to their objective. The MLF was of course canceled before serious negotiations began. But it was certainly not canceled because of fears over its potential harm to these negotiations.

The legacy of East-West relations in the 1970s—SALT, MBFR, the Conference on Security and Cooperation in Europe, *Ostpolitik,* and détente—predisposed the December 1979 decision toward a heavy focus on arms control. As an integral part of the so-called two-track decision, arms control has an importance unique in the history of U.S. attempts to restore confidence in its nuclear guarantee. Some viewed arms control as a way to reduce the threat of the new Soviet theater nuclear deployments. This is certainly one aspect of Schmidt's 1977 speech that is often forgotten. Others viewed arms control as a way to make the deployment program more politically acceptable to the Europeans concerned about halting the arms race.

But NATO governments recognized that modernization and arms control were dependent on each other. If modernization would have no political support without a parallel and credible arms-control effort, arms control would have no real future without modernization. More than mere bargaining chips, the Pershing II and GLCM programs were the *only* chips the West had to offer. Unless NATO clearly resolved to deploy these weapons at the end of 1983, in the absence of a concrete agreement to the contrary, the Soviets would have little incentive to negotiate seriously on comparable systems of their own.

In this particular case, arms control and modernization seem to have been well integrated, at least during the process of reaching the December 1979 decision. Some observers, however, have raised a difficult issue: is this relationship one that NATO should try to preserve as it considers new modernization questions? Need every modernization decision be accompanied by an arms-control effort? Need every arms-control initiative be bolstered by new modernization programs?

There are no clear answers to these questions. Perhaps the first observation should be that arms control is a long, complex process that can boast only the most modest achievements over the past three decades. Tying all modernization programs to arms-control negotiations would seem to risk holding needed military improvements hostage to a fragile, unpredictable, and drawn-out diplomatic process. At the same time, there may be political circumstances in the future that, as in 1979, make modernization without arms control politically insupportable. What this argues for is some flexibility on the part of NATO leaders in linking modernization and arms control. Not all situations will require a link; when such a link is needed, NATO should be prepared to make it.

Continuities: Doctrine and Process

So far this summary has been using history as a data base for deriving analysis, noting similarities, underscoring differences, and pondering implications. This is one use of history, and with some care it can give insight into whether, and how, people learn the lessons of the past. But history has another use. Events of today are a product of past events. By tracing the development of an issue, or a set of related issues, over time, one can gain some insight into why events occurred as they did and what is likely to happen in the future.

Indeed, some aspects of the December 1979 decision are incomprehensible unless this approach is adopted. Take, for example, the implicit NATO decision that a change in doctrine was not feasible. For the armchair strategist, this decision is difficult to explain. If the credibility of the U.S. strategic guarantee comes into question, the credibility of NATO's strategy of flexible response, which is based in part on this guarantee, should in principle also come into question. From a logical point of view, there would be two ways to rectify the problem: either take steps to make the guarantee more credible, or revise the strategy to take into account the decreasing credibility of the U.S. guarantee. A revision of the strategy, however, was never contemplated. In fact, one can read the events leading up to December 1979 as an effort to preserve the doctrine of flexible response at all costs, despite a changing strategic environment that called the doctrine into question. Those familiar with the way NATO handles doctrinal matters have been struck repeatedly by the religious parallels. The doctrine of flexible response is the central tenet of the faith, MC 14/3 serves somewhat the same function as the ten commandments, and NATO nuclear planners are the theologians responsible for interpreting the sacred text for future generations.

But though rigid, this attitude is not all bad. Chapter 6 suggests just how difficult it was to achieve agreement on doctrine, just how difficult it was to reconcile differing interests and perspectives. It also suggests how much MC 14/3 represented a carefully worded compromise that left the most controversial matters deliberately ambiguous. Indeed, one of the strengths of a doctrinal approach is that, unlike weaponry, it is subject to creative ambiguity. Little wonder, then, that NATO is reluctant to tamper with sacred text. To do so would be to reopen old debates that have no better prospects for easy resolution today than they had in the past. Given the choice between doctrinal revision and force-posture revision, NATO will choose the second, and reconcile it with the first.

If there is a danger in this situation, it lies not in the inadequacy of the doctrine, which is, after all, flexible enough to provide a rationale for a wide range of necessary improvements, but in the complacency that reluctance to examine doctrine tends to breed. Force-posture changes are possible in this situation; the LRTNF decision is an example. But refusal to address doctrinal issues can lead to a presumption that the current force posture is adequate, precisely because of the flexibility of the doctrine. In particular, nations can use MC 14/3 as an excuse not to devote necessary resources to conventional defense. The doctrine provides for escalation to the nuclear level if conventional defense fails; this is held by many to be a strong deterrent, and some even argue that so far as conventional improvements reduce the need for nuclear escalation, they lower the risk of aggression to the enemy and thus undermine the deterrent.[45]

Whatever the pros and cons of doctrinal revision might be, it is not surprising that NATO's LRTNF initiative took flexible response as the point of departure, as an inflexible given in the constellation of considerations leading to December 1979. The history of NATO's efforts to deal with nuclear uncertainties had a direct effect on December 1979 in other ways as well. As seen in chapter 5, the MLF experience showed U.S. decisionmakers the dangers of pursuing a multilateral, hardware solution in the absence of a clear consensus both at the working levels and at the highest political levels. The consultative mechanisms that were developed indicated that a lesson from the past had been learned.

Although the United States recognized the inadequacy of the Nuclear

45. Karl Kaiser and others, "Nuclear Weapons and the Preservation of Peace," pp. 1157–70.

Planning Group mechanism for handling the LRTNF issue, it accepted the institutional and political importance of the NPG system created in the late 1960s. Insensitivity to this history might have led the United States to propose a mechanism that would have circumvented the NPG. As it was, the U.S. bureaucracy took the institutional importance of the NPG as a given and appended the HLG process onto the NPG system, making the HLG a creation of the NPG and requiring that HLG conclusions be passed along to NPG ministers for endorsement. Substantively, this relationship did not make any difference; procedurally, however, it gave the HLG a natural, accepted way to have its recommendations considered by NATO ministers. The principal danger of this institutional arrangement has already been mentioned, namely, that NPG ministers may seek to use the HLG to address all future items on their nuclear agenda, thereby overburdening the small nuclear planning staffs in capitals.

Conclusions

The historical perspective of this study shows why the deliberations leading up to December 1979 took the form they did. To leave the analysis at this point, however, would be to miss the forest for the trees. NATO has been wrestling with the same problem for more than three decades and has never developed a permanent solution. Will the December 1979 decision be any different? Will it put to rest the doubts over the U.S. nuclear guarantee? So far as history suggests anything, it suggests that the solution is only temporary.

That said, history also demonstrates that some solutions have been more temporary than others. Some, like the Norstad MMRBM proposal and the MLF initiative, never really materialized. The stationing of Thors and Jupiters did materialize in Europe and may have quelled doubts for a while, but the systems were prone to obsolescence and were soon withdrawn, to be replaced by more explicit reliance on the central strategic arsenal of the United States. Once adopted, the doctrine of flexible response seems to have withstood the ravages of time, in part because of its ambiguity, in part because the battle over it was so unpleasant that no country is eager to reopen the issue. But the doctrine did not forestall concern over new Soviet theater nuclear deployments. The NPG proved to be a useful forum for quieting fears, but it did not forestall concern over new Soviet theater deployments either, nor did it seem an adequate forum in itself to deal with the perceived problem once that problem was articulated.

Because the December 1979 decision is viewed as a response to concerns about the U.S. nuclear guarantee in an era of strategic parity, as a test of U.S. leadership of the alliance, and as a test of alliance cohesiveness and resolve, it has taken on an importance totally out of proportion to the size and scope of the military role the new weapons systems are likely to play in the event of war. Perhaps this development is to be regretted. Nevertheless, it is a fact of life for the alliance. Controversial as the decision may be, the interests it has engaged make its successful implementation imperative. If the arms-control part of the decision can moderate the planned deployment, reduce the threat to the NATO allies, and make deployments less controversial, it can significantly reduce the political costs the alliance will pay in implementing the decision, and moderate the Soviet response to deployments. But the December 1979 decision will not put to rest the basic problem it was intended to address.

Is there a more permanent solution to be found? The history of NATO's nuclear dilemmas suggests there may be one, though one unlikely to be palatable to governments that have grown comfortable with the way in which the debate over flexible response was resolved. As long as the alliance relies on a deterrent based on the U.S. threat to use its nuclear weapons in defense of its allies, doubts will always exist about whether the United States will make good on that threat. Measures that have been adopted since the 1960s have increased the options open to the United States should escalation to nuclear conflict seem necessary. This fact has been, and should continue to be, the basis for reducing the importance of these doubts.

A complementary policy could be built on the observation, inherent in McNamara's original conception of the flexible response doctrine, that the nuclear posture of the alliance, and the U.S. willingness to use its terrible arsenal in defense of its allies, is manifestly more credible if the alliance has a strong enough conventional posture to force the Soviet Union to contemplate using nuclear weapons to achieve its military objectives. This was the goal first put forward by McNamara in his Athens speech of 1962, the goal eventually rejected in the version of flexible response adopted by the alliance in 1967. Whether the alliance is ready to reexamine this goal, and whether such a posture is technically feasible, given the improvements in Soviet conventional and nuclear forces since 1967, must await treatment in another study. Yet only by reexamining that goal can NATO determine whether it is doomed to revisit the problem of the credibility of the U.S. nuclear guarantee time and again, or whether it can place the burden of nuclear escalation on the shoulders of the Soviet leadership, where that burden belongs.

Bibliography

Books and Articles

Acheson, Dean. "The Practice of Partnership." *Foreign Affairs,* vol. 41 (January 1963).

Alphand, Hervé. "France and Her Allies." *Orbis,* vol. 7 (Spring 1963).

Armacost, Michael H. *The Politics of Weapons Innovation: The Thor-Jupiter Controversy.* New York: Columbia University Press, 1969.

Aron, Raymond. "The American Atomic Monopoly and Europe." *Atlantic Community Quarterly,* vol. 1 (March 1963).

————. *The Great Debate: Theories of Nuclear Strategy.* Garden City, N.Y.: Doubleday, 1965.

Ball, Desmond J. *Déjà Vu: The Return to Counterforce in the Nixon Adminis-tration.* Los Angeles: California Seminar on Arms Control and Foreign Policy, 1975.

————. *Politics and Force Levels: The Strategic Missile Program of the Kennedy Administration.* Berkeley, California: University of California Press, 1980.

Ball, George W. "The Nuclear Deterrent and the Atlantic Alliance." *Department of State Bulletin,* vol. 48 (May 13, 1963).

Ball, Mary Margaret. *NATO and the European Union Movement.* London: Stevens and Sons, 1959.

Beam, Jacob D. "A Nuclear Test Ban and Arms Control." *Department of State Bulletin,* vol. 48 (March 25, 1963).

Beard, Edmund. *Developing the ICBM: A Study in Bureaucratic Politics.* New York: Columbia University Press, 1976.

Bechhoefer, Bernard G. *Postwar Negotiations for Arms Control.* Washington, D.C.: Brookings Institution, 1961.

Bell, Coral. *Negotiation from Strength: A Study in the Politics of Power.* New York: Knopf, 1963.

Beloff, Max. *The United States and the Unity of Europe.* Washington, D.C.: Brookings Institution, 1963.

Beloff, Nora. *The General Says No: Britain's Exclusion from Europe.* London: Penguin Books, 1963.

Bernstein, Barton J. "The Cuban Missile Crisis: Trading the Jupiters in Turkey?" *Political Science Quarterly*, vol. 95 (Spring 1980).

Berry, F. Clifton, Jr. "Pershing II: First Step in NATO Theatre Nuclear Force Modernization." *International Defense Review*, vol. 12, no. 8 (1979).

Betts, Richard K., ed. *Cruise Missiles: Technology, Strategy, Politics.* Washington, D.C.: Brookings Institution, 1982.

Boulton, J. W. "NATO and the MLF." *Journal of Contemporary History*, vol. 7 (July–October 1972).

Bowie, Robert R. "Strategy and the Atlantic Alliance." *International Organization*, vol. 17 (Summer 1963).

———. "Tensions within the Alliance." *Foreign Affairs*, vol. 42 (October 1963).

Brodie, Bernard, ed. *The Absolute Weapon: Atomic Power and World Order.* New York: Harcourt, Brace, 1946.

———. *Escalation and the Nuclear Option.* Princeton: Princeton University Press, 1966.

———. "Nuclear Weapons: Strategic or Tactical?" *Foreign Affairs*, vol. 32 (January 1954).

———. *Strategy in the Missile Age.* Princeton: Princeton University Press, 1959.

———. "Unlimited Weapons and Limited War." *The Reporter*, vol. 11 (November 18, 1954).

Buchan, Alastair. "The Multilateral Force: A Study in Alliance Politics." *International Affairs* (London), vol. 40 (October 1964).

———. "The Reform of NATO." *Foreign Affairs*, vol. 40 (January 1962).

———. *Studies in International Security*, vol. 1: *NATO in the 1960s: The Implications of Interdependence.* London: Wiedenfeld and Nicolson for the International Institute for Strategic Studies, 1960.

Bundy, McGeorge. "The Future of Strategic Deterrence." *Survival*, vol. 21 (November–December 1979).

Burt, Richard. "The Cruise Missile and Arms Control." *Survival*, vol. 18 (January–February 1976).

Buzzard, Sir Anthony W. "Massive Retaliation and Graduated Deterrence." *World Politics*, vol. 8 (January 1956).

Cave Brown, Anthony, ed. *Dropshot: The U.S. Plan for War with the Soviet Union in 1957.* New York: Dial Press, 1978.

Cleveland, Harlan. *NATO: The Transatlantic Bargain.* New York: Harper and Row, 1970.

———. "The Transformation of NATO." *NATO Letter*, November 1967.

Cohen, S. T. "Enhanced Radiation Warheads: Setting the Record Straight." *Strategic Review*, vol. 6 (Winter 1978).

———, and Brigadier General Edwin F. Black. "The Neutron Bomb and the Defense of NATO." *Military Review*, vol. 58 (May 1978).

Collins, General J. Lawton. "NATO: Still Vital for Peace." *Foreign Affairs*, vol. 34 (April 1956).

Davis, Lynn Etheridge. *The Cold War Begins: Soviet-American Conflict over Eastern Europe.* Princeton: Princeton University Press, 1974.

Dawson, Raymond, and Richard Rosecrance. "Theory and Reality in the Anglo-American Alliance." *World Politics,* vol. 19 (October 1966).

DePorte, A. W. *Europe between the Superpowers: The Enduring Balance.* New Haven: Yale University Press, 1979.

DeWeerd, H. A. "Britain's Changing Military Policy." *Foreign Affairs,* vol. 34 (October 1955).

Dougherty, James E. "European Deterrence and Atlantic Unity." *Orbis,* vol. 6 (Fall 1962).

Dulles, John Foster. "Challenge and Response in United States Policy." *Foreign Affairs,* vol. 36 (October 1957).

———. "The Evolution of Foreign Policy." *Department of State Bulletin,* vol. 30 (January 25, 1954).

Earle, Edward Mead, ed. *Makers of Modern Strategy: Military Thought from Machiavelli to Hitler.* Princeton: Princeton University Press, 1971.

Eisenhower, Dwight D. *The White House Years: Mandate for Change, 1953–1956.* Garden City, N.Y.: Doubleday, 1965.

———. *The White House Years: Waging Peace, 1956–1961.* Garden City, N.Y.: Doubleday, 1965.

Enthoven, Alain C. "U.S. Forces in Europe: How Many? Doing What?" *Foreign Affairs,* vol. 53 (April 1975).

———, and K. Wayne Smith. *How Much Is Enough? Shaping the Defense Program, 1961–1969.* New York: Harper and Row, 1971.

Erler, Fritz. "Atlantic Policy: The Basis of Partnership." *Foreign Affairs,* vol. 42 (October 1963).

Feis, Herbert. *Between War and Peace: The Potsdam Conference.* Princeton: Princeton University Press, 1960.

Fisher, Robert Lucas. *Defending the Central Front: The Balance of Forces.* Adelphi Paper 127. London: International Institute for Strategic Studies, 1976.

Fox, William T. R., and Annette B. Fox. *NATO and the Range of American Choice.* New York: Columbia University Press, 1967.

Francis-Williams, Edward. *A Prime Minister Remembers: The War and Post-War Memories of the Rt. Hon. Earl Attlee.* London: Heinemann, 1961.

Furniss, Edgar S., Jr. "France, NATO, and European Security." *International Organization,* vol. 10 (November 1956).

———. *France, Troubled Ally: De Gaulle's Heritage and Prospects.* New York: Harper and Brothers, 1960.

Gaddis, John Lewis. *The United States and the Origins of the Cold War, 1941–1947.* New York: Columbia University Press, 1972.

———, and Paul Nitze. "NSC 68 and the Soviet Threat Reconsidered." *International Security,* vol. 4 (Spring 1980).

Gail, Bridget. "NATO, Kissinger, and the Future of Strategic Deterrence." *Armed Forces Journal International,* vol. 117 (November 1979).

Gallois, Pierre M. *The Balance of Terror: Strategy for the Nuclear Age.* Boston: Houghton Mifflin, 1961.

———. "The Raison d'Etre of French Defence Policy." *Atlantic Community Quarterly,* vol. 1 (Winter 1963–64).

———. "U.S. Strategy and the Defense of Europe." *Orbis,* vol. 8 (Summer 1963).

Gavin, General James M. *War and Peace in the Space Age.* New York: Harper and Brothers, 1958.

Geyelin, Philip. *Lyndon B. Johnson and the World.* New York: Praeger, 1966.

Gilpatric, Roswell L. "Present Defense Policies and Programs: United States Does Not Seek to Resolve Disputes by Violence." *Vital Speeches of the Day,* vol. 28 (December 1, 1961).

Gordon Walker, P. C. "The Labor Party's Defense and Foreign Policy." *Foreign Affairs,* vol. 42 (April 1964).

Gowing, Margaret. *Britain and Atomic Energy, 1939–1945.* London: Macmillan, 1964.

Groom, A. J. R. *British Thinking about Nuclear Weapons.* London: Frances Pinter, 1974.

Halperin, Morton H. "The Gaither Committee and the Policy Process." *World Politics,* vol. 13 (April 1961).

———. *Limited War in the Nuclear Age.* New York: John Wiley, 1963.

Hanmer, Stephen R., Jr. "NATO's Long-Range Theatre Nuclear Forces: Modernization in Parallel with Arms Control." *NATO Review,* vol. 28 (February 1980).

Hanrieder, Wolfram F., ed., *The United States and Western Europe: Political, Economic, and Strategic Perspectives.* Cambridge, Mass.: Winthrop, 1974.

Herter, Christian A. "Atlantica." *Foreign Affairs,* vol. 41 (January 1963).

———. *Toward an Atlantic Community.* New York: Harper and Row, 1963.

Hockaday, Arthur. "Nuclear Management in NATO." *NATO Letter,* May 1967.

Holst, Johan J., and Uwe Nerlich, eds. *Beyond Nuclear Deterrence: New Aims, New Arms.* New York: Crane, Russak, 1977.

Hunt, Brigadier K. *NATO without France: The Military Implications.* Adelphi Paper 32. London: International Institute for Strategic Studies, 1966.

Huntington, Samuel P. *The Common Defense: Strategic Programs in National Politics.* New York: Columbia University Press, 1961.

International Institute for Strategic Studies. *The Military Balance.* London: IISS. Annual.

Joshua, Wynfred. *Nuclear Weapons and the Atlantic Alliance.* New York: National Strategy Information Center, 1973.

Kaiser, Karl, and Hans-Peter Schwarz, eds. *America and Western Europe: Problems and Prospects.* Lexington, Mass.: Lexington Books, 1977.

Kaiser, Karl, and others. "Nuclear Weapons and the Preservation of Peace: A German Response." *Foreign Affairs,* vol. 60 (Summer 1982).

Kaplan, Fred M. "Enhanced-Radiation Weapons." *Scientific American,* vol. 238 (May 1978).

———. "Warring over New Missiles for NATO." *New York Times Magazine,* December 9, 1979.

Kaufmann, William W. *The McNamara Strategy.* New York: Harper and Row, 1964.

————, ed. *Military Policy and National Security*. Princeton: Princeton University Press, 1956.

Kelleher, Catherine McArdle. *Germany and the Politics of Nuclear Weapons*. New York: Columbia University Press, 1975.

Kelly, George A. "The Political Background of the French A-Bomb." *Orbis*, vol. 4 (Fall 1960).

Kennedy, Robert F. *Thirteen Days: A Memoir of the Cuban Missile Crisis*. New York: Norton, 1969.

Killian, James R., Jr. *Sputnik, Scientists, and Eisenhower: A Memoir of the First Special Assistant to the President for Science and Technology*. Cambridge, Mass.: MIT Press, 1977.

King, James E., Jr. "Nuclear Weapons and Foreign Policy." *New Republic*, July 1, and July 15, 1957.

Kintner, William R., and Stefan T. Possony. "NATO's Nuclear Crisis." *Orbis*, vol. 6 (Summer 1962).

Kissinger, Henry A. "Force and Diplomacy in the Nuclear Age." *Foreign Affairs*, vol. 34 (April 1956).

————. "Military Policy and Defense of the 'Grey Areas.' " *Foreign Affairs*, vol. 33 (April 1955).

————. "NATO: The Next Thirty Years." *Survival*, vol. 21 (November–December 1979).

————. *The Necessity for Choice: Prospects of American Foreign Policy*. New York: Harper and Brothers, 1961.

————. *Nuclear Weapons and Foreign Policy*. New York: Harper and Brothers, 1957.

————. "Strategy and Organization." *Foreign Affairs*, vol. 35 (April 1957).

————. *The Troubled Partnership: A Re-appraisal of the Atlantic Alliance*. New York: McGraw-Hill for the Council on Foreign Relations, 1965.

Kleiman, Robert. *Atlantic Crisis: American Diplomacy Confronts a Resurgent Europe*. New York: Norton, 1964.

Knorr, Klaus, ed. *NATO and American Security*. Princeton: Princeton University Press, 1959.

Kohl, Wilfrid L. *French Nuclear Diplomacy*. Princeton: Princeton University Press, 1971.

————. "Nuclear Sharing in NATO and the Multilateral Force." *Political Science Quarterly*, vol. 80 (March 1965).

Kraft, Joseph. *The Grand Design: From Common Market to Atlantic Partnership*. New York: Harper and Brothers, 1962.

Le Ghait, Edouard. *No Carte Blanche to Capricorn: The Folly of Nuclear War Strategy*. New York: Brookfield House, 1960.

Leitenberg, Milton. "The Neutron Bomb—Enhanced Radiation Warheads." *Journal of Strategic Studies*, vol. 5 (September 1982).

Lippmann, Walter. "How Many Drivers at the Nuclear Wheel?" *Atlantic Community Quarterly*, vol. 1 (March 1963).

McNamara, Robert S. "The Communist Design for World Conquest: Some

Shift in Our Military Thinking Required." *Vital Speeches of the Day*, vol. 28 (March 1, 1962).

———. "The United States and Western Europe: Concrete Problems of Maintaining a Free Community." *Vital Speeches of the Day*, vol. 28 (August 1, 1962).

Manning, Robert J. "U.S. Foreign Policy: Problems and Challenges for 1963." *Department of State Bulletin*, vol. 48 (January 28, 1963).

Mariska, Captain Mark D. "The Single Integrated Operational Plan." *Military Review*, vol. 52 (March 1972).

Martin, Laurence W. "The Market for Strategic Ideas in Britain: The 'Sandys Era.' " *American Political Science Review*, vol. 56 (March 1962).

Mearsheimer, John J. "Why the Soviets Can't Win Quickly in Central Europe." *International Security*, vol. 7 (Summer 1982).

Mendl, Wolf. *Deterrence and Persuasion: French Nuclear Armament in the Context of National Policy, 1945–1969*. New York: Praeger, 1970.

Moore, Ben T. *NATO and the Future of Europe*. New York: Harper and Brothers, 1958.

Moulton, Harland B. *From Superiority to Parity: The United States and the Strategic Arms Race, 1961–1971*. Westport, Conn.: Greenwood Press, 1973.

Mulley, F. W. *The Politics of Western Defence*. London: Thames and Hudson, 1965.

———. "Nuclear Weapons: Challenge to National Sovereignty." *Orbis*, vol. 7 (Spring 1963).

Murphy, Charles J. V. "NATO at a Nuclear Crossroads." *Fortune*, vol. 66 (December 1962).

Neustadt, Richard E. *Alliance Politics*. New York: Columbia University Press, 1970.

———. "Memorandum on the British Labour Party and the MLF." *New Left Review*, vol. 51 (September–October 1968).

Newhouse, John. *De Gaulle and the Anglo-Saxons*. New York: Viking Press, 1970.

Nitze, Paul H. "Atoms, Strategy and Policy." *Foreign Affairs*, vol. 34 (January 1956).

———. "The World Situation: Strengthening of the United States Armed Forces." *Vital Speeches of the Day*, vol. 28 (October 15, 1961).

Osgood, Robert E. *The Case for the MLF: A Critical Evaluation*. Washington, D.C.: Washington Center of Foreign Policy Research, 1964.

———. *Limited War: The Challenge to American Strategy*. Chicago: University of Chicago Press, 1957.

———. *NATO: The Entangling Alliance*. Chicago: University of Chicago Press, 1962.

———. *Nuclear Control in NATO*. Washington, D.C.: Washington Center of Foreign Policy Research, 1962.

Owen, Henry. "What the Multilateral Force Could Achieve." *European Review*, vol. 14 (Autumn 1964).

Patterson, Gardner, and Edgar S. Furniss, Jr. *NATO: A Critical Appraisal.* Princeton: Princeton University Press, 1957.

Pearson, Lester B. "After Geneva: A Greater Task for NATO." *Foreign Affairs,* vol. 34 (October 1955).

Pfaltzgraff, Robert L., Jr., and Jacquelyn K. Davis. *The Cruise Missile: Bargaining Chip or Defense Bargain?* Cambridge, Mass.: Institute for Foreign Policy Analysis, 1977.

Pierre, Andrew J. *Nuclear Politics: The British Experience with an Independent Strategic Force, 1939–1970.* London: Oxford University Press, 1972.

Possony, Stefan T. "Toward Nuclear Isolationism?" *Orbis,* vol. 6 (Winter 1963).

Quester, George H. *Nuclear Diplomacy: The First Twenty-Five Years.* New York: Dunellen, 1970.

Record, Jeffrey. *U.S. Nuclear Weapons in Europe: Issues and Alternatives.* Washington, D.C.: Brookings Institution, 1974.

Reed, Bruce, and Geoffrey Williams. *Denis Healey and the Policies of Power.* London: Sidgwick and Jackson, 1971.

Richardson, James L. *Germany and the Atlantic Alliance: The Interaction of Strategy and Politics.* Cambridge, Mass.: Harvard University Press, 1966.

Ricketts, Admiral Claude V. "Multilateral Force." *European Review,* vol. 13 (Summer 1963).

Rockefeller Brothers Fund. *Prospects for America: The Rockefeller Panel Reports.* Garden City, N.Y.: Doubleday, 1961.

Rosecrance, R. N. *Defense of the Realm: British Strategy in the Nuclear Epoch.* New York: Columbia University Press, 1968.

———, ed. *The Dispersion of Nuclear Weapons: Strategy and Politics.* New York: Columbia University Press, 1964.

Rostow, W. W. "The Atlantic Agenda." *Department of State Bulletin,* vol. 50 (April 13, 1964).

Royal Institute of International Affairs. *British Security: A Report by a Chatham House Study Group.* London: RIIA, 1946.

Royal United Services Institution. *Does the Strategy of Flexible Response Need Modifying? If So in What Way?* London: RUSI, 1970.

Rusk, Dean. "Secretary Rusk's News Conference of March 8." *Department of State Bulletin,* vol. 48 (March 25, 1963).

Russett, Bruce M., and Bruce G. Blair, eds. *Readings from Scientific American: Progress in Arms Control.* San Francisco: Freeman, 1979.

Scheinman, Lawrence. *Atomic Energy Policy in France under the Fourth Republic.* Princeton: Princeton University Press, 1965.

Schilling, Warner R., Paul Y. Hammond, and Glenn H. Snyder. *Strategy, Politics, and Defense Budgets.* New York: Columbia University Press, 1962.

Schlesinger, Arthur M., Jr. *A Thousand Days: John F. Kennedy in the White House.* Boston: Houghton Mifflin, 1965.

Schmidt, Helmut. *Defense or Retaliation: A German View.* New York: Praeger, 1962.

———. "The 1977 Alastair Buchan Memorial Lecture." *Survival,* vol. 20 (January–February 1978).

――――. "Remarks by Chancellor Helmut Schmidt." *Survival,* vol. 19 (July–August 1977).

Seim, Harvey B. "Nuclear Policy-Making in NATO." *NATO Review,* vol. 21 (November–December 1973).

Slessor, Sir John. "Atlantic Policy: Control of Nuclear Strategy. *Foreign Affairs,* vol. 42 (October 1963).

――――. "British Defense Policy." *Foreign Affairs,* vol. 35 (July 1957).

Sommer, Theo. "The Neutron Bomb: Nuclear War without Tears." *Survival,* vol. 19 (November–December 1977).

Sorensen, Theodore. *Kennedy.* New York: Harper and Row, 1965.

Spaak, Paul-Henri. "The Search for Consensus: A New Effort to Build Europe." *Foreign Affairs,* vol. 43 (January 1965).

"Spaak-Beaufre Debate on NATO and Europe." *NATO Letter,* May 1967.

Spanier, John W., and Joseph L. Nogee. *The Politics of Disarmament: A Study in Soviet-American Gamesmanship.* New York: Praeger, 1962.

"Special Meeting of Foreign and Defense Ministers Communiqué." *NATO Review,* vol. 28 (February 1980).

Speier, Hans. *German Rearmament and Atomic War: The Views of German Military and Political Leaders.* Evanston, Ill.: Row, Peterson, 1957.

――――. "Soviet Atomic Blackmail and the North Atlantic Alliance." *World Politics,* vol. 9 (April 1957).

Stanley, Timothy W. "Decentralizing Nuclear Control in NATO." *Orbis,* vol. 7 (Spring 1963).

――――. *NATO in Transition: The Future of the Atlantic Alliance.* New York: Praeger for the Council on Foreign Relations, 1965.

Stehlin, General Paul. "Atlantic Policy: The Evolution of Western Defense." *Foreign Affairs,* vol. 42 (October 1963).

Steinbruner, John D. *The Cybernetic Theory of Decision: New Dimensions of Political Analysis.* Princeton: Princeton University Press, 1974.

Stockholm International Peace Research Institute. *Tactical Nuclear Weapons: European Perspectives.* New York: Crane, Russak, 1978.

Sullivan, Walter. "Neutron Bomb Is a Modification of H-Bomb with Smaller Blast." *New York Times,* June 27, 1980.

Talbott, Strobe. *Endgame: The Inside Story of SALT II.* New York: Harper and Row, 1979.

Taylor, General Maxwell D. *The Uncertain Trumpet.* New York: Harper and Brothers, 1960.

Taylor, John W. R., ed. *Jane's All the World's Aircraft, 1977–1978.* New York: Franklin Watts, 1977.

"Text of General Norstad's Cincinnati Speech." *NATO Letter,* December 1957.

Treverton, Gregory F. "Nuclear Weapons and the 'Gray Area.' " *Foreign Affairs,* vol. 57 (Summer 1979).

Tsipis, Kosta. "Cruise Missiles." *Scientific American,* vol. 236 (February 1977).

Von Hassel, Kai-Uwe. "The Search for Consensus: Organizing Western Defense." *Foreign Affairs,* vol. 43 (January 1965).

Wells, Samuel F., Jr. "Sounding the Tocsin: NSC 68 and the Soviet Threat." *International Security,* vol. 4 (Fall 1979).

Wiegele, Thomas C. "Nuclear Consultation Processes in NATO." *Orbis,* vol. 16 (Summer 1972).

Wohlstetter, Albert. "The Delicate Balance of Terror." *Foreign Affairs,* vol. 37 (January 1959).

Wolfers, Arnold, ed. *Alliance Policy in the Cold War.* Baltimore: Johns Hopkins Press, 1959.

Government Publications

Commission on the Organization of the Government for the Conduct of Foreign Affairs (Murphy Commission). Washington, D.C.: Government Printing Office, 1976.

Kaplan, Lawrence S. *A Community of Interests: NATO and the Military Assistance Program, 1948–1951.* Washington, D.C.: Government Printing Office, 1980.

Public Papers of the Presidents: John F. Kennedy, 1961. Washington, D.C.: Government Printing Office, 1962.

U.K. Parliament. *Hansard Parliamentary Debates* (Commons). 5th series, vol. 537 (1955).

U.S. Atomic Energy Commission. *In the Matter of J. Robert Oppenheimer.* Hearing. Washington, D.C.: Government Printing Office, 1954.

U.S. Congress. House. Committee on Appropriations. *Department of Defense Appropriations for 1952.* Hearings. 82 Cong. 2 sess. Washington, D.C.: Government Printing Office, 1951.

U.S. Congress. Joint Committee on Defense Production. *Deterrence and Survival in the Nuclear Age (The "Gaither Report" of 1957).* Committee Print. 94 Cong. 2 sess. Washington, D.C.: Government Printing Office, 1976.

U.S. Congress. Senate. Committee on Armed Services. Preparedness Investigating Subcommittee. *Status of U.S. Strategic Power.* Hearings. 90 Cong. 2 sess. Washington, D.C.: Government Printing Office, 1968.

U.S. Congress. Senate. Committee on the Budget. *First Concurrent Resolution on the Budget—Fiscal Year 1978.* Hearings. Vol. 1. 95 Cong. 1 sess. Washington, D.C.: Government Printing Office, 1977.

U.S. Congress. Senate. Committee on Foreign Relations and Committee on Armed Services. *Assignment of Ground Forces of the United States to Duty in the European Area.* Hearings. 82 Cong. 2 sess. Washington, D.C.: Government Printing Office, 1951.

U.S. Congress. Senate. Committee on Foreign Relations. *Mutual Security Act of 1958.* Hearings. 85 Cong. 2 sess. Washington, D.C.: Government Printing Office, 1958.

————. ————. ————. *Nominations of Robert R. Bowie and U. Alexis Johnson.* Hearings. 89 Cong. 2 sess. Washington, D.C.: Government Printing Office, 1966.

———. ———. ———. *SALT and the NATO Allies*. Committee Print. 96 Cong. 1 sess. Washington, D.C.: Government Printing Office, 1979.

———. ———. ———. Subcommittee on Arms Control, International Law, and Organization. *U.S.-U.S.S.R. Strategic Policies*. Hearings. 93 Cong. 2 sess. Washington, D.C.: Government Printing Office, 1974.

———. ———. ———. Subcommittee on U.S. Security Agreements and Commitments Abroad and Subcommittee on Arms Control, International Law, and Organization. *Nuclear Weapons and Foreign Policy*. Hearings. 93 Cong. 2 sess. Washington, D.C.: Government Printing Office, 1974.

U.S. Department of Defense. *Annual Report, Fiscal Year 1980*. Washington, D.C.: Department of Defense, 1979.

———. *The Theater Nuclear Force Posture in Europe*. Report to the Congress in compliance with P.L. 93-365. Washington, D.C.: Department of Defense, 1975.

U.S. Department of State. *Foreign Relations of the United States, 1948*, vol. 3: *Western Europe*. Washington, D.C.: Government Printing Office, 1974.

———. *Foreign Relations of the United States, 1950*, vol. 1: *National Security Affairs; Foreign Economic Policy*. Washington, D.C.: Government Printing Office, 1970.

U.S. General Accounting Office. *Models, Data, and War: A Critique of the Foundation for Defense Analyses*. Report to the Congress by the Comptroller General. PAD-80-21. Washington, D.C.: Government Printing Office, 1980.

U.S. Library of Congress. Congressional Research Service. Foreign Affairs and National Defense Division. *The Modernization of NATO's Long-Range Theater Nuclear Forces*. Committee Print. Report prepared for the Subcommittee on Europe and the Middle East of the House Committee on Foreign Affairs. 96 Cong. 2 sess. Washington, D.C.: Government Printing Office, 1974.

Unpublished Works

Ball, Desmond J. "The Strategic Missile Programme of the Kennedy Administration, 1961–1963." Ph.D. dissertation. Australian National University, 1972.

Buteux, Paul Edward. "The Politics of Nuclear Consultation in NATO, 1965–1974: The Experience of the Nuclear Planning Group." Ph.D. dissertation. University of London, 1978.

Krone, Robert Max. "NATO Nuclear Policymaking." Ph.D. dissertation. University of California Los Angeles, 1972.

Rowny, Edward L. "Decision-Making Process in NATO." Ph.D. dissertation. American University, 1976.

Sigal, Leon V. "The Politics of War Termination in the United States and Japan." Washington, D.C.: Brookings Institution, 1982.

Declassified Government Documents

Acheson Report. "A Review of North Atlantic Problems for the Future." March 1961.

Bowie, Robert R. "The North Atlantic Nations' Tasks for the 1960's: A Report to the Secretary of State." August 1960.

Neustadt, Richard E. "Report to the President: Skybolt and Nassau, American Policy-making and Anglo-American Relations." November 15, 1963.

McNamara, Robert S. Remarks delivered at a restricted session of the NATO Ministerial Meeting (Athens, Greece), May 5, 1962. Released under the Freedom of Information Act, August 17, 1979.

NSC 162/2: A Report to the National Security Council on Basic National Security Policy. Washington, D.C.: NSC, 1953. The report was declassified on October 20, 1977, and is available through the Modern Military Branch, National Archives.

Index